Other Smart Pop Titles

the unauthorized
Glee companion

Filled With Glee

edited by Leah Wilson

SMART
POP

An Imprint of BenBella Books, Inc.

DALLAS, TEXAS

"The Nerd in All of Us" Copyright © 2010 by Bev Katz Rosenbaum
"Musical Promiscuity" Copyright © 2010 by Kristine Kathryn Rusch
"The Alpha *Glee* Male" Copyright © 2010 by Candace Havens
"Who's the Real LIMA Loser?" Copyright © 2010 by A.M. Dellamonica
"Don't Make Me Over: Mercedes and Tina" Copyright © 2010 by Maria Lima
"Minorities R Us" Copyright © 2010 by Janine Hiddlestone
"Not Just a River in Egypt" Copyright © 2010 by Diane Shipley
"The Twisted Love Life of Mr. Schue" Copyright © 2010 by Jonna Rubin
"At the Heart of Sue Sylvester" Copyright © 2010 by Gabi Stevens
"'You Think This Is Hard? Try Being an Antagonist, *That's* Hard'"
    Copyright © 2010 by Jennifer Crusie
"'You're Having My Baby'" Copyright © 2010 by Claudia Gray
"*Glee*'s Most Versatile Character" Copyright © 2010 by Gregory Stevenson
"Getting Out There" Copyright © 2010 by Jamie Chambers
"*Glee* Episode Guide," "*Glee* Cast Biographies," and Trivia Copyright © 2010 by Amy Berner
Introduction and Other Materials Copyright © 2010 by BenBella Books, Inc.

All rights reserved. No part of this book may be used or reproduced in any manner whatsoever without
written permission except in the case of brief quotations embodied in critical articles or reviews.

Smart Pop is an imprint of BenBella Books, Inc.
10300 N. Central Expressway, Suite 400
Dallas, TX 75231
www.benbellabooks.com
www.smartpopbooks.com
Send feedback to feedback@benbellabooks.com

Printed in the United States of America
10 9 8 7 6 5 4 3 2 1

Library of Congress Cataloging-in-Publication Data is available for this title.
ISBN 978-1-935618-00-3

Copyediting by Oriana Leckert
Proofreading by Erica Lovett
Cover design by Faceout Studio
Text design and composition by John Reinhardt Book Design
Printed by Bang Printing

Distributed by Perseus Distribution
www.perseusdistribution.com

To place orders through Perseus Distribution:
Tel: (800) 343-4499
Fax: (800) 351-5073
E-mail: orderentry@perseusbooks.com

Significant discounts for bulk sales are available.
Please contact Glenn Yeffeth at glenn@benbellabooks.com or (214) 750-3628.

CONTENTS

G*lee* isn't perfect.

...which seems like a strange way to begin the introduction to an anthology celebrating the show, but stick with me.

I love *Glee*. Very little lifts my mood like the clip of the McKinley football players dancing to Beyoncé. There's no show I get more excited to watch. But *Glee* doesn't always live up to my (deservedly) high expectations. In those rare moments where I find myself frustrated with the show, it's usually because *Glee* has *too much* going on: Too many subplots to devote the deserved amount of time to any one of them. Too many characters to let us get to know them the way we want to.

Glee packs a lot into a small space. The show pulls songs from more than half a dozen decades and a surprising number of musical genres. The comedy and drama are packed shoulder to shoulder, jockeying for position. Sometimes things tip over too far one way or the other: Certain scenes are so heartwarming as to feel saccharine. Others are so over-the-top that they no longer ring as true and lose their satirical power. Occasionally these two things happen in the same subplot.

But when *Glee* works—when the show hits exactly the right balance and all the various notes come together perfectly? To exploit the opportunity for a good musical pun: it *sings*. When *Glee* harmonizes its sharp tongue and earnest heart, it has a power like nothing else to touch, to inspire, to entertain.

That's the *Glee* millions of viewers have fallen in love with, and that's the *Glee* at the heart of this book: One that's multidimensional and surprising, entertaining and inspirational, outrageously implausible and yet in many ways more real than anything else on television. One that transforms both its characters and its audience on a weekly basis.

But the *Glee* that doesn't always get it right is of interest here, too. Not explicitly—if you're looking for negativity or nitpicking, you're in the wrong place—but implicitly. Because if I had to use just a single word to describe *Glee*, that word would be "inclusive." The show advocates valuing people for who they are, flaws and all. Because those "flaws"— the things others judge or look down on, the things that make others uncomfortable—can also be a source of strength and worth.

Glee lauds the outsider: the talented outcast, the ostracized cheerleader, the underdog high school teacher-turned-mentor. Will Schuester is, unsurprisingly, a fitting poster child for *Glee*. He's a Spanish teacher in an area of the country with a low Hispanic population, which marks him as a bit of an outsider himself (he teaches a subject many other educators consider secondary—or even, as Sue suggested with her trademark bluntness, worthless). But it also marks him as someone who has devoted his career to reaching out and communicating with those who are different from him.

He's also a perfect illustration of the power of pursuing your passion. Will isn't perfect. He makes mistakes. When we first meet him, he's miserable—he's let himself become someone he doesn't recognize. But he remembers who he always wanted to be, and he goes after it: he takes over the glee club, and he changes not just his own life, but his students' as well. He rediscovers what makes him happy—what makes him *Will*—and he's willing to face resistance and ridicule to hold on to it.

Glee is all about that kind of authenticity. It rewards it in its characters and encourages it in its viewers. More than that, it practices what it preaches. Because whatever else *Glee* may be, it is always, totally and completely, itself: quirky, passionate, and larger than life.

Glee may not be perfect, but neither are we. And that's the point. Being perfect—fitting into that Cheerios costume, winning that trophy—isn't the goal. Being yourself—finding what makes you happy and doing it, whether that's singing Barbra Streisand or playing quarterback (or both)—is.

One thing that makes the writers whose pieces you're about to read happy is *Glee*—watching it, and talking about it. Here, they take on topics as diverse as Will's disastrous love life, Puck and Finn's improbable friendship, and how *Glee* changed television, all with the same kind of passion that drives the characters we love to watch onscreen.

Get new perspectives on characters like Rachel, Kurt, and Sue. Revisit particular episodes with our episode guide, and use the song lists to find sheet music or track down other versions of your favorites. Learn a few things even the biggest Gleek may not know. Even find tips for creating a show choir of your own, no matter how old you are. (Writing the piece even inspired its author to get back in action!)

We've also included true stories from *Glee* fans, submitted to our "Share Your *Glee*" contest, about how the show has affected their lives. Because that's really this book's goal: to share what we see when we watch *Glee* and, hopefully, to encourage you to share what you see, too. If *Glee* has shown us anything, it's that the more voices we hear, the richer the song.

Your voice doesn't have to be perfect. It just has to be yours.

Leah Wilson
August 2010

BEV KATZ ROSENBAUM

The Nerd in All of Us

YEAH, SURE, we all know the show choir at William McKinley High School is filled with nerds. The original members of New Directions fit the usual definition of the word: they're interested in things that are unusual for their age (e.g., Rachel Berry and Barbra Streisand), are physically or socially awkward (e.g., all of them), and are routinely excluded from more conventional activities (ditto). But here's the thing: the popular kids at McKinley are just as messed up, lonely, and marginalized as their showbiz-lovin' counterparts. Consider Finn Hudson, the confused, fatherless football player with the impressive pipes who still mourns the loss of his single mom's mullet-headed, power-ballad-rockin' lawn-painter boyfriend. Then there's Quinn Fabray, the pregnant cheerleader who got kicked off her beloved cheerleading team by nasty coach Sue Sylvester, and then out of the house by her mortified parents. Or Noah "Puck" Puckerman, whose family celebrates Jewish holidays by parking themselves in front of the TV. The adults on the show who were once popular (Will and Terri Schuester, April Rhodes) seem pretty dang messed up, too.

At first glance, *Glee* seemed poised, like most TV or film vehicles about teens, to focus on the humongous differences between the geeks and the popular kids. The pilot opened with the popular kids (football players, mostly) getting ready to throw flamingly gay, über-talented, Marc Jacobs–attired Kurt Hummel into a dumpster. We soon learned that this kind of torture (particularly the slushie-in-the-face variety) went on all the time at McKinley. Indeed, there's a regular caste system at the school, as Sue Sylvester, coach of the Cheerios, McKinley's cheerleading champions, told Spanish teacher Will Schuester when she discovered his plans to restore the glee club to its former glory. But barely any time passed before we learned how deeply screwed by circumstances—and therefore how deeply vulnerable and insecure—the perfect popular kids (Finn, his girlfriend Quinn, and his bestie Puck) were.

In "Preggers" (1-4), it became hugely obvious that poor Finn still desperately missed lawn-painter guy (who left Finn's mom for a much younger specimen, natch) or at least some male force in his life. When he found out Quinn was pregnant (poor, gullible virgin Finn bought her I-got-pregnant-in-the-hot-tub story), he collapsed, crying, into Mr. Schuester's arms. Earlier, when he joined glee club (under duress from Will), it was immediately obvious that he loved having the opportunity to belt out those tunes and pound on those drums. Being as messed up as the other glee club members—a big black girl, a cripple, a queen, a narcissist, and a stutterer—he clearly craved an emotional outlet.

And Quinn? She was the quintessential insensitive rhymes-with-witch until her world was rocked when she became pregnant, got kicked off the Cheerios, and was thrown out of the house by her appearances-obsessed parents. In an emotional scene after she got thrown out, she accused the 'rents of never talking about their feelings, particularly the "bad" ones. It seems that when Quinn joined glee club (initially to spy for Sue Sylvester), she finally found out how cathartic it could be to express one's feelings in song. Clearly, she bullied people (ahem, Rachel) in her pre-preggers days out of a glaring sense of insecurity, to make her unloved-for-real self feel better. It took friendship with the glee club peeps, who know from being ostracized, and their unconditional acceptance of her (in contrast to that of cheerleader Santana, who called her "Tubbers" in

"Hairography" [1-11]), to make her a mensch. (In Finn's case, it was Kurt who taught him a thing or two about loyalty, in "Mash-Up" [1-8], when he poured the slushie Finn had been dared to throw at him over his own head since Finn couldn't. Afterward, Kurt told Finn to "take some time to think about whether your friends on the football team would have done that for you.")

Puck blurred the lines between popular and geek over the course of the first season, too, unlikely as that seemed back in the pilot, when we saw him itching to toss Kurt into that dumpster. That he turned out to be as confused as the rest of us came as no surprise to the viewer who watched "Mash-Up," in which Puck's mother told him he was no better than the Nazis in *Schindler's List* because he didn't have a Jewish girlfriend. (Talk about Jewish guilt!) Puck originally joined Acafellas, Will's short-lived a cappella group, to sleep with the eager cougars in its fan base, but he, like Finn, soon came to dig expressing himself. Once he joined glee club, he couldn't seem to care less what people thought of his new hobby, only occasionally bemoaning his loss of status. (At a brownie sale to raise money for an Artie-friendly bus in "Wheels" [1-9], he said mournfully, "Last month I could have sold over fifty of those on fear alone.") Over the course of season one, Puck still did a lot of popular-type stupid stuff, like tell Quinn in "Hairography" that he intended to be with her but still hook up with other girls. But he also said tons of revealing, almost sensitive stuff, like, "My dad's a deadbeat, and I don't roll that way." When he got a slushie in the face in "Mash-Up," his response was to say to Rachel, "I'm really sorry I ever did this to you. No one deserves this feeling...I kind of feel like I could burst into tears at any moment."

Taking a closer look at the popular-in-high-school adults on the show further proves my there's-a-nerd-in-all-of-us thesis (and also that popular kids become healthiest and most whole when they embrace their inner nerds). First, let's take a look at the formerly popular adults of *Glee* who *haven't* embraced their inner nerds. Take Terri Schuester, Will's wife, the former head cheerleader with the absurdly huge sense of entitlement. Terri, like Sue Sylvester, and like Quinn

2010 Emmy Nominations

Glee was nominated for nineteen Emmy awards for its first season by the Academy of Television Arts & Science, giving the show more nominations than any other series in 2010. The nominations included nods for Matthew Morrison (Lead Actor in a Comedy Series), Lea Michelle (Lead Actress in a Comedy Series), Chris Colfer (Supporting Actor in a Comedy Series), and Jane Lynch (Supporting Actress in a Comedy Series), plus guest actor/actress nominations for Mike O'Malley, Neil Patrick Harris, and Kristin Chenoweth. *Glee* was also nominated for Direction, Writing, Art Direction, Casting, Costumes, Hairstyling, Interactive Media, Make-Up, Sound Mixing, and, of course, Outstanding Comedy Series.

Fabray when we first met her, is not above criminally scheming to get what she wants, never once thinking about the possible consequences. (Fake a pregnancy? No problem! She'll just wear a pad, convince Quinn to give her her baby, and Will will never know! Easy-peasy!) But beneath that breathtakingly confident shell is a glaring sense of insecurity. Witness the telling line Terri uttered to Will in "Mattress" (1-12): "Ever since you started it [glee club], you're walking around like you're better than me." Yup, now that the former head cheerleader had nothing but her (fading) looks, she was not about to let hubby have anything else of significance in his life aside from her. (Sorry, Terri, you can't win 'em all!) That sense of insecurity was likely present even back in high school. It's a cinch to imagine Terri as a pre-glee-club-Quinn kind of bully and that a similarly messed-up home life was at the root of her attention-seeking behavior at McKinley. Terri's sister, a semi-regular character in the first half of the first season, is a complete nutbar. (She was the genius behind the blackmail-a-doctor-to-show-Will-a-fake-ultrasound scheme in

"Throwdown" [1-7].) It's not a big leap to imagine these two were spawned by a couple of other crazies. And it's not any bigger of a leap to imagine that Terri is what Quinn could someday have become, if it weren't for glee club.

The fifth episode of the first season, "The Rhodes Not Taken," introduced Kristen Chenoweth as April Rhodes, former glee club star and current disaster. (She was a drunk, a squatter, and a prostitute in that episode. Later in the season she became the mistress of an elderly roller rink magnate.) Glee was a club with status back in April's day, and she was hugely popular, à la Terri, but there are several hints that she too had some, er, problems back then. Well, one big problem—namely, promiscuity. When she was first reunited with Will, she asked if she'd ever slept with him. He laughed and said, no, he was in ninth grade and she was in twelfth. She just stared at him blankly and repeated the question.

When April got a second shot at glee club (she returned to McKinley to finish her high school credits and sang in the club after Rachel stormed out in a diva moment), she wasn't so quick to want to give up stardom when Will decided she was stealing the spotlight from the kids. She was so eager, so desperate to reclaim her popularity—and the illusion of being okay/not messed up—that even getting that status among high-schoolers was better than nothing. Everything that made her a failure in real life (the drinking, the stealing, the promiscuity) was actually cool to the other glee members and high-schoolers in general (including the football team).

Perhaps if glee club then had been like glee club now and April had made empathetic friends who'd taught her the True Meaning of Life (instead of the guy who ended up ditching her in New York, where an attempted showbiz career crashed and burned), and perhaps if, back then, she'd had a glee club mentor like Will who'd taught her about inner reserves and good values, she could have made something of herself after all those disastrous post–high school experiences, and wouldn't have had to resort to stealing roles from high-schoolers to feel successful again. April is yet another version of what Quinn—

or, okay, maybe Santana—could become without misfit friends and a Mr. Schuester in her life.

And speaking of Will...On the surface, he seems to have it all together. He's nice, cute, popular with his students, and married (for a while, anyway) to his high school sweetheart, the former head cheerleader. But those brilliant flashbacks in "Dream On" (1-19) revealed the spectacular nerd he was before he became a glee club superstar (status club back then, remember?). That he was once a capital-L loser at least partly explains his own possibly unhealthy obsession with the spotlight. From the minute he heard, in the pilot, that Sandy Ryerson, head of glee club, had been let go, he was determined to take over the club and lead it to glory again, despite the fact that the club's budget had been slashed to nothing in favor of Sue Sylvester's ESPN-starring Cheerios. Maybe Sue was on to something when she said, in "Showmance" (1-2), "You wanna be in the spotlight? You wanna be me?" Certainly, Principal Figgins thought Sue had a point. In "Vitamin D" (1-6), he accused Will of being obsessed with winning and passing on his unhealthy obsession to the gleeksters. Even Will himself seems to realize this is a problem for him. Although generally his values are A-1 and he's a terrific role model, he did apologize to the New Directions kids several times over the course of the season for emphasizing winning over having fun.

Will's former status as a nerd could also explain why he married crazy, rhymes-with-witch Terri. As a former nerd, Will probably couldn't quite believe it when the head cheerleader fell for him. And since he identified as a nerd for the majority of his school career—when our identities are cemented—he likely always retained a certain level of nerdish insecurity. His involvement with McKinley's current glee club and his newfound closeness with its misfit participants and supporters, including mega-germaphobe guidance counselor Emma, puts him well and truly back in touch with his inner nerd and helps him put a finger on his own feelings and needs. By the end of the first season, Will had left his beautiful (but psycho) wife, declared his love for super-nerd Emma, and made his peace with not winning

Regionals. In other words, he'd embraced his inner nerd, as each of the popular kids did over the course of the first season.

Even Sue Sylvester, the win-at-all-costs mentor of the popular cheerleaders, came to identify with the glee club nerds—and embrace her own inner nerd—by the end of the first season. (And hey, if Sue Sylvester can identify with the glee club kids, you *know* there is well and truly a nerd in all of us.) In the season finale, she was relentlessly insulted by her fellow Show Choir Regionals judges ("true" celebrities Olivia Newton-John and Josh Groban), who also took cruel shots at the New Directions kids. Sue realized (we could tell by the look in her eye) that from where Olivia and Josh were sitting, *she* was the pitiful nerd. She lives in Ohio, not L.A.! She travels economy, not first class! She may be a local celebrity, but to them she was a joke, a loser—just an older New Directions kid! We saw the light go on, and the determination in her eye when she confidently wrote "New Directions" in the first-place slot on her judge's sheet. Despite her vote, the McKinley kids ended up losing Regionals, which, according to the deal Will made with Figgins, meant that Glee was to be disbanded. But it was none other than Sue who ended up talking Figgins into giving the club another chance—one more year.

The fact that this transformation is a pivotal aspect of the first season's finale confirmed my suspicion is that one of *Glee*'s most important messages is that there's no such thing as a winner or a loser, a popular kid or a nerd—we're all just gloriously human. When *Glee* won a Golden Globe award for Best Comedy/Musical, show creator Ryan Murphy dedicated it to "everyone who ever got a wedgie in high school," but IMHO, one of the show's main points (as I've just been trying to prove) is that there's a nerd in all of us. Or, in the immortal words of Finn in the pilot, "Dontcha get it? We're *all* losers."

•   •   •

Bev Katz Rosenbaum, a former fiction editor, is the author of the Penguin young adult novels *I Was a Teenage Popsicle* and *Beyond Cool*, as well as a pop culture junkie. She loves that she càn use her Smart Pop essays (this is her third) to justify watching TV. Bev lives in Toronto with her husband and two teenage kids, who provide endless inspiration.

KRISTINE KATHRYN RUSCH

Musical Promiscuity

The Music of *Glee*

YOU KNOW HOW THE BEST EPISODES of *Glee* follow the same trajectory? The show establishes a theme and the characters who best express that theme, and then mashes them together with something awful. The characters have a dark night of the soul but come out of it singing, and with the right song, everything winds up perfect, or at least uplifted, in the end.

Well, that trajectory also describes my personal relationship with *Glee*.

Listen to my story, and you'll probably see why, in those "Which *Glee* character are you?" internet quizzes, I always come out as Rachel.

I saw the previews for *Glee* during the last few episodes of the Adam Lambert season on *American Idol* (he was robbed, by the way). I set up my DVR to record because, clearly, *Glee* was my kind of show. My DVR, traitor that it is (and it figures as strongly in this story as Sue Sylvester does on *Glee*), recorded only half of the premiere episode, so I decided to wait until the re-airing in the fall.

I had all summer to anticipate. In fact, I even discussed *Glee* (several times) with the local high school's musical director, who was looking forward to the show as much as I was.

The date finally came. I watched the first episode, then the next three, and then I—

Quit.

That's right, you heard me, Gleeks. I quit watching *Glee*.

I couldn't take it. Or, to be blunt, I couldn't take Terri's fake pregnancy, Sandy Ryerson's inappropriate touching (and the cast's tolerance of it), and the references to Coach Tanaka's hygiene. (Okay, I could have taken the hygiene stuff without the other two elements.)

I would, however, have stuck it out through more than four episodes if only my DVR, the Sue Sylvester of my life (can't live with it; can't live without it), hadn't deleted episode five.

I saw that as a sign and deleted the remaining episodes all by myself. My high school musical director friend had quit watching the moment Sandy Ryerson got rehired at the school, and our Gleek friends kept making understanding sounds, without really agreeing with us. (Rather like the *Glee* kids themselves in conversation with the Cheerios.)

But...

I had already downloaded "Don't Stop Believin'" onto my iPod—both the *Glee* version and the original Journey version, which I have always loved. And strangely, on my daily run, I found myself listening to the *Glee* version. It had more energy. Or maybe it felt fresher. I dunno. Maybe (heresy!) I liked it better.

I snuck to my computer and opened iTunes. I downloaded "Somebody to Love," because I adore that song (the Queen version) and I trusted *Glee* not to murder it. They didn't murder it—they *killed* it, and I mean that in a good way.

Somehow I ended up with "Can't Fight This Feeling" and "Take a Bow," too, and when I looked at my iPod's playlist, I realized that someone (gosh, me?) had played the *Glee* songs more than any other songs in my music library.

So I ordered *Glee: The Music, Volume 1* and asked my Gleek friends if the fake-baby subplot had gone away yet. It hadn't. But somehow the mashup of "Don't Stand So Close to Me" and "Young Girl" ended up on my iPod (who downloaded that? Me? Really?), and after a few listens, I had to see who sang it. I figured Matthew Morrison—and I was right—but I wondered if maybe Cory Monteith had taken a few of the vocals (wrong).

That's when I found myself in front of the *Glee* music videos, watching all of them.

And that's when I ordered the first *Glee* DVD: *Season 1: The Road to Sectionals*, promising myself I would only watch the music and nothing else.

Well, we all know how that ended up. The episode I'd skipped, "The Rhodes Not Taken" (1-5), charmed me, but "Vitamin D" (1-6) nearly chased me away again. As I look at the music list, I realize that "The Rhodes Not Taken" had six songs, and "Vitamin D" (in which, in case you forgot, Terri briefly became the school nurse) had only two.

And as I look back on my song list, by episode (thank you, Wikipedia), I realize that the episode that allowed me to escape my impending Gleekness was "Preggers" (1-4), which had only three songs. "Vitamin D" and "Preggers" had the fewest songs of all of the episodes (except for "Wheels" [1-9], which also had three songs—but three *brilliant* songs, along with a kick-ass storyline).

Someone in the *Glee* hierarchy had finally realized that the show is the music, and the music is the show.

Let's deconstruct, shall we?

The All-Important History

Glee's creators—Ryan Murphy, Brad Falchuk, and Ian Brennan—call *Glee* a musical comedy/drama. Whenever you see them interviewed, they use the word "musical" first. And *Glee* is, first and foremost, a musical.

What is a musical?

The dictionaries I checked called a musical a lighthearted movie or play that uses music (singing and dancing) to develop the story and/or portray the emotions of the characters. I take exception to the lighthearted part. Clearly the writers of the dictionaries have never seen *Miss Saigon*.

So let's go to an authority to find out what a musical is. The site Musicals101.com has all you ever wanted to know about musicals (and more!). Here's the definition given by the site's creator, John Kenrick:

> **Musical** (*noun*): a stage, television or film production utilizing popular-style songs—dialogue optional—to either tell a story (book musical) or showcase the talents of the writers and/or performers (revue).

Okay. By this definition, *Glee* is a "book musical," although I'd love to see a revue (actually, that's what *Glee* did this summer, when the cast went on the road).

But even better than the overall definition, Kenrick adds this in his article on the site titled "What Is a Musical?":

The best musicals have three essential qualities—

- **Brains**—intelligence and style
- **Heart**—genuine and believable emotion
- **Courage**—the guts to do something creative and exciting

Check, check, and check.

Oh, my. We have a musical here.

But a musical on TV is not easy. There are several problems, the first being the cameras themselves. As a friend of mine who used to be a professional ballet dancer pointed out, television directors often don't know how to film choreography. If you don't believe me, watch the Tony Awards some time, or PBS productions of popular musicals, or, hell, even the Oscars. Dancers get truncated or the dumb director films only their feet or pans back so far that the dancers look like fringe blowing in the wind.

Then there's the issue of sound mixing. Most TV directors—again—have no idea how to mix music so that it sounds good. Even *American Idol* screws this up on occasion, particularly when they bring in guest musicians. Either the background voices are too loud or the lead voice is too shrill.

Once television went stereo—somewhere around 1975 (no, I didn't look that up; I remember. I'm *old*)—the variety show (which featured revues) died. Music didn't sound better on a stereo TV set; it sounded worse. No one knew how to engineer it. And don't cite the rise of MTV, either, because music on MTV, even in the early days, was the music from an album, not a difficult-to-film live performance.

It seemed, for a very long time, that TV and music had stopped being a good mix—pun intended.

And for a very long time, TV was a vast musical wasteland. Yes, there were music channels and music videos, but music on prime-time shows? Nope. None. Any attempt to revive the variety show failed.

But musicals on Broadway, after a rough patch in the 1970s, were staging their own revival, led mostly by Stephen Sondheim. And TV execs, thinking they could make money on musicals in a television format, devised a show called *Cop Rock*.

For my sins, I remember *Cop Rock*. I was excited about it, too. All music, all original to the show, which happened to be a *Law & Order* cop drama.

You think it sounds bad? Really? Well, it was worse.

Musicals and TV do not mix. Period.

But...

A few things happened, and they happened almost simultaneously: *Moulin Rouge*, *Cold Case*, and *American Idol*.

Let's take *Moulin Rouge* first.

Baz Luhrmann decided to make a musical without hiring anyone to write the music. In other words, instead of finding a modern Rogers and Hammerstein (or hoping he'd found a modern Rogers and

Hammerstein), he did the music himself, inserting popular songs like "Diamonds Are a Girl's Best Friend" into a story set in 1900s Paris.

Everyone said it wouldn't work. Everyone said it would be stupid.

To make matters worse, he cast Nicole Kidman and Ewan McGregor, neither of whom were known for having a stellar singing voice. Still, they sang and danced their way into a successful film—a film that inspired a cult following of those who happened to love the pop covers and the irreverence at the heart of the musical.

Then there was the TV show *Cold Case*. *Cold Case*, part of Jerry Bruckheimer's early *CSI* trifecta (with *CSI* and *Without a Trace*), decided to have a budget for music permissions. In the past, television shows were unwilling to pay artists to use their originals songs, although WB asked new artists to write songs for a few shows and featured the playlists at the end—mostly to help the musicians sell their CDs, since the music market was (at that time) imploding.

But *Cold Case* hopped timelines—solving old murders from different time periods. If the show was set in 1955, the show's musical director chose songs that were popular in 1955 to help with the flashbacks. The show's use of these songs often led to a small revival of the songs' popularity—all for a new audience. As the original artists (and the music industry) realized that *Cold Case* was providing good advertising for moribund titles, they were a lot more willing to license songs to the show.

Then add *American Idol* to the mix. *American Idol*—which was billed as a reality show because that was the only way Fox would buy it—is really (as Randy Jackson says almost every week) a singing competition. The dirty little secret of *American Idol* is that it reached back to *The Original Amateur Hour* from the 1930s and 1940s—the show that unleashed Frank Sinatra onto America. (Yes, Sinatra won his generation's equivalent of *American Idol*.)

While *Idol* had to have some smarmy reality show bits (like all the clips of wannabe Idolettes sobbing during Hollywood week), it mostly focused on the performances of the contestants each and every week.

And it became a juggernaut.

And *still* television didn't know how to capitalize. A few other channels tried *Idol* wannabe shows—*Nashville Star* comes to mind—but they were merely pale imitations.

Television needed something. But what?

It had no idea it was waiting for *Glee*.

But there were hints. *Hannah Montana* stepped into *The Partridge Family* vibe. And then there was *High School Musical*, a loving parody of the form.

The creators of *Glee* like to say that it's the anti–*High School Musical*. Others have said that it's a real-life-based *High School Musical*.

It's neither, honestly. Because *Glee* isn't one long musical told in episodic sections. It's a different musical each and every week.

The Importance of High School as a Setting

Glee's musicals are set in high school, because, well, high school is a perfect setting for a musical. Reviewers get the reason for this wrong. They think that it's because the characters in *Glee* are in a glee club, so it makes sense for them to sing about their emotions.

But it's more than that.

High school is a universal American experience. We know, even if we're middle-aged, where we fit in our high school years. We were jocks or theater geeks or cheerleaders. We were misfits or nerds or outcasts. We were too fat, too thin, too smart, or too stupid. We were all pretending to be beautiful while feeling ugly inside.

And yet we all had moments, moments we still remember, things that define us even now—and most of those moments revolved around music. I, for instance, can never hear "Hey, Jude" without thinking of one particularly miserable high school dance. I agreed to dance the next song with a guy I didn't like to get him off my back, and the next song was "Hey, Jude"—which is, I swear, the longest song in the known universe, especially when someone you dislike is groping you to the "na-na-na-nananana"s.

And then there are all the times when high school kids semi-spontaneously burst into song. Just about everyone picks up a hairbrush and uses it as a pretend microphone at some time in their teenage lives. Many people sing in the shower. If someone starts singing in public, often others will join in.

Let me give you an example of one of those musical moments from my own high school life, the kind of example that *Glee* critics (dang those grumpy people) call "unrealistic" and say would never actually happen.

On a ride back from an acting competition that my drama class participated in in the "big city," three hours away, someone in the back of the bus started singing the opening to "Bohemian Rhapsody." Other kids joined in and—in my memory, anyway—we created an impromptu, beautiful, *Glee*-worthy rendition of the song (well, without the childbirth noises and the phenomenal dancing).

If life actually had playback and I got to watch that moment from the outside, I have no doubt that I'd have seen how out of tune and overly theatrical we were. Most of us weren't even in choir. But we created a moment, one that most of us still remember, one in which we felt like the kids on *Glee*, bursting into perfect unrehearsed song at the drop of a chord.

And then there's the emotion. Studies have shown that we feel things more intensely when we're in high school. And the music of high school embodies those emotions. We even formalize the music/emotion connection. For example, every couple has "their song." Even the jocks have music—whether it's the school song, or the song that the cheerleaders always perform to.

Music—rehearsed and impromptu—will always be an important part of high school life.

So: Having cops burst into song while making an arrest is ridiculous, but having high school kids burst into song is normal.

Most kids don't sing as they walk down the hall, but I bet all of them sing in their cars, or in their bedrooms, or in the privacy of their own minds.

Musical Promiscuity

In "Bad Reputation" (1-17), Rachel used the term "musical promiscuity" to refer to her music video in which she fooled Jesse, Finn, and Puck into believing they were all playing the male lead. But *Glee* practices its own musical promiscuity—a much better kind.

Unlike *Cop Rock* or even *High School Musical*, *Glee* does not rely on the talents of one songwriter. In this, *Glee* takes its cue from *Moulin Rouge*. *Glee* uses music that's *appropriate*, regardless of when it was written, when it became famous, and whether or not it has fallen out of favor. *Glee* mines music from a diverse array of artists, from Kanye West and Rihanna to Barbra Streisand and Louis Prima. Yes, there are show tunes from real Broadway musicals like *Cabaret*, just like there are real Broadway performers dancing their way through the episodes, stars like Matthew Morrison, Lea Michele, Kristin Chenoweth, and Idina Menzel. But show tunes aren't all of it, and neither are the pop songs. *Glee* adds its own delightful twist to the modern phenomenon: the mashup. *Glee*'s use of mashups illuminate the show's characters very well. The beautiful combination of "One Less Bell to Answer" with "A House Is Not a Home" created a heartbreaking look at loneliness. But the show's most brilliant mashup was "Don't Stand So Close to Me" with "Young Girl."

Gary Puckett and the Union Gap's version of "Young Girl"—a song about the seduction of an underage girl—has to be one of the creepiest songs of the rock era. The Police's "Don't Stand So Close to Me" is about a schoolgirl's attraction to her teacher and the teacher's disgust about it. (The Police's version even references the novel *Lolita*.) The mashup of these two songs helped *Glee* deal with an underlying concern—the closeness between Will Schuester and his students and the way it could be misunderstood. As Schuester sang the song to Rachel with Emma looking on, his performance let the show heal its earlier mistake—playing creepy Sandy Ryerson for humor. In this way, *Glee* acknowledged, without actually saying it, that non-platonic adult/teenage relationships are inappropriate and a serious problem.

Glee used music to address another issue later in the season. About the time I was thinking I should write an essay about the show's mistreatment of the female characters—Rachel is abrasive, Sue is a villain, Santana is snarky mean, and Brittany is unbelievably stupid—the show redeemed itself with "The Power of Madonna" (1-15).

As the male characters acknowledged over and over, you can't sing from Madonna's catalogue without dealing with feminism. Although no one actually used that word in the episode, it floated through as a subtext that all the men had to deal with at some point. And the female characters reveled in the music.

But the best part of that particular episode was another surprise—Madonna's most powerful statement on being a woman, "What It Feels Like for a Girl," was sung by the guys, as they discussed their bad behavior.

Glee uses music to surprise, touch, and empower. When *Glee* takes iconic songs, like John Lennon's "Imagine," it manages to make the song even more iconic. Having the *Glee* kids join the deaf choir's performance of that song could have been a train wreck. The show could have played the deaf choir for laughs. It could also have had the *Glee* kids "interpret" "Imagine" so that we would understand what the deaf choir was singing.

Instead, the moment—a sharing of a love of music—was one of the best moments on any television show this season.

By the Decades

Here's a breakdown of the number of songs performed in the first season of *Glee* from each decade:

1920s	1
1930s	4
1940s	0
1950s	5
1960s	19
1970s	25
1980s	29
1990s	13
2000s	29

Brains, Heart, and Courage

Glee's writers know they're doing a different musical in each episode. They determine their theme. Then they get a list of songs that might fit the theme. Ryan Murphy selects songs from the list for the episode with an eye to characterization and emotion.

Each song either reveals character, adds emotion, or helps our understanding of the situation. The best episodes use a variety of songs from different time periods to work with the theme.

Musically, "Hell-O" (1-14) was particularly brilliant, coming as it did in the first episode after sectionals—and after a four-month hiatus. The show had to reintroduce itself to viewers, reset the plot as the characters moved to Regionals, and remind us of what we loved about *Glee*. It did that with "hello" songs, originally performed by the Doors and the Beatles and the All-American Rejects. (Okay, that last one wasn't a hello song; it was, as Rachel said, a song that used only the first four letters of the word.)

From the beginning, *Glee* has had heart and courage. The show itself is courageous, but its willingness to take risks in both the characters and the music is what endeared it to viewers. Even though I disapproved of Sandy Ryerson, I adored another controversial moment—when Vocal Adrenaline sang Amy Winehouse's "Rehab." The song set up Vocal Adrenaline as a dark, unethical group that would be our heroes' greatest rivals. It was brilliant, just like "Imagine" was brilliant, just like the *Glee* kids' version of "Proud Mary," done in wheelchairs—during an entire episode done in wheelchairs—was brilliant.

The show's initial problem was the first part of Kenrick's musical formula—brains. In the early episodes, everyone was dumb or crass. Will was too stupid to see that his wife was manipulative, Terri mistreated Will for no reason, Principal Figgins tolerated behavior that would have put everyone in jail. Sue Sylvester, horrible as she is, became a popular character because of the talents of the marvelous Jane Lynch. But it wasn't until "Hairography" (1-11) that Sue became a real, *understandable* character with the introduction of her sister.

By the middle of the first season, the show finally added brains to the mix. The characters evolved. We learned that they were more than stereotypes—Kurt wasn't just the gay kid and Mercedes wasn't just the fat kid and Artie wasn't just the understanding, handicapped kid. They were real human beings with real human emotions, and their depth gave the individual episodes depth.

It would have been easy to keep the kids as stereotypes throughout the entire season. It would have been easy to allow the broad characterizations to continue to define the show. But the show's writers chose the harder route. They chose to make each character real, and the reality added to the emotional depth, showed a lot of courage, and took brains to pull off.

The Finale

I'm back, and millions of others have joined me. *Glee* has become a phenomenon—not just as a TV show, but as a musical force. As of May 4, 2010, *Glee* has released sixty-nine songs as singles. There are three albums—*Glee: The Music, Volume 1*, *Volume 2*, and *Volume 3*—as well as an extended play called *Glee: The Music, The Power of Madonna*. *Volume 3* hit the top of the album charts (something a TV soundtrack has never done) and held the position for more than two weeks.

But most impressive is this statistic: In 2009, the *Glee* cast had twenty-five singles on the Billboard Hot 100. That's the most songs on the Billboard Hot 100 held by any one group since 1964...when some group called the Beatles had thirty-one songs on the chart.

Is *Glee* a phenomenon? Oh, yeah.

Does it deserve to be? Yep.

Will it continue? As long as it remembers the secret formula: brains, heart, and courage.

• • •

Kristine Kathryn Rusch, a former editor and journalist, has written non-fiction since she was in high school. These days she mostly writes fiction. Her internationally bestselling Fey series has just reached audio through Audible.com. WMG Publishing is in the process of putting her entire backlist into electronic books. Pyr will publish *City of Ruins*, the next book in her Diving universe series. Sourcebooks will publish *Wickedly Charming*, a paranormal romance that she wrote under the name Kristine Grayson. Two more Kristine Grayson books will follow. She also writes award-winning mysteries as Kris Nelscott—and she still finds time to watch waaaaay too much TV.

Music Appreciation

s h a r e y o u r G l e e

I have a terrible singing voice. It's very flat.

This has not, however, kept me from singing—karaoke, *Rock Band*, in the car, while drunk. I love music and I love to sing. I love watching musicals—I remember watching *South Pacific* on HBO when I was in high school and that feeling of excitement that swept over me when Nellie Forbush washed that man right outta her hair, or when Bali Hai was calling me.

I loved that feeling, and I would sing along whenever I could. I still break out into song—I sing opera-style for my daughter when I want her to do something or want to emphasize what I'm saying. I sing to myself when I'm anxious or frustrated, reminding myself that it'll all be okay. I sing to make sense of my life.

My life is a musical, and I love the fact that *Glee* lets me in on a bit of that each week for each character. I can't wait to see each new episode, to see what songs they'll pick and how happy they'll be to be singing, even if they're singing something sad or angry.

And the dancing—my goodness, the dancing! Who doesn't love to break out into dance? We have disco days at home, where my daughter and I will start dancing when a good song comes on. Sometimes I can even get my husband to join in.

Glee makes me happy because for about forty minutes a week, I get to see people enjoying themselves, expressing themselves, through song and dance. That uplift I feel, the way my heart jumps up—really, it does—when Mr. Schuester starts singing and dancing, when Puck and Rachel sing to each other, when Kurt expresses himself...I love it all.

When Will and Emma danced while she tried on her wedding gown? Painful and beautiful.

When Mercedes sang with the Cheerios? Empowering and heart-rending.

When they all sing and dance? I'm excited to be able to watch people really showing how they feel—showing that life and love and pain and heartache are sometimes best expressed through music or dance.

I remember, distinctly, being at band camp in seventh grade (I know, so cliché, right?). There was a dance, and I had never been to a dance before (sheltered, sheltered girl). I remember, distinctly, how free I felt when I was whirling around to the music. I know people thought I was weird. That I was a freak for really just letting go and dancing and expressing myself. But I didn't care.

I didn't care then and I don't care now. I never care when I dance or sing. I am expressing myself. Expressing the emotions that are generally so wrapped up in the day-to-day, inside myself, that they can't come out in any other way. *Glee* reminds me that it's okay to do that. Not just okay, that it's *important* to do that.

And that's why I love *Glee*.

SUZAN HYSSEN
Livonia, MI

CANDACE HAVENS

The Alpha *Glee* Male

'LL BEGIN THIS ESSAY with a confession: I'm a complete and total Gleek. Every week the show takes me to my happy place, and I like it there. The music, quirky characters, and storylines help me feel better about life. I also like the idea that not everything on the show is what it may seem on the surface. The biggest nerd might have the coolest tone to his voice. The young woman of size might have the best self-esteem. And the strongest man on campus—the alpha male—could be someone you would never expect.

It's interesting to examine specific traits of the alpha male in relation to the characters on *Glee*, as there are many of them who have these behaviors, though not generally in the way one might expect. The show constantly challenges stereotypes and proves that it's okay to be unusual. That makes the role of the alpha male in the musical series a little different from what we would otherwise expect. Follow me as we go in search of the alpha male on *Glee*. You might just be surprised by what you discover.

First we must understand what an alpha male is. In the animal kingdom, the alpha is the dominant male in a social group. He gets the best food and usually has a multitude of mates from which to choose. Most of the time he determines his status by fighting for it and showing off his physical prowess, and must constantly fight other males in order to maintain his position. It is the survival of the fittest.

When it comes to humans, what we mean by the term *alpha male* has less to do with social position and more to do with having a certain type of personality. An alpha male does tend to assume a dominant role in social or professional situations, but he does not have to do so through physical ability. More importantly, the alpha male must possess the qualities and confidence to be a leader. He is secure in himself and his decisions, and he leads by example, guiding others without losing his temper and commanding respect through his actions. He is brave, he strives for the best for his tribe, and he often makes difficult decisions in order to keep his group together. He keeps his feet on the ground, but he also dreams big and can see the big picture, even when no one else does. He doesn't let trivial things set him back, and he always listens to his instincts.

So who is *Glee's* biggest alpha? Let's peruse the tribe that is New Directions and see.

"Courage is grace under pressure."
—Ernest Hemingway

At first glance, McKinley High School glee club coach Will Schuester and lead singer Finn Hudson would seem to be the two prime candidates for the title of alpha male. They are capable, athletic, and handsome, and women love and lust after them—they are key elements in many of the show's love triangles. In many ways, Finn and Will share the same journey on the show. Unfortunately, this journey is fraught with obstacles that keep them from being true alphas.

Will was the one who brought the group of talented singers together in the first place, and he is always willing to do whatever it takes to make the glee club successful. In the pilot, Will offered up his soul to Principal Figgins to get the glee club started, and he did whatever he could to involve the most talented kids in the school. He made great sacrifices in his personal life, incurring the wrath of his wife, to keep the group together. From the beginning, Will always put the good of the glee club ahead of his personal needs. This is prime alpha behavior.

Finn shares many of these characteristics. Like his glee club coach, he is often the glue that holds the club together. He began the first season of *Glee* as the high school quarterback and one of the most popular kids in school. He had the beautiful and equally popular cheerleader Quinn Fabray as his girlfriend. She was absolutely a dominant female, and a fitting partner for such a strong young man. They were a golden couple who could do no wrong. Finn was forced into joining glee club, but not just because he would have gotten in trouble otherwise: if he hadn't agreed to Will's blackmailing scheme, the football team would have suffered. Finn couldn't let his team down, so he joined glee club even though it caused his reputation to take a serious hit. That made him good alpha male material.

This was also the first chink in Will and Finn's alpha male armor: A real alpha male doesn't need to use coercion, as Will did, to get what he wants, and an alpha would never submit to coercion in any form, as Finn did. In the end, the blackmail worked for the good of New Directions, but both men failed to display true alpha male traits.

It was on the second episode, "Showmance," where Will's alpha male status really began to slide. His high-maintenance, nagzilla wife Terri insisted that since she was pregnant, they had to buy a house— even though she knew as well as Will did that there was no way they could afford it. To give his wife everything she wanted, Will was forced to take on a second job as a janitor at the school. While looking out for his family (even though part of that family was a lie) is a good alpha male trait, when it came to Terri, Will broke one of the alpha male rules: No one tells the alpha male what to do. He might listen to and incorporate ideas from his tribe, but the ultimate decision is up to him.

Will's slide down the slippery slope continued in "Acafellas" (1-3), when Terri told him he was a better mentor than performer—and

he believed her. Terri couldn't stand that other women were interested in her husband, so—in true Terri fashion—she did everything
she could to make Will feel bad about himself, destroying his hopes
and dreams.

Throughout the first thirteen episodes, Terri continually duped
Will with her fake-pregnancy antics. He fell for her tricks and became a weaker man by trying to fulfill her many demands. When,
during "Mattress" (1-12), he finally grew a pair and confronted Terri
after finding her fake pregnancy pad, he became so angry it looked
like he might hit her. (I don't advocate any kind of violence, but if
ever there was a woman to smack...) A true alpha male would *never*
strike a woman in his effort to dominate. He is strong and can fight
for his tribe, but he doesn't use brute force on those weaker than
him. It's to Will's credit—and that of his alpha male potential—that
he walked out instead. In fact, by the end of the first half of the season, Will had reversed many of his earlier less-than-alpha attributes.
He had dumped his horrible wife, stood up to his nemesis, Sue Sylvester, and done what was necessary to insure the success of New
Directions. He had, in short, achieved alpha status.

Finn, while a good leader, isn't always the brightest bulb in the
room. Intelligence and an intuitive nature are important aspects of
an alpha male, and unfortunately, Finn, for all his good qualities,
lacks both. Like Will with Terri, Finn let himself be ruled by Quinn's
many demands. Then again, also like Will, Finn put taking care of
his family first. He worried about nabbing a football scholarship so
he could provide for his child, and he took a job in the interim to
help pay for doctor bills, showing a strong character and a willingness to do what's right. When Quinn's family kicked her out, Finn
was there to take her in.

Unfortunately, Finn's baby was just as much a lie as Will's, and
when Rachel told Finn that his best friend Puck was the father of
Quinn's child, Finn jumped to the dark side. And who could blame
him? He broke up with Quinn, beat up Puck, and quit glee club.
With Sectionals upon them, and no leading man, the gleesters had
no idea what to do. Their chances were further foiled when their

song list was leaked to the other schools. The club's routines became useless as they watched the other schools perform them. When it seemed all was lost, Finn swooped in to save the day. He brought the glee kids a new song to sing, and they found a way to work around their other numbers. By the end of the first half of the season, Finn, like Will, had achieved alpha status.

That is, until the second half of the season. Will's relationship with Emma, the school counselor, was almost immediately felled by his soon-to-be-ex-wife Terri. Will allowed Terri to interfere in his life once again, and he didn't fight back when he should have. What he should have done was given Terri a tongue-lashing and swept Emma off her feet, reassuring her that he cared for her.

Finn, who was exploring his relationship with Rachel, suffered a similar fate. Though Rachel's overbearing ways were already wearing thin, if he had stood up for himself and given their relationship a chance to adjust, rather than breaking up with her to date some manipulative cheerleaders, he could have saved himself a great deal of trouble later on. Will and Finn learned nothing from their past mistakes with the fairer sex, and that's one thing alpha males do: When they make mistakes, they learn from them and move on.

I've spent a great deal of time on these two, because there is hope for them. They share many of the traits we expect from alpha males. They are good leaders, they stand up for their beliefs, and they take great care of their tribe. They just aren't there yet.

"Some people change their ways when they see the light, others when they feel the heat."
—*Caroline Schoeder*

Waiting on the sidelines of the alpha male parade is Noah "Puck" Puckerman. Though he definitely has dominant traits, most of the time he expresses them by being a bully—and as mentioned, an alpha male doesn't have to use brute force to get what he wants. Puck is far from the ideal alpha male. So far, his days have been spent thinking about the next girl he can sext or actually get horizontal. While a strong sex drive may be a strong male dominance trait—alpha males in the animal kingdom do need to procreate—unfortunately, Puck lacks leadership skills and has a problem looking out for anyone other than himself.

When he learned that he was the father of Quinn's baby, he told her that he wanted to provide for his child to prove he wasn't a loser. Yet he was in no way willing to give up his deviant behavior. He also refused to take a leadership role with the glee club. He participated, but unwillingly. Even when he was down and out after his haircut, he never learned his lesson. He'll do anything to keep his position of power, and he was only interested in restoring his status. Puck simply doesn't make the alpha male cut, and it's doubtful he ever will.

> **"Character is that which reveals moral purpose, exposing the class of things a man chooses or avoids."**
> —*Aristotle*

Some would argue Sue Sylvester is an alpha male. She may be a female, but she certainly does exhibit alpha tendencies. She does whatever it takes to make sure her Cheerios win, and she never backs down from a battle. While she often uses unorthodox methods, she gets the job done. Her Cheerios are incredibly successful, and most days Sue rules the roost at McKinley High. There are even moments of goodness in Sue, never more evident than in "Wheels" (1-9), in which we discovered she has a sister with Down syndrome for whom she cares a great deal.

While it isn't necessarily an alpha trait, Sue's voting outcome on the season finale also showed more depth than we'd come to expect from her. But anyone who has ever seen an episode of *Glee* knows that, despite her better moments, Sue is nothing but an insecure bully. She may talk tough, but she's no alpha.

"Those who wish to sing always find a song."
—*Swedish proverb*

Moving on, we take a look at an unlikely alpha male candidate: Kurt Hummel. Courage is an important aspect of the alpha male, and that's something Kurt has in abundance. On a daily basis, he was dumped in trash bins and slammed into lockers, but he took it all with a quiet determination. He was proud of his talent, and he wasn't afraid to make bold choices, whether in fashion, music, or life.

In "Preggers" (1-4), Kurt came out to his father Burt (and, in one of my favorite and most tearful moments on *Glee*, Burt accepted him and let Kurt know he'd been of his aware of his sexual preferences since he was a tot). Few things are more difficult than coming out to one's parents, and Kurt did it with great aplomb and courage.

He's also not afraid to take one for the team, whether that team is glee club or his family. After Will agreed to allow both Rachel and Kurt to audition for "Defying Gravity"—traditionally a song with female vocals—in a diva-off, Kurt was on his way to wowing the crowd when he threw the audition by not hitting the high F. Kurt later told his father that he'd made the mistake on purpose because, though Burt had backed Kurt up in his desire to sing the song, Kurt knew others were giving Burt a hard time, and it didn't seem fair to make his father suffer the consequences of Kurt's choices. Kurt also realized with Rachel singing the song, he wouldn't embarrass his glee team.

Kurt was one of the first on the team to call someone out if they weren't doing what was best for New Directions. There were times when his performance ambitions ended up getting in the way of what was right, but he usually had the best intentions.

All of this makes Kurt great alpha male material. He's always strong in his beliefs, and he isn't afraid to stand up for what's right. Unfortunately, his need for acceptance, though it makes him relatable and very human, often leads to less-than-alpha-worthy behavior, whether at school or home. Never was that more evident than in "Home" (1-16), when he and Mercedes made the Cheerios and Kurt encouraged Mercedes to do whatever it took to fit in, even if that meant starving herself. Mercedes and Kurt came to their senses, but not before some damage was done to Mercedes' self-esteem.

Though Kurt showed he could hold his own as the place kicker for the football team in "Preggers," he didn't do it for himself. It was an attempt to please his father, and to prove they could have something in common. By the end of the episode Kurt learned the best thing he could do for everyone was to be true to himself, but it was a lesson he had to re-learn several times during the first season.

Kurt continued to try to be someone else in "Laryngitis" (1-18). Jealous of his father's relationship with Finn as they enjoyed their boys' nights out, Kurt tried to man up. He put on a ball cap and flannel, and worked desperately to become something he wasn't. Like being on the football team, he only did it to please his father.

He seemed to have learned his lesson in "Theatricality" (1-20), when he refused to back down and wouldn't change out of his crazy Lady Gaga costume. He stayed strong in his beliefs, and didn't let the bullies have the last word—even though they almost killed him. But so long as Kurt keeps forgetting one of his best traits—being proud of who he is—he still has too much emotional growth to do before he can be considered a true alpha male.

"The world knows nothing of its greatest men."
—*Henry Taylor*

There is one young man in *Glee* who goes through his days with a quiet strength—a young man who possesses all the qualities of a true alpha male. That young man is Artie. Artie is a voice of reason, and someone who isn't afraid to speak up for what's right. He is stalwart and kind, and while he may have a disability, he doesn't focus on it and never uses it as an excuse to not go after his dreams.

In "Wheels" (1-9), Will wanted the group to understand what Artie went through, so he demanded that they spend a few hours a day in wheelchairs. Not only did this episode make kids aware of what it was like for disabled teen on a daily basis, it also showed how much of a hero Artie was. (During an interview I did with the *Glee* cast, they said that using the wheelchairs made "Rollin' on the River" the single hardest musical number they had to do all season. It gave them all a new respect for what those in wheelchairs go through.) Every day Artie faces great adversity and does so with dignity. He doesn't blame anyone for his troubles; his life is what it is. He doesn't let the chair keep him from performing in glee club, and his wheels don't define who he is. This shows a great strength of character, which is imperative for an alpha male.

In this same episode, Tina and Artie finally had a date. After they kissed, she confessed that she didn't really have a stutter. Artie was disappointed with her for lying to him. He'd believed in her and thought they had their disabilities in common. Unlike the other males on the show, when he learned he'd been lied to, he didn't turn over and play dead, or explode with uncontrolled anger. He calmly explained that while she'd only pretended to have a handicap, he was always going to be stuck in his chair, and then they temporarily parted ways. There are some who might argue he was too harsh toward her, but this was his way of standing up, so to speak, for his beliefs. He had every right to be angry at her deception. The rest of the guys on the show could take a cue from Artie.

Importantly, unlike Finn and Will, who at the end of the season were still allowing their anger at the women who'd betrayed them to rule their lives, Artie eventually forgave Tina. In "The Power of Madonna" (1-15), he even realized he might have been objectifying Tina in some ways. All the boys realized they had been treating the girls poorly, and Artie was one of the first to apologize, promising

Tina that he would be more respectful of her in the future. It takes a real man—and a real alpha male—to admit when he's wrong, and to learn to appreciate those around him.

Though his presence is sometimes overlooked, Artie played a part in many of the most important decisions for New Directions. In "Hell-O" (1-14), Artie, Tina, Kurt, and Mercedes were the ones who confronted Rachel about dating Jesse, one of their rivals from Vocal Adrenaline. Artie helped them to be a united front when they gave Rachel an ultimatum: either she had to end her relationship with Jesse, or she would be out of glee club permanently. This was a difficult situation, but Artie was never afraid to speak out about what was right for the team. His ideas might make him unpopular at times, but he's obviously earnest in his desire to ensure glee club is the absolute best it can be. He also isn't afraid to fight for his fellow gleesters.

Artie shared his deepest secret in "Dream On" (1-19), when viewers learned he wanted to be a dancer. The episode ended with him realizing he probably wouldn't ever see that dream come true. Though he had a few low moments, he was okay with letting the dream go. He did what he always does—instead of whining or complaining, he dealt with his disappointment gracefully. He told Tina that while he might never be a dancer, he would come up with a new dream. Artie may have his sad times, as he did in "Funk" (1-21) and "Journey" (1-22), but he is usually one of the first to bounce back to his usual positive self.

This journey of discovering the alpha male on *Glee* comes with an important lesson: Don't always trust what seems obvious. New Directions tends to look to Will and Finn for leadership, but they'd do better to look to Artie. Will and Finn are great guys, but they don't necessarily have the strength of character Artie does. While he has strong leadership qualities, he doesn't beat people over the head with them. And though he has faced great adversity, he keeps a positive outlook and he never stays down for long. There isn't anything he won't do for New Directions and the people he cares about. He's a guy who has his wheels on the ground but isn't afraid to dream. I vote Artie Abrams the alpha *Glee* male.

• • •

Bestselling author **CANDACE HAVENS** has written six novels for Berkley, including *Charmed & Dangerous*, *The Demon King and I*, and *Dragons Prefer Blondes*. Her new venture is writing for the Blaze line of Harlequin. Those books include *Take Me If You Dare*, and the upcoming releases *She Who Dares*, *Win*, and *Triple Dare Ranch*. Her books have received nominations for the RITA's, Holt Medallion, and Write Touch Reader Awards. She is the author of the biography *Joss Whedon: The Genius Behind Buffy* and a contributor to several anthologies. She is also one of the nation's leading entertainment journalists and has interviewed countless celebrities. Her entertainment columns are syndicated in more than six hundred newspapers across the country. Candace also runs a free online writing workshop for more than sixteen hundred writers. She does film reviews with the Dorsey Gang on The Big 96.3 and also serves as a mentor for young writers.

A . M .   D E L L A M O N I C A

Who's the Real LIMA Loser?

The Curious Friendship of Finn Hudson and Noah Puckerman

N THE FIRST SEASON OF *GLEE*, one thing was crystal clear: if Finn Hudson had it, then Noah Puckerman wanted it. Despite their longstanding friendship, Puck couldn't seem to keep from sabotaging a good thing. He had sex with Quinn, then pursued her behind Finn's back. Later, he made a move on Rachel, Finn's not so-secret crush.

Cheating, lying, and competing for the affections of women are all ancient human behaviors, of course, and if he were called upon to explain himself, it seems more than likely that Puck would say he was letting his groin make his choices for him. But on *Glee*, nothing is ever so simple. Fans of Puck's bad-boy mystique have to ask whether poor impulse control is the whole story.

If not, what's the alternative?

"You think either of us is gonna give a damn about Finn in three years?"
—Puck, "Journey" (1-22)

During their fateful sexual encounter, Quinn raised the question of Finn. Puck's response—that neither of them was going to care about Finn after high school—was immediate, callous, and made him sound like an immoral jerk, someone with nothing to lose. After all, messing with someone's girlfriend is no big deal if you're just hanging out with the guy to kill time until graduation.

It is only natural to ask if the boys' friendship is a sham, a façade without any depth. Puck's behavior aside, the question of true friendship—real intimacy, as opposed to shallow social alliances—is one that arose repeatedly on *Glee*.

This is a show where people constantly pretend to like each other. Terri Schuester and Sue Sylvester are masters of feigning friendliness with an exploitative agenda. Will took a page from that same playbook when he came on to Sue in "Funk" (1-21), and of course there's Jesse St. James and his romance with Rachel.

Even the kids we generally think of as good or nice on the show made occasional decisions to run with people they didn't like. Mercedes was very matter-of-fact when she weighed the pros and cons of dating Puck, despite her reservations about his personality. When Rachel asked to Quinn to return to New Directions in "Vitamin D" (1-6), she didn't pretend the two of them were chummy, or that they ever would be. Her argument was all tactics, no emotion: she pointed out that the Cheerios were sure to reject Quinn, while the glee club wouldn't.

The complicated politics of high school friendship reflect the fact that it is something of a shaky proposition to begin with. In this stratified social environment, the pool of possible friends for any given individual is small. (As Will tells us in "Dream On," [1-19]: "Those kids get labeled the second they walk in the door freshman year. Geek. Punk. Jock. Queer.") Even in schools with hundreds of students, kids are corralled into small groups, separated by class, race, religion, talent, academic ability, and extracurricular interests. It isn't just on TV that cheerleaders only hang out with other cheerleaders. Traveling in a herd of like-minded teens is crucial to surviving adolescence.

Once students have eliminated the kids they *can't* hang out with, odds are good that they will be left with only a handful of likely possible friends. If those few options include one or two people they truly connect with, it is something of a miracle.

In "Ballad" (1-10), Suzy Pepper pointed out to Rachel how similar they were. Yet it was obvious that the girls wouldn't become friends; their core identities were completely different. Whatever Suzy is, it's not a glee clubber.

So, are Puck and Finn BFFs—part of the lucky few who do find meaningful friendship in high school—or, as Puck's statement to Quinn suggested, simply frenemies?

On paper, Puck and Finn are a match made in heaven. Their common ground is so vast, they're practically the same person. As season one opened, their identities were completely bound up in their shared identity as popular high school jocks—kings of the social pecking order. They're white, straight, decent-looking, and they share an abiding interest in teenage-boy passions: girls, sex, sports, sex, video games, sex, and music. Neither boy is academically minded, but they're willing to work, at least for a while, to achieve the things they want.

The biggest difference between the two is temperamental. Finn is disciplined, well-mannered, craves approval, and aims to please. Puck is impulsive, self-serving, uninterested in the good opinion of others, tactless, periodically mean, and a rule-breaker. In the opening episodes of *Glee*, they had the school at their mercy. Finn presided over the student body like a benevolent god, while Puck kept the riffraff, notably Kurt, in line through bullying. As Puck put it later in "Funk": "Revenge, fear, the merciless infliction of pain—these are my kingdoms."

This kingdom was a shared monarchy. Finn wasn't just aware of the bullying; he participated from the sidelines. By doling out small acts of mercy, he earned affection and a nice-guy reputation. Puck's violence, meanwhile, dissuaded challenges to that status quo. The team effort secured their popularity—it was a good-cop, bad-cop routine that benefited them both. It also allowed Finn, conveniently, to give rein to his darker impulses, to explore his inner jerk without getting his hands dirty.

Did this symbiosis mean that the boys' relationship was, indeed, just a convenient alliance? No. Though neither boy is overly emotionally demonstrative—they're dudes, after all—the evidence shows that the two share a real bond of affection. They need each other, and their storyline makes this obvious time and again.

There's no questioning that Finn is sincere in his fondness for Puck. Sure, he was jealous when Puck sang "Sweet Caroline" to Rachel, and the boys came to blows in "Wheels." But Finn is no Jesse St. James—he doesn't pretend. Before the traumatic revelations of "Sectionals" (1-13), his friendship—like his heart—was offered without strings. It was only after he learned the truth about Puck and Quinn's hookup that Finn lost a morsel of this generosity. In "The Power of Madonna" (1-15), he warned Rachel that her dating Jesse might ultimately endanger their friendship. He had become someone who could imagine his friends causing painful problems within their relationship, you see, and he wanted Rachel to know that if she did damage the glee club, or him, she shouldn't expect to skate on it.

Even as he guarded himself against further hurt, Finn found himself incomplete without Puck. Deprived of his more aggressive partner in crime, Finn played with expressing his darker impulses directly. He told Rachel he wanted to play the field, hooked up with Santana, wooed Rachel behind Jesse's back, and let Kurt have it in the memorably homophobic outburst of "Theatricality" (1-20).

If he was more selfish and less tactful, he was also even more honest. His dramatic expressions of grief over his dead father were what allowed him to come, eventually, to a painful understanding of his mother's loneliness. The pre-Sectionals Finn might have swallowed those feelings, letting his distress show but at most airing only a few quiet objections to his mother's stepping out. Instead he erupted, Puck-style, and thereby brought matters to a head.

In most cases, though, when Finn experimented with behaving badly, it cost him more than he was willing to pay. Losing Rachel to Jesse was bad enough, but the dressing down given to him by Kurt's father must have been utterly agonizing for someone with such an investment in his good-guy mythos. Consciously or not, he was a bit lost without his wingman.

And what about Puck? It was easy to relate to Finn's feelings...because he was not the one who cheated and lied. Did Puck care about the friendship at all?

The answer is yes. In "Preggers" (1-4), he offered Finn a chance to vent when he was visibly depressed...and before he knew what had Finn so upset. He saw that his friend was troubled, and he offered himself. He didn't let himself get brushed off. Despite Puck's general insensitivity to others, he insisted that Finn confide in him, just when he needed it most. This was, indisputably, an act of concerned friendship.

After Puck learned of Quinn's pregnancy—and despite his own turbulent feelings—he remained at Finn's side, listening to his complaints and backing his play in joining glee club.

These weren't moves Puck made lightly. When Finn joined New Directions, Puck's first response was to try to re-establish the existing social order through intimidation. He struck at the weak point he knew so well—Finn's desire to fit in—by bringing in the other football players, making a paintball attack into a ritual shaming.

Peer pressure worked...briefly. Then Finn remembered that their mutual popularity was riding on his star qualities. He told the team that it needed him—to win games, he meant, but in Puck's case it seemed to identify a need that went deeper than football. Having failed to bully Finn back into his comfort zone, Puck made the startling decision to follow his best friend into Acafellas.

Puck hung in with Finn, in other words, even when it cost him socially. Logically, he should have cut his losses, recruiting the other football goons to ostracize Finn and reforming the social order to suit himself. But instead of staging a coup, Puck moved with Finn into the socially hazardous waters of the glee club. As their cred in the school sunk, he stood firm, taking his slushie facials like a man.

After "Sectionals," Puck's social status even within New Directions plummeted...and this time, his confidence wasn't unshakeable. Like Finn, he was suddenly flying solo. Nobody had his back, and it made him vulnerable. Rachel appealed to Puck's desire to rehabilitate his rep when she convinced him to appear in her "Run, Joey, Run" video. When his head got shaved and the unpopular kids chucked him in the dumpster, he took it to heart. Instead of toughing it out, he pursued Mercedes. Without Finn's companionship and support to make the social cost of being in glee club worthwhile, he jumped at a chance to restore his former social status as a popular guy and fearsome bully.

So if Puck and Finn's friendship is real—if Puck really does care about Finn—why did he sleep with Quinn? Was it just a lack of sexual self-control? A need to slip one past his alpha male?

"I try to be good. I tell myself, 'Be cool, Puck, be nice.' But by second period I've got a fire extinguisher in my hands and I'm spraying some dweeb with it, and I don't know how I got there."
—Puck, *"Bad Reputation" (1-17)*

Like the trickster god for whom he is named, Puck is very much a creature of impulse. It's easy to imagine that his initial seduction of Quinn was unplanned. He loved her, they were drinking, and he's used to getting what he wants.

What is unusual isn't that Puck had an opportunity for sex and took it—that barely seems noteworthy. The more significant betrayal came after both boys learned of Quinn's pregnancy, during the episodes between "Preggers" and "Sectionals," when Puck couldn't quite bring himself to confess to Finn. By declining to speak up, he ended up making Finn's hurt that much worse, without gaining anything for himself. Puck is a straight-talking guy, and he wants Quinn for himself...so why conspire with her to hide the truth? Had he come out with it up front, when Finn was still reeling at the news that he'd fathered a child, Puck might have minimized the damage to both of them.

The reason behind his self-destructive behavior lies in a troubling comment Quinn threw at Puck. "You're a LIMA loser. You'll always be a LIMA loser," she told him in "Preggers." She said it in a moment of rage, as she was beginning to embark on the painful process of admitting her pregnancy to herself, not to mention exposing it to others. And though later she recanted, there is no doubt in my mind that she meant it.

LIMA. Lost in Middle America. The name of the town where *Glee* takes place is also an acronym for a particular type of hell. To be a LIMA loser is to be stuck, dead-ended in a place where nothing happens, where nobody has any real prospect of success, where your horizons do not stretch beyond those established in high school. Speaking of men a decade older than he is, guys who had children in their teens, Finn put it like this: "They're caged. They got no future" ("Preggers").

"LIMA loser" is a deadly insult. It means you peaked in high school and your life is over before you're twenty.

Getting out of Lima is an overriding concern for almost all of the New Directions kids. When Quinn revealed her pregnancy to Finn, she told him about having believed she might get out of town. Kurt's talk of escape is wrapped up in a very real need to survive small-town homophobia and get to a bigger, safer, and more culturally diverse pool. Rachel dreams of her Grammy Award, and Finn's desire to lead a life that will make his mother proud includes the idea of attending college. Sue Sylvester's fame as a local celebrity is built on her status as a nationally successful cheerleading coach.

When *Glee* began, Will Schuester was a poster boy for LIMA loser-dom—he was marking out the end of a troubled marriage to an un-happy former cheerleader, and the only certainty in his life seemed to be that while some things might get worse, nothing was going to get better. We even saw him moping over the trophy he won as a kid, looking back to better days.

Most of the adults in town seem to think they have failed by stay-ing in Lima. Sue had always basked in her fame, for example, but she was seriously set back when she was mocked by Olivia Newton-John and the other judges at Regionals. Ironically, Will would kill to have that same stature, or that of the indisputably successful coach of Vocal Adrenaline, Shelby. But Shelby only saw that she had given up a baby, failed to make it in New York, and been forced to return to Ohio.

Glee is populated, in other words, by adults who are struggling to give their stuck-in-Lima existences some meaning, and students who are scared as hell of becoming them.

"My old man's a deadbeat, but I don't roll that way."
—*Puck, "Preggers"*

Puck is one of the few characters who doesn't seem to have done the "LIMA loser" math. He never talks of leaving town or having big dreams. He all but embraces the working-poor lifestyle—bussing tables, pumping gas—that Finn speaks of with such horror. Though he intends to support Quinn and the baby, Puck has no real idea of what that means. His idea of ambition is exceeding the low bar set by his father, who was "too crazy and rock-and-roll to be there for his kid" ("Theatricality").

Puck *already* thinks of himself as a winner, you see. He is so secure in this idea of who he is that, unlike Finn, he doesn't cast his mind ahead a few years to consider what having a baby young and staying in Lima forever might mean. When Quinn called him a LIMA loser, it was because of his inability to look forward.

By embracing Finn as a suitable father for her child, Quinn was explicitly saying that he was the winner: whatever it was, this undefined thing Puck had lost, Finn had earned it. By casting them thusly, as loser and winner, she threw Puck's whole identity into question.

Winning. Being a winner. If *Glee* could be said to be about any single thing, it's about that. Everything in this show is a contest. We don't see the kids putting together a yearbook or fundraising for a trip to the Louvre. Everything they do—Cheerios, sports teams, glee club, the fight for popularity, and various romantic rivalries—is a competition. Lima is a war zone, where Will and Sue duke it out for school funding, Will and Ken compete for Emma's heart, and Emma and Terri fight for Will himself.

To the kids in the glee club, winning and getting out of Lima are the same thing. Winning is about expanded horizons, about reaching for opportunities beyond their small slice of America.

Quinn's insult cast Puck as the loser in what he could only see, subconsciously, as a zero-sum game. To be a winner—to get the ill-defined success he had always expected as his due, to be the person he had always believed himself to be—he has to take victory away from his best friend.

It's ironic that Puck let Quinn define winning in these terms. She craves an escape he's never dreamed of, and from what we see of her home life, there's no mystery as to why. But she was speaking to him as someone who had already made the deadliest of LIMA missteps: getting pregnant out of wedlock.

Before the pregnancy, Puck was comfortable in Lima and with himself. Quinn challenged him to be better, to *win*, without specifying what that meant. It's hardly surprising that in the absence of a definition, and not being a deep thinker, he decided it was to become Finn.

Quinn's insult struck at the heart of the boy's friendship. In response, Puck declared war on Finn, immediately razzing the couple about Quinn's pregnancy. It was the first of many attempts on his part to shove the truth into the light, in order to show that he'd gotten what Finn couldn't have—Quinn herself, sexually—and to challenge him for the right to be her partner and the baby's father. But Finn stood up to him and he backpedaled—following the established pattern of their relationship—making this the first of his failures to come right out with it. Puck is selfish, but he's not ruthless. He loves Quinn, but he loves Finn, too. He had just enough remorse that he could not deliver the coup de grâce.

Instead he backed down, waited for the inevitable revelation, and convinced himself that Finn would forgive him.

But why did Puck buy into Quinn's insult so completely? In many ways, he's not second-banana material. Finn is a demonstrably better human being, but Puck has it over him on any number of fronts: he's more athletic, a better musician, and provably smarter. He shows flashes of sensitivity that rival Finn's kindest moments. He's more self-confident and decisive, and better at standing up for himself. As for looks...well, the boy's certainly not lacking for admirers.

As I've said, Finn is the nicer of the two; that's the big difference between them. But there's more to this temperamental gap than meets the eye. What it comes down to, ultimately, is a sense of entitlement.

Finn has grown up knowing that nothing gets handed to him. Puck may have a deadbeat dad, but Finn has no father at all. He has worked since boyhood to make his mother proud of him. His initial response to Quinn's pregnancy is to seek a way to preserve his imagined future as a college student while somehow providing for a family. This goal is selfish and selfless at the same time—he wants to avoid the cage he speaks of to Will, but he knows that by doing so, he will also ensure a better quality of life for his child. If he can pull it off and go to college, he might even keep his unspoken promise to his mom.

Finn is a stand-up guy. He wants to do the right thing *and* be happy, and he understands that getting both these things right will be hard, punitively so. Puck, pre-"Preggers," was content to get away with the wrong thing, figuring that success would fall into his grasp as easily as Quinn had.

One of the first times we saw Puck upset was when he told Mercedes that he was the baby's father—and what was getting under his skin there? Was it that he might never have a relationship with his daughter? No: those feelings came later. What distressed him in that moment was that Finn was winning attention and support that belonged, as Puck saw it, to him.

It is Finn's understanding of the realities of life and his corresponding strength of character that Puck lacks. Deep down, Puck senses this. He finds himself in situations of his own making and wonders if he's out of control; he feels the cost of his lack of restraint, even if he can't quite articulate what's gone wrong or how he screwed up. It is this, more than any star quality of Finn's, that keeps Puck in the number-two position within their dynamic.

Another thing Puck feels entitled to, ironically, is something Finn doesn't have—sex. Getting laid regularly is part of what makes him feel like a winner. He has older lovers. He succeeds in seducing a girl Finn can't get into bed. He literally cannot be bothered to have a conversation with Rachel if he doesn't think there's a chance to get to second base in the offing, and he told Quinn that, pregnant or not, if she wouldn't put out, he was entitled to hook up with any hot, willing girl who came along.

It's a circular argument: I get laid, therefore I'm a winner. I'm a winner, therefore you should sleep with me.

Unlike Finn, who consciously identifies his goals, examines the obstacles, and works to defeat them—all while recognizing that, as the Stones put it, "you can't always get what you want"—Puck just assumes he'll get what he wants. He's a winner, remember?

> ## "Isn't that what you've been drilling into their heads all year? That (the joy of doing what you love) is way more important than winning or losing?"
>
> —Emma, "Journey" (1-22)

It isn't whether you win or lose, we're told as schoolchildren, but how you play the game; and in the season one closer of *Glee*, Emma echoed this advice to Will. There are a million other clichés about winning, too, like "virtue will prevail" or "cheaters never prosper." Even so, the one we saw in action much of the time on *Glee* seemed to be "good guys finish last." As all the competitions and interpersonal battles played out, whether we saw New Directions go up against Vocal Adrenaline, sweet, sensible Emma confronting take-no-prisoners-Terri, or the Puck/Finn smackdown for Quinn's heart, viewers were continually challenged to evaluate whether any of these truisms were, in fact, true. Would the cheaters come out ahead? Were guys like Will and Finn doomed to the shame and humiliation of eternal loserdom, merely because of their good nature? They didn't win Regionals, after all, not even with Sue on their side.

It would be easy to tackle this question in a simple, black-and-white way. Instead, *Glee* took us down a delightfully messy path. Will flirted with his own dark side when he brought in Kristen Chenowyth as a glee club ringer, and when he sabotaged Sue before Nationals. When Puck used "lying and crime" to get money for Quinn in "Wheels," Finn was barely a step above him on the moral high ground; he too faked a disability, and the only difference was that he did so to get a legitimate job.

This may seem like cynicism at first, this idea that the show's nice guys are only *slightly* better people than their competition. But *Glee*'s characters are all human, and flawed, and inconsistent. The difference—in Will's case, in Emma's case, and in Finn's—is in their strength of character.

When the truth about the baby's paternity came out, Finn didn't rejoice at being off the hook. He didn't see the revelation as a chance to go to college without baggage and obligations. He lost a daughter, a lover, and a friend all in one blow, and the only choice he had left was between bailing on Sectionals and sucking up his humiliation— taking a big hit for his team. If anyone was entitled to let New Directions down at that point, it was Finn.

Instead, he did what he always did: dug deeper, worked harder. He powered through. He showed grit, to a heroic degree: the quality that Puck lacks, the one that Quinn's insult had caused Puck to fully recognize and envy, the thing that has always drawn Puck to him.

Self-worth and a knack for doing the right thing have their upside, but they don't do anything to combat loneliness. If the boys had merely been frenemies from the start, Finn would have been better off after he'd jettisoned Puck. But as Puck's star fell, as the reality of fatherhood and facing the consequences of his behavior started to come crashing in on him, Finn too began to suffer, to perceive that void I mentioned earlier, and to behave more Puckishly, as it were, in response. That didn't bring back his missing other self; mostly, it just got him into trouble.

A strange and wonderful chain reaction played out in this first season of *Glee*, and its spark was Terri Schuester, of all people. Will told Emma that Terri was always pushing him to become something more, though he wasn't sure what she meant. It's the same vague challenge that Quinn set for Puck when she called him a LIMA loser.

Will's response to the gauntlet Terri threw down was a far cry from what she probably imagined. Instead of becoming more devoted to her, more financially successful, and more materialistic, he grew from a gifted teacher into a great one. He became the best possible version of himself . . . and along the way, he cast her aside. He also scooped up Finn, whom he saw as a younger version of himself. Will set himself up as a role model, and Finn took him up on it. No matter what happened, no matter how hard he tried to be bad, Finn returned, time and again, to the nice-guy values he shares with Will. By the season's end, he could even say out loud that the father figure he needed was his glee club coach.

And Puck? It was the bad boy himself who stood to benefit most of all. As the season unfolded, he began to show signs of restlessness, a possible desire to grow. Trying to steal Finn's girl led Quinn to belittle him, and that in turn drove him to the failed attempt to steal Finn's identity. By "Laryngitis" (1-18), he was already flailing, and then Mercedes hit him with a new, startling accusation: she told Puck she thought he didn't like the self he'd always seemed so comfortable with, the misbehaving, people-using, thoughtless jerk. And she was right. After a lifetime of thoughtlessly doing as he pleased and thinking well of himself by default, Puck was given just enough opportunity for self-reflection to finally find himself wanting.

After the club's loss at Regionals, Puck made two key admissions: he expressed shame over his bullying of other students, and he told Quinn he loved her. Just as Finn became more solidly like Will, Puck became more like both of them. This maturation was rewarded: Quinn let him witness his daughter's birth, and then name her.

But can he redeem himself in Finn's eyes?

Sometimes when a friendship is broken, there's no fixing it, and it remains to be seen whether there are limits to Finn's nobility. Being hurt affected him, but it didn't destroy his underlying selflessness. He welcomed Jesse into New Directions for Rachel's sake. He tried to set aside his feelings about his dead father to allow his mother a chance at happiness. After the ugly scene with Kurt and Burt Hummel in "Theatricality," he did his best to make it up to him.

As the season and the school year wound down, Finn was facing a lonely summer. The path to dating Rachel might finally be clear, but his mother might yet move in with Burt Hummel, and his former friends on the football team have made it clear that they're looking for a chance to put all the glee kids—and especially their top dog— in their place. If anyone needs a friend, someone to watch his back, it's Finn.

There's still room in his life for a surrogate bad boy. Puck—newly awakened to his own shortcomings, but still far from perfect—was visibly waiting for a chance to reconnect. By the end of the season, the two were slashing tires together, and doing penance for it together. Their issues might be unresolved, the road back is there if the boys care to take it.

Will Finn forgive Puck? The ability to let bygones be bygones is a key indicator of strength and maturity, but few viewers would fault Finn for hanging on to a grudge. There's no compelling reason for Finn to forgive Puck.

But taking a hard line isn't in keeping with his personality. And there's nobody to fill that gap in his life. It was no accident that it was Puck he looked to, instinctively, when Kurt sang a ballad to him in "Home" (1-16).

It seems likely that Finn will let Puck back into his orbit—perhaps not unconditionally, but he'll do it. It's who he his, deep down—not a basketball star, not a glee stud, but an emotionally generous person.

Besides, New Directions has bigger fish to fry: they failed to place at Regionals, and only survived because of Sue's sudden act of mercy. They have yet to triumph, other than morally, at a major competition. The McKinley High Glee Club is going to need all the solidarity it can muster if it's going to keep on singing.

That is what it's going to take, after all, for these kids to come out winners.

• • •

A.M. DELLAMONICA's first novel, the ecofantasy *Indigo Springs*, is on the 2010 Short List for the Sunburst Award. Her short story "A Key to the Illuminated Heretic" was short-listed for the 2005 Sidewise Award and was also on the preliminary Nebula Award ballot. A 2006 Canada Council Grant recipient, Alyx teaches writing through the UCLA Extension Writers' program (www.uclaextension. edu) and writes book reviews for Syfy.com. Dellamonica maintains a website at www.alyxdellamonica.com.

True Colors

share your Glee

Growing up isn't easy, especially for women. The media bombards girls with images telling them how they should look, how they should act, and what they should say. Billboards, commercials, magazines, and television all tell young girls to wear provocative clothing and heavy makeup, never speak too much but always sound sexy, know what you're talking about but don't be too smart. It can be confusing being told that you're beautiful just the way you are, only to have someone add that you'd look even better if you just cut your hair, added lipstick, lost ten pounds, and wore nicer clothes. As girls, we're told it's what's on the inside that counts, but if you're heavy or have acne, you're always going to be alone.

I've never fit in. In primary school I didn't have a ton of friends because I could never find the courage to make them, and by the time high school came around I'd already been labelled a hermit. I'd try to dress differently so I would stand out, but I'd only make myself more transparent. I've never seen myself as exceptionally beautiful, and I've definitely never considered myself to be a catch. I've spent most of my life being overweight, or dealing with acne so severe that I've singlehandedly kept Clearasil in business. I'd like to say I'm smart, but trying to get me to understand anything with numbers is like trying to teach a cow to sing opera: it's not going to happen. I never had the grace or agility other girls my age had, and to this day I'm still a klutz with asthma. If I was asked to use one word to describe myself, up until about six months ago, it would have been "invisible."

I was home late one evening, channel-surfing to kill time, when I heard the opening notes of Journey's "Don't Stop Believing" being belted by some girl. Curious, I hit the return button on my remote and prepared to be disappointed. I doubted anyone could ever do that song justice, so I wanted to get a good look at whoever it was that was making the attempt.

After sitting through the song—and finding myself pleasantly surprised— I watched the whole episode on a different channel a couple hours later. Needless to say, I was hooked on *Glee*, and on two characters in particular: Rachel Berry and Mercedes Jones.

They were smart, they were talented, and, like me, they were single.

Week after week, I'd tune in to see if they'd find someone, because, for a while, that was all that mattered to me. Would they end up with someone special? Would they finally be loved by someone else? Could they get the men of their dreams? I didn't care if they were successful in their glee club, because what did it matter if they were alone?

The more they sang, and the more they got rejected, the more interested I became. I couldn't help but wonder what was wrong with them. Didn't they understand that it didn't matter how many solos they had? If Mercedes just lost some weight and Rachel just learned to stop talking so much, they'd finally be happy. For such smart women, why couldn't they see what they were doing wrong?

Continued next page

Then one Tuesday night, something clicked. All episode long I'd watched Rachel Berry try to change who she was and how she looked so Finn would finally notice her. She swapped her skirts and knee-high socks for a skin-tight outfit, and I thought she was finally going to get the man she loved. But it turned out that the real Rachel was the one Finn liked best.

And you know what? I was relieved. While New Directions was singing "True Colors," as cliché as it might sound, I realized why I'd been so obsessed with Rachel and Mercedes.

They knew they weren't perfect, they knew they could change to be like every other girl, but they chose not to. Why? Because they were beautiful just the way they were, and they shouldn't have to change for someone else to love them. Because if they had, then they wouldn't have been themselves anymore, and isn't that what's important? If we can't be happy with who we are, then how are we ever going to be happy with someone else? Maybe the moral of the story isn't that to find happiness, we need to find a boyfriend. Maybe it's that to be happy, we need to find ourselves.

I still don't consider myself to be exceptionally beautiful. Because of *Glee* I haven't miraculously found the key to fitting in or getting rid of acne. I haven't fallen in love with some white knight, or suddenly found the courage to get on-stage and burst into song. But I know who I want to be: myself.

And I'm pretty okay with that.

Acne and all.

CAITLIN MARCEAU
Montreal, Quebec, Canada

MARIA LIMA

Don't Make Me Over:
Mercedes and Tina

"The whole point of the club is about expressing
what's really inside you."
—*Mercedes "Acafellas," (1-4)*

FELL IN LOVE WITH *GLEE* on the first airing of the original
pilot, several months prior to the actual airdate for the show.
For me, no matter how much I enjoyed the dynamics among
the four major teen players, the show wasn't about Rachel, the
over-the-top Jewish American Princess diva with two dads; nor
was it about Finn, the jock turned choirboy, nor even about Puck
and Quinn and their baby drama. It was about the others, the ones
singing backup: Kurt, Artie, Mercedes, and Tina, the ones who truly
embodied the role of the outsiders. *Glee* is about identity. Whether
it was Will Schuester (a.k.a. Mr. Schue) discovering his own self-
expression by coaching the show choir, or Sue Sylvester, award-
winning coach of the Cheerios, finding that trophies could be cold

bedfellows, the show's first season was about discovering one's true individuality and one's place in the world, whether that world is McKinley High or the adult world. It's no coincidence that the show started with a Journey song ("Don't Stop Believin'" in "Pilot," 1-1), ended with a Journey medley ("Journey," 1-22), and used road metaphors in several episode titles. This entire season's theme was one of exploration and pilgrimage, of finding out who each character really was—though also ostensibly about striving to win Regionals and take home that pretty, pretty trophy.

By exploring the unexpected depths of each of its characters, *Glee* illustrates how easy it is to misperceive others. But the show also illustrates how the lure of the gold star sticker or a ridiculously enormous trophy can deceive us, too. Winning isn't really what life or happiness is all about. The hot boyfriend and the prestigious place on the cheerleading squad can all disappear in a moment, leaving a person broken and alone, like Quinn. The gorgeous shiny trophy can be smashed against a wall to lie in pieces, like a broken heart. The questions *Glee* tried to answer in its first season were: Are you strong enough to stand on your own? Can you be proud of yourself without needing the prop of those ephemeral emotional crutches? For two of my favorite characters, that answer is "Hell, yeah."

Sure, at first glance, all the audience saw was the stereotypes for the backup characters: the gay kid, the boy in the wheelchair, the fat and sassy black girl, and the shy Asian girl. But as with everything about *Glee*, there was much more to those characters than what we saw on the surface. The writers gave us backstories, episodes focusing on more than just the cool kids (Quinn, Puck) or the ones singing solos (Rachel, Finn); in fact, it was the cool kids who got their comeuppance (but eventually learned real lessons), while the sidekicks blossomed and ended up in places of strength.

From the very beginning, my faves were always Mercedes and Tina, who shone from the sidelines and made a place in my heart. They're definitely my girls, the ones I (and probably most viewers) can relate to. Most of us were never pregnant cheerleaders or overly ambitious budding starlets in high school. We weren't the top of the heap, nor were we homecoming hotties—we were just people, with issues and problems, and, especially during those school years, most of us had no clue how to leverage the talents we did have. We were the ones often overlooked and "trotted out to wail the last note" ("Power of Madonna," 1-15), but never the lead. In the story of our lives, we, like Mercedes and Tina, were often the Zeppos—a term coined by *Buffy the Vampire Slayer*'s popular girl Cordelia Chase to describe Xander Harris' non-essential sidekick role, and taken from the name of the fourth, often overlooked, Marx Brother. We were never the stars. But without the Zeppo—just ask Xander—the world would be a different and less interesting place. Without these two talented young women, *Glee* would be just another boring *High School Musical* of a TV show, featuring too-pretty-to-be-real teens, always popular and well-liked. Mercedes and Tina are the "everyman"—the ones who epitomize the struggle for identity, the fight to discover one's true self that every one of us goes through, no matter our own ethnic and cultural backgrounds.

Both girls spent the season as works in progress, growing into themselves in ways that were even more valuable to me than the more obvious transformations of Rachel, Finn, Quinn, and even Will Schuester, because Mercedes' and Tina's struggles to be more than what they thought they were were more realistic, more personal, than the others' advancement. Mercedes' and Tina's growth was, for many episodes, almost behind the scenes, as they began the season as the invisible girls—something that, if it hadn't been for their unique styles and their gradual path into the limelight thanks to glee club, they probably would have remained. By the end of the first season, both girls shone, no longer generic sidekicks but valued members of the choir, both of whom were accepted and supported by the rest of the gang; no longer invisible, but each a necessary part of the larger whole.

A lot of viewers will remember how Joss Whedon wrote *Buffy* as a quintessential high school metaphor: high school is hell. In *Glee*, and for Mercedes and Tina, the monsters aren't vampires or demons but their fellow students, their reputations, the usual pressures of high school, as seen through the lens of this over-the-top show choir. Mercedes and Tina are more Willow and Xander than Buffy and Cordelia: they're the quintessential sidekicks fighting for identity, for their own well-deserved place in the sun...or at least on the auditorium stage.

During the most difficult time of life, when fitting in is absolutely essential, Mercedes and Tina, already a bit off the beaten drum path, exposed themselves to even more possible humiliation to do the thing they each love. (And Buffy thought *she* had it hard fighting demons! At least when she killed a demon, it generally didn't come back the next day to fight her again.) But no matter how hard Mercedes and Tina tried, especially in the first half of the season, they were still not part of the "in" crowd. Question is, did they really want to be? In the second half of the season, the answer to that seemed to be in the affirmative—especially as we viewers experienced Mercedes' meteoric rise to popularity...and then her almost immediate decision to dump the trappings and return to being who she was meant to be. Tina's growth was less obvious, but by the end of "Theatricality" (1-20), she, too, had attempted and then rejected the idea of changing herself to fit in.

But why them? What makes each of these girls so unique and her path so illustrative of the show's overarching message?

Mercedes Jones: Rhythm and Blues

"In some of us, there is a spark...we call it drive."
—*Mercedes-Benz ad*

Her name says it all—Mercedes: a classic luxury brand standing for consistency and absolute class; Jones: an everyman's name, not quite as generic as Smith, but pretty darn close. It's hard to remember, now, the Mercedes we met in *Glee*'s pilot. Our gal Mercedes was a walking contradiction in the first part of the season: sassy, savvy, and not afraid to show it, but at the same time afraid that there was no one out there for her (so much so that she sometimes missed the obvious, such as Kurt's sexual preference, misunderstanding his offer of friendship). Mercedes was the girl who so many of us were in school, bravado tempered by insecurity. She was confident about her singing, but unsure about almost everything else. When she joined the Cheerios, her eagerness to fit in overwhelmed her brilliant "I am woman" attitude, and she bought into the "you must lose weight; you must suffer to look great, to fit in" mantra so many teens (and still many adult women) buy into in today's Western society. Thank goodness that an unlikely rescue by Quinn Fabray brought Mercedes back to herself and led to her performance of "Beautiful" in front of the entire school ("Home," 1-16). This bold and brilliant action moved the once-reviled glee club nerd into the spotlight she so longed for: popularity. In fact, a couples of episodes later, Mercedes supplanted Quinn's place as the "it" gal, and her popularity was so shiny and bright that Puck (after the loss of his trademark mohawk) decided to date her to get some of his mojo back in "Laryngitis" (1-18). She'd gained the ground she wanted, without having to compromise her sense of self (or so she thought, for a few episodes). Instead of being downtrodden and put upon, Mercedes rose beyond the slushie facials to become someone to lean on—to become the person with the hard answers.

In "Home," Mercedes completely changed the dynamic in her friendship with Kurt, becoming the hard taskmaster who held him to a higher standard. As *Glee* fan Sanj said in her post-episode blog entry:

> Enter Mercedes, who is thank GOD a moral compass for him. And for herself. So when Kurt's messed-up priorities (power, popularity) screw up why they've joined the Cheerios (more performances, representing for themselves), it's Mercedes—with a very crucial assist from Quinn—who remembers that her and Kurt's job is not to buy into the system, but to speak truth to power. It's Mercedes who would have to rewrite herself, in this

case, to fit in. (In much the same way, Kurt resents feeling like he's made to do with his father, actually.) But Mercedes doesn't and won't—even when she's not actually sure that Kurt has her back.[1]

It's this version of Mercedes that won in every way: she grew from the extremely shy gal who hid her shyness behind the sassy exterior, asking for only a little R.E.S.P.E.C.T. (in her audition song in the pilot), to the young woman who now knows who she is and how to be that person—and who can now help others, like Kurt and like Puck (dissatisfied with his regained position at the top of the high school heap), discover who *they* are and want to be. "It was fun, I guess, but when I put the uniform on, I didn't feel like myself. It's not who I am," she told Sue when she turned her Cheerios uniform in, adding, "Glee club's taught me something very important...You have to be true to who you are" ("Laryngitis"). Mercedes embodied that wish of every high school girl in existence—to grow up and grow through the self-doubt, the angst, the yearning to be someone you're not— and survived. She climbed that first road, completed that first part of the journey to adulthood, to self-realization.

Tina Cohen-Chang: Color My World

**"It's my thing that makes me cool. You know,
that makes me unique. I'm Car Guy. Guy with the car."**
—*Xander, Buffy the Vampire Slayer,* "The Zeppo" (3-13)

Even more than Mercedes, Tina was an invisible girl, hiding in the shadows. In glee, as we can assume in the rest of her school life, Tina's presence is often overwhelmed by the overbearing egos of others. Yet her desire to stand out is clear. Choosing goth dress in

---

[1] See http://sanj.dreamwidth.org/427209.html.

Middle America and faking a stutter to mask her shyness don't help her blend in; they make her stand out. Before glee club, there was no crowd that Tina was a part of, and unlike Mercedes, it's hard to imagine Tina giving up her personal style to be popular. But is that because she doesn't want to be one of the cool kids, or because she is afraid of being rejected? Her dark clothes scream "ignore me." The only really colorful things about her are the streaks in her hair and the occasional splash of a colorful shirt or leggings. It is as if that choice of intermittent brightness is trying to accentuate the part of her that badly wants out and is begging to be seen, but instead just emphasizes the shadows she lives in.

When she did get a chance to stand out in "Preggers" (1-4), she freaked. With Mr. Schue wanting to shake things up, Tina was given a chance to solo, to sing the quintessential love song "Tonight" from *West Side Story*. At first happy, then unsure, finally Tina told Mr. Schue to give the song to Rachel—that Tina would, as she put it, "take one for the team." Though Mr. Schue ended up giving the solo back to Tina, despite Rachel's threats to quit, we never got to see Tina perform the entire song in front of an audience or as part of a production number.

In fact, the only other time Tina led a song was in "Hairography" (1-11), where she sang "True Colors," a song about empowerment and inclusion...yet still a quiet, mellow tune, far from the power ballads and strong vocal statements of Mercedes or Rachel. Even in leadership, Tina remained somewhat in the background, less a leader and more a uniter. She continued to stand slightly to the side of everyone else, meshing beautifully with the ensemble but never really carving out her own place.

There was a slight glimpse of a more actively rebellious Tina in her audition song, "I Kissed a Girl" ("Pilot"), but it was obvious that her performance in the audition was no more than onetime bravado—the musical equivalent of her stutter or the streaks in her hair, another way to keep people at a distance so they couldn't reject her. She actively chooses to be an outsider. In fact, the only two songs she did get to lead underscore her very sense of being an outsider.

In "Tonight," as performed in *West Side Story*, the character of Maria, a Puerto Rican foreigner, sings about how on this night, she's going to finally be happy. She's cut off from her homeland, her people are derided by the other residents of New York, but this night (waiting for her love) is different. How appropriate this song is for Tina, the goth Asian, who, in getting her own solo, is finally getting "her night." In "True Colors," a song first made popular by Cyndi Lauper (one of the eighties' sartorial trailblazers), Tina sings about how "the darkness inside you / can make you feel so small." The songs *Glee*'s characters sing often convey their innermost thoughts; was this Tina's cry from the heart? One can only assume that it is truly how she sometimes feels—small, lost, outside of the accepted norm, yet wanting to include and be included. Both of Tina's lead numbers resonate with hope, yet both also speak of yearning for something, someone, to allow their singers to shine.

"She's really quiet, really shy," says Jenna Ushkowitz, the actress who plays Tina, in an interview on fancast.com. "You see her smile when she's performing because that's really where her happiness lies. I think she's got a lot of layers—people may say, 'Oh, she's the gothic one, she's not going to be happy,' but I think there's a lot of happiness underneath." And that's exactly where Tina's personality shone for me. The happy places underscored by the quiet, shy parts make her so much more interesting and complex than if she'd just been the rebellious goth gal her audition song and dress indicated her to be.

But it wasn't until "The Power of Madonna" that Tina really began to break out of her shell—and stand up for herself. Her incredible speech to Artie was nearly a 180-degree attitude change from "Wheels" (1-9), when she admitted to him that she'd faked her stutter to get out of doing a speech in sixth grade: "My eyes...are up here. I am a person with feelings. Get out of my grill. I am a powerful woman, and my growing feminism will cut you in half like a righteous blade of equality."

In "Theatricality," she first went along with Principal Figgins' new edict regarding her goth gear, but found that dressing like all the other kids (for those values of "all" that equal hoodies and jeans) made her feel like an "Asian Branch Davidian." As with Mercedes' own epiphany—first joining Cheerios to be popular and fit in, then rejecting the costume for her own style—Tina also had her identity stripped from her. In Tina's conformist clothing, it was as if she were diminished, a part of the cult of high school, nothing more than another cog in the machine led by the quintessential "don't rock the boat" man, Principal Figgins. It wasn't until the show choir expressed their Lady Gaga selves that Tina finally clued in to what she really wanted and who she really *was*. Only by having her outward self (her signature clothing) taken away was she able to realize that this was authority she couldn't bow to. No longer the shy girl, she used Principal Figgins' inferred fear of vampires to scare him into letting her wear her "lady-demon clothes," once again donning the outward plumage that made a bold and very strong statement: "I am who I am."

I get the feeling that Tina wants to be...not popular, exactly, but genuinely liked and appreciated for her uniqueness—which explains her style. She doesn't want to be like all those other kids from the fly-over states—or, at least, what many of us think people like them are like: white, middle-class, boring. Tina wants to have her own style, her own purpose, just like Mercedes; but opposite to her choir colleague, Tina's style isn't as easily embraced by the mainstream. Like her hair, it's dark, with just a touch of color. In an interview with the *New York Post* in April 2010, Jenna Ushkowitz confirmed: "No, Tina knows who she is, and the goth thing is a part of how she expresses herself. So that won't go away...She's still shy, and her clothes are one of the only ways for her to show who she is."

The Road Goes On

Mercedes and Tina began the show as stereotypes: the sassy black girl and the quiet Asian. But as we've come to know them, and they've come to know themselves, they've risen above their own stereotypes, their fears, and their insecurities to find inner strength and purpose of soul. They don't need trophies or popularity. They stand tall, flying their freak flags proudly. They've accepted their uniqueness, risen above the need to worry about what other students think, and begun a new journey—to shaping the adults they'll become.

At the GLAAD awards, *Glee* creator Ryan Murphy said, "We are using the show in a great way…We have a great responsibility…" For me, and I'm sure for many happy Gleeks, the show has lived up to that responsibility. As we watched our favorite characters change, grow, and become more, we rejoiced in their triumphs and reveled in their happiness. *Glee*, by showing us Mercedes' and Tina's journeys, along with the journeys of all the main cast members, illustrates that important message: sometimes the uncool kids get to win, too—not the gold-colored trophy that's really just cheap plastic, but instead the immeasurable but oh-so-important prize of self-esteem, self-respect, and a sense of one's own place in the universe. That kind of win beats the heck out of all the gold stars in the world.

• • •

MARIA LIMA is a writing geek with one foot in the real world and the other in the make-believe. Her Blood Lines series (Pocket Books) is set in the Texas Hill Country—a fabulous place for things that go bump in the night. Maria loves to read, write, and watch genre TV and feels very lucky that people actually pay her to do at least one of these things. Even though her last name is Lima and she once lived in Ohio, she's never participated in show choir, though she's been known to let her own freak flag fly. Visit her at www.marialima.com.

My Life to the Tune of *Glee*

Even though I'm in my thirties, *Glee* appeals to that teen hiding somewhere inside me. The first time I watched the show, it not only validated the way I viewed my entire high school existence—it was hard, unfair at times and just plain awkward—but also made my teen years look like a total breeze.

Instead of sticky slushies, mean-spirited teachers, and unplanned pregnancies, my threats were spitballs, glued lockers, bad hair days, and unreciprocated crushes. One saving grace was that, like Quinn, in addition to loving my time in glee club, I found myself on the varsity cheerleading squad.

Part geek, part cool.

More importantly, *Glee* has made me realize my life, like a movie or an episode of the show, has a unique soundtrack that symbolizes the important events: a personal musical. Today, when I look back, I can pinpoint a song that represents each important milestone for me. Lyrics that describe my individual journey.

Basically, I can sum up my life in less than a thousand notes.

When I was little, it was Kermit singing "The Rainbow Connection." As a teen, it was "Let's Hear it for the Boys." When I started college, it became "Welcome to the Jungle." My first job could only be summarized as "Opportunities" by the Pet Shop Boys. When I got married, "Someone Like You" swept me off my feet. Now, as I embark on my dream of being a published writer, "The Climb" strikes just the right chord.

Every day, every event in my life, can be summarized in a few bars. Played to the perfect note. Expressed by the right lyrics. Having this montage of songs reminds me of the good and the bad times in my life. It highlights the things that have defined my journey. The moments that truly matter.

Glee has taught me that life is like a song. A few bad notes here and there, but a great tune in the end.

S.R. JOHANNES
Atlanta, Georgia

JANINE HIDDLESTONE

Minorities R Us

"New Directions" in Diversity

YOU GUYS look like the world's worst Benetton ad!" declared glee club newcomer April Rhodes, looking at the group members seated in a row in "The Rhodes Not Taken" (1-5). (They looked perturbed, unsure whether to be offended, probably unaware that it was a cutting reference to the multicultural advertisements popular with the fashion house during the 1990s.) She wasn't wrong: New Directions boasts at least one member each of multiple racial minorities, in addition to representatives of several other less commonly addressed groups that are routinely discriminated against in society. Like Benetton ads, anti-racist social statements that are also intended to sell fashion, the mixed nature of the ensemble serves a dual purpose: the characters' diversity allows the show to comment on social issues while also providing the chief source of its humor and drama.

The idea of choosing to base a show around a school show choir must have been as risky as it was inspired and original. (One can only imagine how *that* pitch went: "...and every ten minutes they burst into song!") While there is no doubt that the popularity of *High School Musical* and *Hannah Montana* demonstrated the existence of a market for music-centered productions, it was surely a different matter to move away from the Zac Efron/Miley Cyrus/Disney style to a more mature view of high school and society in general. In *Glee*, life is messy, confusing, and often challenging—and not just for the students. It is difficult not to love these characters, even when we hate their behavior, because deep down we are all a lot like them: complicated, lonely, and desperate to sing show tunes. Their sense of their own difference, driven by sex or race or other factors, is one of the reasons we are able to identify with them so easily. And while that hasn't prevented *Glee*'s writers from using racial, sexual, and other stereotypes to drive the show's humor, the use of stereotypes is better understood as a way for *Glee* to poke fun at itself while also dealing meaningfully with the complex issue of stereotyping in minority representation.

It's easy to take *Glee*'s more stereotype-oriented humor at face value—as mean-spirited, or even as a gesture toward equality (as Sue protested when Will accused her of being too mean to a Cheerio with Down syndrome in practice, "I bully everybody"). But that would sell *Glee*, and its approach to minority issues, short. At first glance, it seems as if the show was attempting to create a diverse cast of characters through tokenism. The initial incarnation of New Directions in the pilot includes a token African American, Asian American, gay person, disabled person, and, well, Rachel. But it soon became clear that *Glee* would not be so easily defined. What appeared to be tokenism was soon shown to be satirizing that very idea.

From the very first episode, the glee club is established as a group of "social misfits." They were desperate to get Finn Hudson, captain of the football team and all-around jock, to join and stay in the group—not just because of his talent, but because he is popular and mainstream; they hoped he would raise their profile and attract other students. He was, for all intents and purposes, their "great white hope"—a token minority himself, thanks to his popularity as well as his race. His joining the group ultimately did bring in more participants, but it did nothing to improve the group's popularity, and it actually created even more diversity (only two of the new members, Quinn and Brittany, are white).

In "Throwdown" (1-7), the club's diversity was put front and center. Sue—having manipulated herself into position as co-director of New Directions with Will—split the club, choosing all the minority members to be in her group, in an effort to create division and tension after Quinn (head cheerleader and Sue's spy) reported to Sue that "the minority students don't feel like they're being heard." Sue's announcement of her group was both horrible and hilarious: "Santana, Wheels, gay kid, Asian, other Asian, Aretha, Shaft." She then proclaimed piously that "I won't be part of a group that ignores the needs of minorities." (She rather undermined this last statement by concluding, "I like minorities so much that I'm thinking of moving to California to become one," obviously a jibe aimed at the state's growing Hispanic population.) Her ploy to divide the club was initially quite successful, and, taking things to comically bizarre lengths, she even coaxed Puck and Brittany into her group by convincing them that Will wasn't sensitive to Puck's Judaism or Brittany's Dutch heritage—leaving Will with only three students (one of whom, Rachel, is *also* Jewish). Ironically, Rachel, Finn, and Quinn had become the actual minority.

The glee club is more diverse than the average Ohio population; this is obviously done intentionally and has a satirical quality: the town and the school are very mid-western in character, but the glee club is not. A glance at the 2010 census statistics for Ohio illustrates the liberties taken in the composition of the club. Ohio's population has a higher proportion of whites than the U.S. average (84.8 percent versus 79.8 percent), and although the parity in those identified as black is almost identical, the story for Asians and Latinos/Hispanics is very different. Asians make up an average of 4.5 percent of the U.S. population, but that figure falls to 1.6 percent in Ohio; despite this, there are two Asian Americans in the glee club. (And apparently the only two obstetricians in the town—Dr. Wu and Dr. Chin—are also of Asian descent. Another satirical stab at stereotypes?) But the biggest difference is in those of Hispanic or Latino origin, with Ohio having only 2.6 percent, against the national figure of 15.4 percent. In this regard, *Glee* does seem to reflect reality, with Santana as the sole Hispanic character. Even the school's Spanish teacher, idealistic glee club director Will Schuester, is white.

Will's job is of course derided by Sue, who believes that the students only need Spanish "if they want to become dishwashers and gardeners," once again taking a satirical stab at the stereotypes common in media representations. Jokes like Sue's highlight and then make fun of minority status, and the ability to do so is a difficult—and frequently controversial—balancing act. But *Glee's* ability to deliver the wink and nod manages to be charming even when the viewers feel that they should be cringing. Football coach Ken Tanaka's plea to Emma Pillsbury that he is worthy dating material in part because he will never lose his job due to his minority status tugged at the heart strings while simultaneously producing an awkward smile. Cheerleading coach Sue Sylvester's blackmail of Principal Figgins over a video advertising pressure stockings for Mumbai Airlines—which made fun of his Indian origins—was both cringe-worthy and hysterical. The storylines featuring the competition between McKinley High, the Jane Addams Academy girls' reform school, and the Haverbrook School for the Deaf struck a similar balance. While both were mocked to some extent ("Speak up! Deaf in this ear—scarlet fever as a child" ["Hairography," 1-11]), the issues faced by these groups were also acknowledged and embraced with respect and dignity, allowing *Glee* to avoid accusations of insensitivity or ridicule.

However, the way *Glee* most often gets away with using minority status for humor is, as with its treatment of tokenism, by pushing its minority representations to extremes. The show's characters are often stereotyped to the point of satire, as with Kurt Hummel's gay theatrics ("Get me to a day spa—stat!") and Mercedes Jones' loud-black-girl, soul-singer street smarts. Puck's mother berated him for not having a Jewish girlfriend (during their annual viewing of *Schindler's List*), sending him into fellow Jew Rachel's arms for a short, nonsensical fling and reiterating the cliché of Jewish mothers and guilt. Brittany's dumb-blonde persona almost defies belief ("I'm pretty sure my cat's been reading my diary"). But by pushing the minority stereotypes in particular so far that they become ridiculous, *Glee* turns the joke around, making fun instead of those who assign and believe those stereotypes to begin with. Just as the stereotyping tips into the ridiculous—"It's bad enough that my Sue's Kids are living in squalor and probably on food stamps"—it swings back to reality. "My dad's a dentist!" Mercedes interjected in response to Sue's non-sensical claim in "Throwdown." The show is just as likely to defy stereotypes in pursuit of humor as it is to employ them. And both tactics prove equally effective in highlighting those stereotypes' fundamental inefficiency, as they often mislead, locking people into categorization and denying the possibility of individuality.

After all, in *Glee*, things are rarely as straightforward as they seem. Even Sue's overly aggressive ambition and villainy is occasionally in question—never more obviously than in "Wheels" (1-9). Having been forced to hold open tryouts for the Cheerios, Sue accepted Becky, a teenager with Down syndrome, who appeared to have little talent by Sue's usual measures. We, like Will, were suspicious, convinced that Sue was up to something vile. Will thought he had caught her out when he overheard her pushing Becky during training, but Sue silenced him by saying that Becky just wanted to be treated like a normal student. At the episode's end we saw Sue visit her sister Jean—who also has Down syndrome and is living in an institution—and witnessed Sue's obvious affection and lack of condescension toward her. It was a short but significant deviation from Sue as the stereotypical villain.

This was not the only moment of revelation in "Wheels," or the only message about the struggle for understanding and acceptance for those with disabilities. Although the club appeared to treat and accept the wheelchair-bound Artie Abrams as an equal, "Wheels" highlighted the everyday difficulties that both his fellow glee club members and most of us watching at home take for granted. Because the bus they'd planned to take to Sectionals wasn't equipped for a wheelchair, Will told the club that Artie would have to travel with his father rather than with the rest of the team. The rest of the club seemed content with this inequitable situation—until Will forced them to spend some time in wheelchairs and they came to understand what Artie has to deal with every day. The show mined this situation for entertainment (even having New Directions perform a number in wheelchairs), while also showing the growth in understanding of the other glee club members. (Still, just in case the audience was being lulled by the good vibes and message of inclusion, the show managed a knowing wink when Rachel helped Finn get a job by pretending he was wheelchair-bound and threatening to get her gay lawyer fathers to sue the establishment for discrimination if they didn't hire him.)

While Artie's disability is an obvious one, the show highlights other characters' less overt struggles, such as Tina's stutter (which proved to be fake, but based on a pathological shyness) and Emma's mental health issues. Emma's struggles might be part of a series of running gags (my favorite of which is the grape polishing), but *Glee* focuses on the more serious side of living with OCD as well: Emma realized her illness was getting in the way of attaining a fulfilling relationship and eventually began to go to counseling. However, despite her challenges, Emma has a career she loves and at which she excels, demonstrating that a mental illness need not prevent one from living a full life any more than Artie's inability to walk does.

Generally, when *Glee* defies stereotypes, it does so for dramatic effect (as with Emma) more often than for humor. In television and film, characters with disabilities (particularly physical ones) are often portrayed as strong and accepting of their situation—either that or self-destructively angry. The former is certainly the manner in which the audience saw Artie, at least for the first eighteen episodes. However, in "Dream On" (1-19), Artie revealed that he dreamed of one day being able to dance. Tina attempted to help by showing him research about advances in stem cell research and choreographing a dance number for the two of them to perform; Artie became caught up in the idea, and his dream sequence, in which he danced, ran, and jumped with so much energy and spirit, was only fractionally less heartbreaking than the final scene in which he could sing but only watch as Matt took his place and danced with Tina. Artie's ongoing struggle to deal with his disability is complex and, in "Dream

On," very relatable in a way that lends his experience more dramatic weight.

Another of the shows poignant scenes dealing with a minority-based issue—this time the more controversial issue of sexual preference—occurred in "Preggers" (1-4), after Kurt's triumphant football debut, when his father Burt came to congratulate him. Kurt gathered his courage—fed by adrenaline and his father's pride—and announced that he is gay. To the surprise of the audience (not to mention Kurt), his father didn't seem at all shocked: "Oh, I know. I've known since you were three—all you wanted was sensible heels." Burt made it clear he'd prefer it wasn't so, but that he still loves his son. Here, the break with stereotype was not Kurt's, but his father's. Up until that point, Burt had been the very embodiment of the blue-collar "man's man," almost the anti-homosexual prototype. He owns and runs a garage. He

> **Art Imitates Life**
>
> Zack Weinstein, who played quadriplegic Sean Fretthold in "Laryngitis" (1-18), is paralyzed himself. He suffered a spinal cord injury during a canoe trip in college that left him without the use of his legs or hands. He still hopes to be a working actor; *Glee* was his first professional role.

loves football. He is taken aback by his son's approach to fashion, his love of the theater, and his attitude toward skin care, and he has made attempts to discourage these. But, ultimately, Burt knows who his son is, and he supports him no matter what—whether that means going to bat for him by convincing Figgins and Mr. Schuester to let Kurt challenge Rachel for a "female" lead vocal (despite threatening phone calls at the garage) in "Wheels," or putting his son ahead of his romantic hopes with Finn's mother by evicting Finn from his home for behaving offensively about Kurt's sexuality in "Theatricality" (1-20). Burt was even the one to put an end to Kurt's attempts to seem more masculine when Burt and Finn bonded over their mutual love of football. Burt told Kurt to be true to himself, and that he would always love him, regardless of his choices in life.

Being true to oneself—and finding acceptance for that—is a continuing theme in *Glee*, and perhaps the show's most important one. Often, the characters' search for acceptance takes the form of the search for popularity—the desire to be one of the "cool kids." This is particularly true for Finn and Quinn, who began the season at the top of the social ladder. After joining New Directions, Finn's position in the school hierarchy was threatened, and by the middle of the season he and Quinn had fallen so far that they ended up getting slushie facials alongside the rest of the club. They even visited guidance counselor Emma for tips on reviving their popularity. (Emma suggested that being popular might not be as important as being accepted for being themselves, but when this advice was rejected, she proposed they wear dark sunglasses like celebrities—a poke at the capricious nature of popularity.) Puck, too, found that his social worth had plummeted, so much so that he decided he should date then-popular Mercedes in order to regain it (though with him, as with Quinn, there were other factors involved—hairstyle change and pregnancy, respectively).

The show deals with this misconception—that acceptance will bring popularity and vice versa—over and over again. Mercedes herself found a degree of popularity through joining the Cheerios, but could not find acceptance: in "Home" (1-16), she struggled to fulfill Sue's expectations in regard to her weight, and when she decided to leave the Cheerios in "Laryngitis" (1-18), she told Sue that "It's just not who I am." Like Quinn, Mercedes learned that being a cheerleader came at a cost—not remaining true to herself.

While being oneself always seems to come at the expense of one's popularity in *Glee*, the show emphasizes its other benefits, including the value of being accepted for who you really are and not having to pretend. Being a Cheerio may come with strings attached, but belonging to glee club does not.

What does this have to do with minority issues? While more than half of the club could be identified as members of standard minority groups, I would argue that all of them, through their roles as social outcasts, reflect the challenges faced by minorities. They are discriminated against because they're in glee club, because they are members of an unpopular group. But they are still a group, one that does not condition membership on conforming to society's definition of who or what (or what color or orientation) they should be. In "Acafellas" (1-3), when the club hired famous choreographer Dakota Stanley, he immediately rejected those who are "different"—or, as he stated so eloquently, "misfits, spazheads, and cripples." The group stood up to him (Finn and Rachel in particular), and ultimately fired him. The situation, which Sue had engineered in order to divide the glee club kids, instead brought them closer together—united against a common enemy (normalcy?). They realized that they're a group not *in spite* of their differences but *because* of them. Who they are, whether that makes them popular or not, is the source of their strength, not just as individuals, but as a whole.

The idea of strength in unity and diversity was demonstrated again in "Theatricality," when the group came together—dressed in various hysterical incarnations of Lady Gaga and Kiss—to support Finn and Kurt against bullies. (Imagine explaining being beaten up by teenagers in sequins, makeup, and platform heels!) Despite that triumphant moment, Rachel voiced regret that they were still outcasts. But Mercedes proclaimed, "We are freaks," and it was concluded that this was a good thing, a positive outcome (as Finn said, "All freaks together.") Will highlighted this issue in "Throwdown," admitting to Sue that "in hindsight, you were right to shine the spotlight on the fact that these kids are minorities," and telling the kids, "You're *all* minorities—you're in the glee club. There are only twelve of you, and all you have is each other."

Herein lies the premise behind *Glee's* attitude toward minority groups. What at first glance looked like tokenism and stereotyping became a lesson in inclusion and acceptance. Whether it is Dr Wu and his bonsai plants, bitchy cheerleaders, or the dumbest blonde to ever grace television screens ("I forgot how to leave"), *Glee's* stereotypes aim not only to amuse, but also to educate—with the rare talent of not becoming preachy in the process.

There's nothing new about highlighting minority issues on television; inclusion has become a common theme in recent years. But few television shows have managed to successfully avoid "issue of the week" sermonizing, and it's even rarer that shows have been able to make fun of themselves and their attitudes toward minorities without either causing offense or becoming too edgy for mainstream viewers. *Glee* takes on serious issues, but never forgets that its main reason for being is to entertain, somehow managing to be satirical, lovable, occasionally dramatic, and always a lot of fun. While the satirical style of *Glee*'s various approaches to attitudes and representations does not conceal the sweetness of its heart, the show retains enough biting humor and adult sensibility to avoid the treacle trap.

By questioning the standard television norms, by leaving no sacred cow untouched, by flouting the accepted differences and similarities of the marginalized and the mainstream, *Glee* manages to break through the barriers created by minority stereotypes. This is expanded further by the notion that minorities are not just about race, gender, sexuality, or ability—but are also the basis of inclusion and belonging. We are all minorities in some way, just as we all are part of the human race.

Creator Ryan Murphy freely admits that *Glee* delights in challenging ingrained social ideas. Discussing "Wheels," which he referred to as a "game changer" episode in a November 2009 interview with the *Los Angeles Times*, he highlighted the point that "this is a comedy, first and foremost. But we see the obligation to go deeper. This isn't just a genre show to me. It's about the desperate need for a place in the world and how we all fit in and how hard it is for some people to get by."

Despite the fondness that the members of the McKinley High glee club have inspired, and the considerable Gleek culture already sweeping viewers, *Glee* is still in its infancy in television terms, with only one season under its belt. We fans can only hope for a continuation of the catchy tunes and sharp wit that has catapulted the show

to such popularity. But equally as important is a continued empha-
sis on diversity and acceptance. The more we learn about those who
are different than us, the more we see how much we are really all the
same. Ultimately, whatever our origins, lifestyles, beliefs, or abilities,
what we all want most is to belong. And that's a tune to which we
can all hum along.

• • •

JANINE HIDDLESTONE is a lecturer and tutor in politics, history,
and communications at James Cook University in Australia. She
has a PhD in political history and has published articles about the
place of war in culture and history, and how pop culture became
the centerpiece of so much of the public's understanding—and
misunderstanding—of events. She has explored the influence of
technology on pop culture and vice versa, and its pedagogical
uses in encouraging students to develop an interest in political
and historical issues. She has also attained infamy among her
colleagues as a pop culture tragic.

Not Just a River in Egypt

L IKE MOST MUSICALS, *Glee* portrays a heightened reality. To enjoy the show is to suspend our disbelief and accept that we cannot take everything we see literally. When Kurt performed "Rose's Turn" ("Laryngitis," 1-18), for example, he began singing in the school hallway, was magically transported to a stage that featured his name in lights, and then returned to (so-called) reality, where his dad applauded him. Other songs take place inside characters' imaginations: when Mercedes smashed Kurt's windscreen in anger in "Acafellas" (1-3), the school carwash became the scene of an impromptu performance of "Bust Your Windows," with the Cheerios as improbably well-rehearsed backup dancers. Then we saw Mercedes, the cheerleaders, and the car all transported to a spot-lit auditorium before cutting back to the parking lot, where only a few seconds had elapsed. In "Dream On" (1-19), Artie, who is paraplegic, appeared to break into a dance routine in the middle of a mall, but he was actually just daydreaming. These logic-defying multi-location performances and dream sequences help define the show as surreal, tongue-in-cheek, and unapologetically escapist.

Most of the show's characters are larger-than-life, from mini-diva Rachel to the nefarious Sue Sylvester, who is Machiavellian out of all proportion to her role as a high-school cheerleading coach. Important storylines are a bit bizarre—head of the celibacy club Quinn expecting her boyfriend's best friend's baby, Will's wife pretending to be pregnant, and Rachel's long-lost mother turning out to be the coach of Vocal Adrenaline, New Directions' biggest rival. Subplots are even more incredible: Josh Groban attended an Acafellas concert to implore Sandy to stop stalking him; Howard Bamboo was arrested after Terri made him buy enough cold medicine to start a meth lab; Olivia Newton-John asked Sue to star in a new video for "Let's Get Physical," which became a cult hit. The characters accept these events as somewhat surprising but not beyond the realm of possibility, indicating that the audience should do the same, and defining the parameters of the show as a little beyond those of the real world.

As the show plays with reality, its characters play with the truth. They tell lies, manipulate each other, and, in some cases, inhabit elaborate fictions of their own design. Denial is a recurrent theme, and the show uses different storytelling techniques to emphasize this. Voiceovers often play over a visual representation of the events they describe, allowing us to compare (and usually contrast) the two versions, or to feed us information the narrator may not be aware of. As well as making us laugh, this allows us to comprehend each character's relationship to reality.

Several episodes explicitly addressed honesty: "Acafellas" explored how hard it can be to tell the truth, "Ballad" (1-10) highlighted songs as a way of revealing feelings, and "Bad Reputation" (1-17) focused on the disparity between how characters feel and the way they're perceived. Many of the characters also express emotions that threaten to overwhelm them through song, both intentionally and—more interestingly—inadvertently.

While the show is not grounded in a world we can directly relate to, and much of the characterization and storytelling is ironic, the emotions and relationships of the characters are treated with sincerity and sensitivity, which allows us to become invested in them. This is a show that is very keen to explore the consequences of not coming to terms with reality. In fact, it's not an exaggeration to say the show is obsessed with truth. But who is clueless about reality, and who is simply using denial as a survival strategy? Let's take a closer look at six characters to discern how their differing approaches to the truth are challenged over the course of the first season.

Rachel Berry

Rachel may initially seem to be the character who is the least tethered to reality but in many ways she actually has the closest relationship with the truth. Because she longs to be a star, she sees her life as a Broadway musical (she even described herself to Finn in the pilot as "the dashing young ingénue"). She made a poster of her future Grammy for her wall and adds a gold star after she signs her name to denote her future fame. This might make her seem delusional but she is actually far from it: her assessment of her singing ability is accurate, and she definitely has the determination to succeed. In fact, her clear-eyed view of the world allows her to serve as a reality check for other characters, zeroing in on truths that they are unable or unwilling to admit. In "Showmance" (1-2), she told the celibacy club that "girls want sex just as much as guys do," and in "Mash-Up" (1-8), she filled Puck in on his flaws. She also realizes that Finn is attracted to her, even though he's dating Quinn.

The problem with Rachel's tendency to be honest is that she is often over-optimistic and unable to accurately interpret or predict the way people treat her. Because she rarely lies, she assumes others are the same, and this means that she is frequently manipulated. Other characters exploit her lust for fame and for Finn to serve their own agendas. In "Acafellas," Santana and Quinn convinced her to hire an expensive and divisive choreographer in an attempt to sabotage the club, and "The Rhodes Not Taken" (1-5) saw Finn use Rachel's feelings for him to convince her to return to glee club after she left to join the school musical. She didn't learn from those experiences: in "Hairography" (1-11), Kurt manipulated her into looking stupid when she tried to seduce Finn, and in "Hell-O" (1-14), she couldn't understand why the rest of the glee club was so suspicious of her new boyfriend—despite the fact that he was Vocal Adrenaline's star soloist. In order to appease the other students, she even pretended not to be dating Jesse at all, but they instantly saw through her attempt to deceive them. Despite her claim that she is psychic, people easily keep secrets from her—she was one of the last people to discover Quinn was pregnant (and, later, that Puck was the father).

Even as she becomes better acquainted with the reality of other people's motivations, Rachel never readjusts her expectations in light of past disappointments. This means she is repeatedly hurt—when she developed a short-lived crush on Will and he rejected her ("Ballad"), when Finn strung her along, or when she confirmed that Jesse did have an agenda ("Funk," 1-21). But perhaps because she sees a therapist, and perhaps because of her almost unshakeable self-confidence, she bounces back each time with renewed vigor. Her ability to slough off criticism, rejection, and self-doubt is a testament to the inner strength that just might make her a star.

Kurt Hummel

Kurt is similar to Rachel in both his desire to be famous and his confidence in his own talent. But he is much more pessimistic, both about his future and in anticipating the behavior of others. Kurt expects far less from people than Rachel does, believing that the world can be very cruel and that most people act primarily out of self-interest. His fantasies of stardom are not a continuing narrative, but short bursts of escapism. His worldview is shaped by the fact that his mother died when he was young, leaving him to be raised by a very traditionally macho father, which made it difficult for Kurt to admit to his homosexuality. He is bullied at school because he stands out, and his negative experiences of other people make it difficult for him to trust anyone.

While Rachel believes her life can be one big musical, Kurt uses music as a distraction from reality, and his self-confidence is all bravado. What saves his sanity is his sense of humor, which allows him to relate to others and to deflect his pain using self-deprecation when he feels vulnerable. Because he takes himself less seriously than Rachel, he is much more popular with the other glee kids. As he became good friends with some of the girls, he was able to be himself with them, even telling Mercedes he was gay before he came out to his father. Though he auditioned for glee club in the pilot by singing "Mr. Cellophane"—a song about being invisible—as the show progresses, Kurt's true personality emerges and he finds he is more complex and interesting—and, to his relief, more accepted—than he ever expected. He undergoes some of the most dramatic changes of any character between the pilot and the season finale as he begins to take risks and challenge his understanding of reality.

When his lie to his father about joining the football team became fact, and he discovered that his dad knew he was gay and accepted him anyway ("Preggers," 1-4), Kurt began to be freed from the self-limiting belief that he should hide the truth about himself. No wonder he was so keen to sing "Defying Gravity" ("Wheels," 1-9)—by pushing against what he once thought were his constraints, he began to soar.

But reality—or rather, his tendency to interpret reality in a negative way—repeatedly brings him back to earth. When he saw how upset his dad was after receiving a homophobic phone call, Kurt blew the top note of "Defying Gravity," effectively gifting the solo to Rachel in order to avoid causing controversy that might further embarrass his father. When he realized that Finn's social status was at stake unless Finn threw a slushie in Kurt's face ("Mash-Up"), Kurt did the deed himself. While this demonstrated Kurt's maturity (no one else in the program is so selfless), it also showed what low expectations he has of others. He believes that by pre-empting pain, he is protecting himself from further hurt, but he is actually pushing people away.

Kurt is not a naturally cruel person, but the depth of his feelings for Finn leads him to try to manipulate others. Perhaps because he subconsciously knows that doing so is wrong, he only ends up hurting himself. In "Hairography," he gave Rachel a makeover to make her repellent to Finn, but it only encouraged an honest conversation between the couple and reminded Kurt that Finn would never return his feelings. When Kurt brought together his dad and Finn's mom in an effort to get closer to Finn, he felt sidelined as his father and Finn bonded over basketball ("Home," 1-16). Because the people he loves mean so much to him, he keeps pretending to be someone he isn't: in "Laryngitis," he tried to be more like his father, even dating Brittany, until his dad reassured him again that he loves and accepts Kurt as he is. In "Theatricality" (1-20), when Burt confronted Finn on Kurt's behalf, proving the depth of his pride in his son, Kurt finally got the message that he is more supported than he realized, and that the world may not be such a lonely place after all. That forced him to realize that he is loved unconditionally, and that it is safe for him to be fully himself.

Finn Hudson

While Kurt becomes aware of how much he has been hiding the truth from himself, Finn must come to terms with the lies that surround him. At the start of the series, he was rarely able to recognize when he was being lied to. In fact, it sometimes seemed that he went out of his way to deny reality: he was blackmailed into the club after Will planted drugs in his locker, he thought that Quinn got pregnant after he ejaculated in a hot tub, even though they were both wearing swimsuits, and despite Puck's increasing (and disproportionate) anger toward Finn for his inability to support Quinn and her fetus, he continued to believe that she was going to have his baby. In addition to being frequently manipulated, Finn's naïveté made him a terrible liar, at least initially. When he missed football practice to attend glee club rehearsal in the pilot, he blamed his absence on his mom's "prostate operation." As his life became more complicated and he juggled the competing pressures of glee club, football, Quinn's pregnancy, and his attraction to Rachel, he became better at playing with the truth, leading him to make some questionable decisions. For the most part, though, his deceptions were based on what he considered to be justifiable motives.

In "Wheels," he got a job by pretending to be a wheelchair user in order to contribute to Quinn's medical expenses, and in "The Rhodes Not Taken," he used Rachel's feelings for him to convince her to come back to glee club, in the hope of one day winning a musical scholarship. When a horrified Rachel discovered that he had manipulated her, he justified it by saying, "I haven't been totally honest with you, but that's different from lying." However, his guilty expression showed that he didn't really believe that. In fact, because they have an emotional connection, he and Rachel hold each other to a higher standard of honesty: he is often able to tell when she's lying, and she understands his motivations better than anyone else. Even when Finn is telling the truth, his communication skills could use some work. Scared to tell Quinn's parents she was pregnant, he instead serenaded her with "You're Having My Baby" in their presence—which just infuriated and devastated them ("Ballad"). He did this on the advice of Kurt, who was only advising Finn so they could spend time together. Finn is slow to recognize that people have their own agendas. If someone seems confident in their advice, he believes them.

By the end of season one, the betrayal of his trust by Quinn and Puck, his mother's new relationship, and his increasing awareness of his own feelings mean that Finn's attitude toward the truth has gone from obliviousness to uneasy acceptance. Unfortunately, this means he has become more adept at lying. In "The Power of Madonna" (1-15), he told Rachel that he didn't have sex with Santana. However, unlike his earlier mendaciousness, this was not because he wanted to manipulate Rachel, but because he didn't want to hurt her. He was also lying to himself, preferring not to think about truths he found uncomfortable (in this case, that he'd had meaningless sex that he didn't enjoy). Either sensing his dishonesty or keen to seem experienced, Rachel lied in return, claiming to have had sex with Jesse. In a relationship defined by honest communication, this was the moment when Finn and Rachel were the furthest apart.

Rachel is important to Finn in part because she is usually the only one of his peers who pushes him toward the truth. While the other club members kept the fact that Quinn was actually having Puck's baby a secret, as soon as Rachel found out, she told him. Finn needs other people to force him to confront reality—Will became his mentor largely because he makes Finn realize the consequences of his decisions, his mom makes him admit that grieving for his dad has stopped them both from moving on, and Burt points out his unintentional bigotry. Even Puck and Quinn, although they betrayed him horribly, did Finn a favor, because he might otherwise never have seen them for who they really are. While his worldview was shaken by these awakenings, he learned a lot. Being so deeply hurt made him let go of his complacency and naïveté, and as a result, he became much more willing to be honest about his feelings.

Emma Pillsbury

When Emma said in the pilot that she doesn't cope well with "the messy things," she wasn't just talking about spills and stains. Rather than enter into a real, intimate relationship, she halfheartedly dated Ken while mooning over married man Will, preferring to fantasize about love rather than experience it. In fact, Emma shares with Rachel a tendency to use fantasy to escape reality. But whereas for Rachel this is a survival technique that allows her to put a positive spin on past and future events, giving her the courage to embrace new experiences, Emma is desperate to cling to her safe status quo, using denial as a shield against much-needed change.

While Rachel's self-delusion only extends to her optimism about other people's motivations and future behavior, Emma's extends to her physical reality, as when she tried on a dress for her wedding to Ken and ended up dancing around the room with Will, dreamily singing "I Could Have Danced All Night" as if he were the man she was marrying ("Mash-Up"). As she obsessively organizes the pamphlets in her office, so she tries to organize events in her mind, repressing anything she doesn't want to believe. When Will suggested that her aversion to mess was a problem ("Showmance," 1-2), her love for him prompted her to open up about the fact that she'd developed obsessive thoughts and behavior after falling into the runoff lagoon at a dairy farm when she was eight. Although she admitted that she'd restricted her life ever since (and we saw her wearing plastic gloves in order to handle food, and later discovered that she'd never had an intimate relationship), she was so mired in denial that she insisted it wasn't an issue.

Despite being a guidance counselor and presumably having some training in the concept of boundaries, it took Emma a long time to

Helpful Advice

Brochures found in Emma's office:

o Ouch! That Stings!
o I Can't Stop Touching Myself
o Radon: The Silent Killer
o My Mom's Bipolar and She Won't Stop YELLING
o Congratulations, You're Pregnant!
o Help! I'm in LOVE With My Stepdad!
o I Still Breastfeed...But How Old Is Too Old?
o Wow! There's a Hair Down There!
o So You Like Throwing Up: Understanding and Overcoming Bulimia
o Divorce: Why Your Parents Stopped Loving You

understand that her close, flirtatious friendship with Will was inappropriate. In fact, like Finn, she needs other people to point her in the direction of the truth. However, she only takes action in response to firm prompting. Ken asked Emma out several times, but she only agreed to date him after Terri forcefully reminded her that Will was married and encouraged her to give Ken a chance ("Vitamin D," 1-6). Only when Ken dumped her on their wedding day because of her feelings for Will did she realize she had been wrong to drag out their sham of a relationship for so long ("Sectionals," 1-13). And she didn't begin seeing a therapist until Will suggested she seek treatment after they began dating and she found herself too inhibited to have sex ("The Power of Madonna").

In return, Emma pushed Will to accept the truth about his own behavior—never letting him off the hook for his bad decisions, but not condemning him for them either, believing in his vision of himself as a good person and thus helping him achieve it. However, by the end of season one, she was much less in awe of him than she'd been at the start, and was much more in touch with reality in general. The episode "Bad Reputation" marked a turning point for Emma, as she not only criticized Will for jerking her around (calling him "a slut"), but also publicly admitted to her OCD for the first time. As much as Will betrays her in his dalliances with other women, his presence is a catalyst in her life. Perhaps she didn't only fall in love with him because he was a fantasy, but because she sensed that he would challenge her to accept the truth about herself. Deep down, she does want to confront reality—she just doesn't want to do it alone.

Terri Schuester

Terri not only has a warped view of reality, but is deluded about her own behavior and how unforgivable it often is. A nervous disposition combined with disappointed expectations has left her self-centered and status-obsessed, convinced that the trappings of an upper-middle-class marriage (a baby, a big house, and a husband who makes a lot of money) will bring her joy. She is so focused on grasping for what she thinks will make her happy that she overlooks how fortunate she really is. But she's not the only one to blame for this delusion: she is more vulnerable than she appears, and may even be mentally ill—"Ballad" featured a flashback to two years prior, when Terri claimed she was taking Prozac. Her sister Kendra and Will, the only two people with whom she has close relationships, rarely challenge her ridiculous assertions (such as that she works hard or that nothing good ever happens to her). Kendra not only dissuaded Terri from telling Will her pregnancy wasn't real, but choreographed the elaborate deception. Meanwhile, Terri's fear that her husband was slipping away from her was not unjustified, and it was perhaps guilt that caused Will to ignore the worst of her solipsism.

In addition to her loose grip on reality, Terri's moral code is pretty ambiguous. She seems to think that by presenting something as fact, she can make it true. She had no qualms about telling complete strangers about her "pregnancy," perhaps because she once thought she was pregnant and does intend to have a baby, if not her own. But sometimes her dishonesty is more calculated. While she is often ignorant of her own issues, she instantly spots insecurities in others and is always willing to exploit them to suit her own agenda. She played on Emma's fear of loneliness to talk her into dating Ken, distracted Will from her faux pregnancy by buying him a vintage car, and tried to put Quinn off keeping her baby by having her babysit Kendra's kids. The more her schemes prospered, the more confidence she had to keep trying to reshape reality. But these tactics only worked in the short term; eventually people chose what was best for them, not what was best for Terri. Worse, she was so busy trying to make life measure up to her goals that she didn't face up to the reality of her situation until far too late, and even then, she found it hard to admit to her mistakes. She only confessed her pregnancy lie when Will found a fake belly, and even then she tried to justify her deceit. She finally admitted how much she had messed up in "Sectionals," telling Will, "I'm weak and I'm anxious and I let my anxiety rule my life." Sadly, her marriage (and the security she thought it represented) was what she had to sacrifice in order to know the truth.

Will Schuester

"I didn't mean to hurt anybody," Will told Emma in "Bad Reputation." But throughout the first season of *Glee*, he hurts a lot of people, albeit unintentionally. He seems to believe that because his intentions are honorable, his actions can be excused. But a lot of Will's actions border on unforgiveable. He brought a forty-year-old alcoholic into the group and was surprised when she corrupted everyone; he put his singers under so much pressure that they began abusing over-the-counter medication; and when he ended his marriage, he immediately began dating Emma, and then just as suddenly cheated on her. Yet he still seems to think of himself as a moral person, perhaps because in each case he is able to identify the wrong decision—but always after the fact.

Will could be accused of being as delusional as Terri and as in denial as Emma, at least some of the time. In fact, it is with the women in his life that he shows the worst judgment of all, acting as if the time he spent with Emma was entirely innocent, despite the chemistry between them and the longing looks they exchanged. Terri betrayed him horribly, but for Will, too, lying to his spouse was an automatic response. In the pilot, when Principal Figgins told Will he had to pay the glee club's $60-a-month running costs, Will's voiceover informed us that hiding the expense from his wife would be difficult. He only saw what an untrustworthy person Terri was when he was ready to leave her, letting her get away with her lies for a long time because it was easier than admitting the truth about their relationship.

One way Will expresses his suppressed feelings is through his choice of songs. In "Acafellas," when Terri was desperately trying to conceive so she would no longer have to lie about being

pregnant, he and his a capella "boy band" performed Bel Biv Devoe's "Poison," which includes the lyric, "it's all so deadly / when
love is not together from the heart," and in "Showmance," when
Terri put him under pressure to get a second job, it was surely no
coincidence that he picked "Gold Digger" to sing with his students.
He associates performing with happiness, perhaps because of the
approval he gets for being good at something and the ego boost
this brings. One reason he likes Emma is that she is impressed by
his talent. But sometimes his egoism turns to egotism: in exchange
for how good Emma's attention made him feel, he tried to return
the favor by "fixing" her. In "Showmance" (1-2), he challenged her
mental health by putting chalk on her nose for ten seconds (despite
not having any therapeutic training), and in "Hell-O," he called
her neurosis "adorable." Only in "The Power of Madonna" did he
wake up to the fact that she has a serious mental illness (and only
when it had implications for him). As unsettling as it can be to see
someone for who they really are, perhaps the fact that Emma and
Will finally did so means that they will be able to form an honest
relationship.

Relationships based on honesty are the only ones that succeed in
Glee; those based on lies (Quinn and Finn, Terri and Will, Emma and
Ken, Rachel and Jesse) all crumbled over the course of the series,
whereas honesty about their feelings and their flaws led Finn and Rachel and Will and Emma to fall in love. After going to great lengths
to manipulate her biological daughter, only when Shelby was honest with Rachel about her feelings (and failings) were the two able to
share a true moment of emotional connection.

Despite its cynicism and subversion, *Glee* is a show with strong
moral values, and it champions the idea that honesty and true human connection ultimately make people happier than any external
success. However, the show also recognizes that honesty is often the
hardest option, and thus portrays characters who all struggle to come
to terms with the truth to some extent—and who lie to themselves,
each other, and us in the process. While the characters are not always
honest, the songs they perform usually are—they reveal emotional

insecurities that are often not expressed in any other way. (It is telling that the least sympathetic character, Terri, is the character who sings the least.) The fact that we like and relate to most of these people despite their flaws shows that their challenges in accepting who they are and where they belong are an important and universal part of the human experience.

Terri's story is a cautionary tale of what can happen when a person is out of touch with the truth for too long, but we can be inspired by Emma's willingness to challenge her delusions and Rachel's capacity to believe in herself even when no one else does. While Will is ostensibly the moral center of the show, he is perhaps the most ethically ambiguous of all, although like Terri, Emma, Finn, Kurt, and Rachel, he has both a closer grip on reality and a firmer realization of his own limitations by the end of the first season. All the characters learn that, as painful as the truth can be, ultimately it is more rewarding than denial. But none of them should feel bad for taking some time to come to terms with reality—pushing against what society encourages us to believe, experimenting with how we relate to the world, and discovering the truth for ourselves is surely a necessary part of growing up, which they are all doing for the first time.

* * *

DIANE SHIPLEY is a freelance writer and pop culture obsessive who will never utter the words "it's only a TV show." Her idols include Brenda Walsh, Lorelai Gilmore, and Veronica Mars. When not writing or obsessively tweeting (@dianeshipley), she can usually be found eating pizza with a box set by her side (scheduled programming is for amateurs). Her website is www.dianeshipley.com.

JONNA RUBIN

The Twisted Love Life of Mr. Schue

What Happens When a Man-Whore Leaves His Marriage and Ignores the Consequences

HERE'S WHAT YOU NEED TO KNOW up front: I'm not a big fan of Will Schuester. In fact, whenever he comes on the screen, I sort of cringe inwardly and hope against hope that he's not going to regale us with old-school hip-hop.

Sadly, I am usually disappointed, and I've suffered through everything from Bel Biv Devoe to (oh, Heaven help us) Vanilla Ice from behind a pillow on my sofa. Watching him play a romantic lead is even more cringe-worthy, as I'm also of the firm belief that he really seems like a bad kisser—all closed-mouthed, unnatural, and full of strange smooching sounds that are anything but sexy. I want to shake him and loudly inform him that he's kissing Idina Menzel, one of the hottest women on Broadway—no, I'm sorry, *in America*—and I'm sure she'd appreciate a little *effort*, for crying out loud, so please, get your fake libido up off of the couch.

Naturally, I can't make any assumptions about Matthew Morrison's kissing abilities—for all I know, his awkward lip-locks could be

a hidden strategy in his portrayal of Mr. Schue—and I'll try to with-
hold judgment unless presented the opportunity to test the goods
myself, perhaps as a guest star in an upcoming episode. You know,
for the sake of research.

Distaste for the man does not impact my enjoyment of the show,
however. If nothing else, it's made it easier to simply sit back, relax,
and watch his romantic escapades unfold without being clouded by a
celebrity crush. (I was unable to properly stomach an inch of the Rachel Berry–Jesse St. James subplot without wringing my hands and
clutching my chest, so deep and inappropriate is my futile crush on
Mr. St. James.)

Certainly, one of the central conflicts in the first season is the romance between Will and…well, at this point, it seems like no one
is safe. Will Schuester has had some sort of romantic link, requited
or otherwise, with everyone, from the obvious (his wife Terri) to
the wildly inappropriate (his student Rachel Berry). No one is safe
from Will's tangled web of love, not even his longtime nemesis Sue
Sylvester.

Even his now ex-wife Terri, whose machinations can be described
as questionable at best, has been caught in the crossfire of Will's misguided attempts at love. Without a doubt, much of Terri's behavior is
indefensible—she faked a pregnancy, made a vulnerable high school
student an accomplice in her deception, and betrayed her husband
in the most hurtful way possible, among myriad other vile things—
but as anyone who's ever been married (and plenty who haven't)
knows, marriages are not merely the sum of their transgressions, and
there's always more than meets the eye. I have a hard time believing
that Terri's actions stemmed purely from selfishness or, worse, were
entirely unwarranted. Marriage—particularly one where the parties
involved were together in youth—is anything but black and white,
and our Jheri-curled hero is hardly an innocent bystander in the train
wreck that became Terri Schuester.

And then there's his work-spouse-turned-sort-of-girlfriend,
Emma. Oh, Emma. The doe-eyed guidance counselor with impeccable taste in cardigans and perfectly coiffed red hair seems just right

for Will—at least at first glance. Delightfully quirky, retro-chic, and hopelessly in love with our intrepid rapper, she seems tailor-made for him, and there's little doubt that the characters (and actors) have an undeniable chemistry. And with Terri's behavior eclipsing even the worst of the ladies on *Real Housewives*, Emma's sweet demeanor and wholesome crush—you get the feeling her fantasies involve nothing steamier than his-and-her ice cream cones—make her the perfect anti-Terri. She appears, if nothing else, to be the ideal antidote for what seems to be years of toxic emotional manipulation, lies, and abuse at Terri's hands.

After an entire season of flirting and lighthearted hijinks, and especially now that Will's marriage to Terri is over, these star-crossed would-be lovers seem perfectly set up for a delightful romp of "will they or won't they?" in the grand tradition of Meredith Grey and Derek Shepherd (*Grey's Anatomy*), Maddie Hayes and David Addison (*Moonlighting*), and, if we want to go there, Tony Micelli and Angela Bower (*Who's the Boss?*), likely culminating in a highly satisfying (re) union event, á la Jim Halpert and Pam Beesly (*The Office*). A few dramatic kisses and makeout sessions followed by several episodes of on-again, off-again merriment, and finally a cliffhanger involving the most awkward declaration of love in the history of television, have all but cemented this inevitability.

. . . Or have they? Who will Mr. Schue end up with? Who *should* he end up with? I'm here to tell you: it isn't Emma. Though she saw a bit of redemption in the latter half of the first season, she's still a hotbed of mental illness on par with Terri, with a terrifying dose of hero worship. Qualities that Will, in his infinite cruelty, will no doubt exploit, leaving her more damaged than ever. But at this point, Terri seems beyond the realm of possibility, for who could forgive such deplorable acts of malice . . . right?

Thanks to Will's unusually prolific romantic escapades in the first season, there are many options before us. So really, who should it be? Rival choir director Shelby Corcoran, played by the inimitable (and smokin' hot) Idina Menzel? Kristin Chenoweth's April Rhodes, a former classmate and longtime crush of Will's? Both women have enough in common with him, certainly, and there's plenty of sexual chemistry to keep the flames burning through those cold Lima winters.

Alas, no. Shelby's hardly commitment material—she admits to making out with nearly every show-choir director in the area, and with a renewed focus on her family, she's likely not looking to start a relationship with a confused playboy—and April is barely sober, making Emma look the very picture of mental health by comparison.

No. He needs someone who sees and loves him for what he really is, isn't afraid to call him out on his own B.S., and is willing to sacrifice everything to be his partner. And while Sue Sylvester fits part of the bill (she certainly isn't afraid to call him out), the thought of them as a committed couple is…well, no.

Yes, folks. Will needs Terri, fake baby bump and all. And if you'll hang in there a moment, I promise I'll explain.

The (Sur)Reality of *Glee*

Before we go any further, however, it's important to note that *Glee* and its characters are archetypes. Part of what makes the show so successful is its over-the-top portrayal of events and characters we can all relate to, done in a way that is exaggerated enough to reassure us that they aren't real. It's glossy, slick, and cheerfully packaged—and although the show deals with some pretty uncomfortable concepts, the obviously unrealistic details make it easy to swallow.

Emma is adorable, isn't she? Oh yes, she's simply *adorable*, with her crippling obsessive-compulsive disorder and complete inability to tolerate any physical contact whatsoever. A true portrayal of this life would be, I'm afraid, interminably sad and heartbreaking to the point of becoming intolerable. But package it up in a cute twinset with a matching handbag and impeccable shoes, and instead of being sad, it's actually funny and endearing.

And Will, ever the handsome do-gooder earnestly making his way through life, bringing kindness, joy, and even salvation to many, if not all, he encounters. A humiliating seduction doesn't seem so bad when it's inflicted on a character as evil as Sue Sylvester...does it?

Of course, who can forget Terri Schuester, the Eye of Sauron to Will's merry Fellowship? Her cruelty is so exaggerated that it becomes comical—masked by such an extraordinary portrayal, it's easy to miss that in reality, such a mean spirit is usually borne of neglect and a real need for attention and yes, a little love.

The students, too, fall into the same pattern. We've all known a driven, ambitious drama geek like Rachel Berry—heck, some of us *were* Rachel Berry—but everything from her wardrobe to her Broadway-caliber talent is emphasized for effect.

Let's be honest: Most real-life kids like Rachel don't have pipes like that, and aren't beautiful enough to pass for "sneaky-hot," as Jesse St. James put it. Nerdy girls are always secretly beautiful on television, otherwise how could we possibly root for them? And as every nerd, both present and former, will tell you: it's just not that way in reality. But to watch such a realistic portrayal would be boring at best, and discomfiting and disturbing at worst. It's a tack taken with nearly every character: Kurt's flamboyant homosexuality is tempered by his refreshing sense of self, thus preventing the audience from feeling too uncomfortable as he is persecuted time and time again.

So while *Glee* is a version of reality, it's not a place where you and I live, and it's definitely not a place where things are precisely what they seem. So with that in mind, let's take a look at things how they probably *really* are.

Oh, Will Schuester. Not So Innocent, You.

One of the more irritating things about this love...pentagon, or whatever it is at this point, is that Will quite happily paints himself in the role of victim when, frankly, he's as responsible as anyone for how mightily things have fallen apart.

During the first half of the season, he seemed the consummate good guy. A phoenix rising from the ashes of his faded high school glory days, he returned for redemption when he resurrected his alma mater's glee club from certain death. He's a hero figure of sorts, gathering together a merry band of misfits to restore the club to its former luster, fighting tooth and nail for resources from the Cheerios, the nationally ranked cheerleading squad, led by Will's archenemy Sue Sylvester. Through it all, he empowered a group of outcasts to realize their full potential and transcend stereotypes through teamwork, song, and personal achievement.

I mean, it's a savior's bio, right? Furthermore, he was married to his high school sweetheart, Terri, and toiled thanklessly, day and night, to pursue his passions while keeping her happy, even in light of her incessant demands and terminal laziness. ("I'm on my feet four hours a day, three times a week!" she lamented about her work schedule at Sheets-N-Things in the pilot.) And when Will learned Terri was pregnant, he redoubled his efforts to satisfy her desire for the finer things—including a McMansion, complete with a grand foyer and pricey Pottery Barn toilet brushes—by logging extra hours as a night janitor for the school where he taught by day.

Ah, yes. The basic facts present an innocent, irreproachable soul. A closer look, however, demonstrates that he spent his days—and later, his janitorial nights—flirting shamelessly with his crush-worthy coworker (Emma, of course), to the point that his colleagues and even the students took note, and Emma actually believed she stood a chance. And worse, as the season played out, her belief proved correct. In fact, as Will admitted to Ken Tanaka later, he did little to discourage this belief, effectively leading her on—far enough, even, that she felt comfortable confronting Terri with the notion that Will "deserves a lot better than you." And although it turned out to be false, perhaps we may remind the peanut gallery that at that juncture Terri was pregnant—at least in the minds of Will and Emma.

Nice, Will. Really nice. Is it any wonder that Terri ended up in such a paranoid state that she enacted desperate measures to keep him from straying? Who knows how many more women there were before this—given the ease with which he moved on from Terri— and later, Emma—it's hard to imagine that this was his first foray into infidelity, at least emotionally. Terri may have suffered in silence for *years*. And it's obvious that she loves him, poor thing, however twisted her actions may be.

As for Emma, who can blame her, really? Well, I can, but we'll get to that later. The point is, she's hardly been dissuaded. In one scene during the pilot, Emma stepped in gum and panicked, unable to control her horror at the sticky mess. Will interceded, ever the gallant gentleman, and she sat like a princess on a throne while he delicately caressed her leg, removing the offending gum with his credit card. While the gesture was done in an exaggerated romantic fashion, suggesting it was tongue-in-cheek, there was just enough subtext (a lingering touch here, subtle eye contact there, not to mention that her foot was still *in* the shoe) to pretend that it was purely friendly.

Will was inappropriate with Emma from the very start—it was in the very first episode that he confided in her that Terri was hard on him and that their marriage was not what it appeared to be. "She wants me to be better, but better at what?" he fretted.

Gee, I don't know, Will. Not sharing intimate details of your marriage and disparaging your wife to a flirtatious coworker might be a good place to lay that first stone on the road to personal improvement.

Beyond the obvious moments, like when Emma removed the mustard from his chin dimple and the sexual tension was so palpable it practically pulled up a chair and made a sandwich ("Vitamin D," 1-6), there wasn't a scene where both actors were present that wasn't bubbling over with flirtation. Yet, throughout much of it, Will remained married, with a baby on the way, apparently oblivious to the fact that this was anything but on the up-and-up.

When Will invited Emma to help him with his nightly janitorial duties (why she would want to is beyond comprehension…oh, wait), he didn't simply ask; he was borderline salacious as he invited her to meet him in the boys' bathroom in the science wing later that night. This, after things had been taken to the next level the night before—a playful dot of chalk on Emma's nose gave way to hushed tones and a near kiss, the spell broken only by Emma's panicked departure. This behavior from a man who thought he had a pregnant wife at home waiting for him!

It's easy to pretend that Will is oblivious to the consequences of his actions—after all, in many other facets of his life, he is a good person. He's an excellent teacher with a remarkable ability to understand and motivate a difficult group of students with wildly divergent personalities. Like most of us, Will is not all bad or all good. But it's safe to say that, when it comes to being entirely faithful in romantic relationships, Will is definitely bad.

Later events made it patently clear that Will was anything but unaware of his effect on other people, and worse, that his behavior with Emma was not a onetime case of star-crossed lovers, bound by duty to a higher power to bring their love into the light of day. In "Ballad" (1-10), he seemed hyper-aware of his magnetism, almost to the point of arrogance. He sighed with mock frustration as he recounted the numerous student crushes he'd endured over the years, and although Suzy Pepper's reaction was extreme (eating the world's hottest pepper in a fit of lovelorn despair), instead of treating it like an anomaly, he assumed that women were "too fragile" to handle being let down by him.

And who can forget the infamous (and supremely uncomfortable) Sue Sylvester seduction? After seeing Rachel's devastation following Jesse's betrayal, instead of focusing on helping his student (which, to his credit, is unlike him), her heartache only served to spur him to endear himself to Sue by way of one cringe-inducing rendition of "Tell Me Something Good" involving...butt-wagging and grinding. Yes, *grinding*, up on Sue Sylvester, and for no other reason than he assumed that his seduction and subsequent rejection would all but destroy her, rendering her ineffective at any sort of subterfuge—and he was rewarded with exactly that.

He uses sex, and his own magnetism, as a means to feed his ego and get what he wants. And who's better suited to serve him than Emma, a woman who was so starry-eyed by his creepy mashup of

"Don't Stand So Close to Me"/"Young Girl," ("Ballad") that she completely lacked the presence of mind to dissuade Rachel from playing Lolita to his Humbert?

It was almost impossible to question his motives when, after he was publicly called out by Emma for his dalliances with April and Shelby, one of the first things he said to her was that he "wants [her] to look at [him] like she used to." That's it, Will? You don't miss her sparkling personality or even her good looks? You miss the way she looked at you, as though you were the irreproachable hero of her life?

Oh, Will. Do you even listen to yourself anymore? It's no wonder he's all but left a trail of heartbroken women in his wake—the man courts female attention more easily than Rachel alienates her teammates. He cruises through life, leaving behind a trail of confused tears, all the while shrugging his shoulders and asking, "Who, me?"

And we're supposed to be *rooting* for him?

Emma Pillsbury: The Cleanest Mess We Ever Did See

Like Will, Emma appears the very picture of saintly innocence, and also like Will, she has moments of true kindness. Sadly, unlike Will, her moments of good intent, at least throughout the first half of the season, were almost entirely selfish, influenced by an unstoppable crush.

In fact, for much of *Glee*, Emma's life was almost entirely defined by how she felt about Will. From the first moment we met her, she was dull and lifeless until he entered the room, whereupon she lit up, eyes wide and hopeful, with a special hello saved just for him. At first it was almost endearing—who hasn't had a crush on an unattainable guy, right?—and it was hard not to root for her to find a love of her own.

Moments later, the innocence had left the building and boarded a plane for Dubai as Emma brooded wild-eyed over the sign-up sheet for a weekend chaperone on the glee club field trip. Her focus was so intent, and her breath coming so rapidly, that she seemed possessed as she made a beeline for the bulletin board, and before you could say "OCD," the pencil was sanitized and her name rested neatly at the top of the list. Calculated alone time with (married) Will? Check.

Her obsession with him continued unabated and, frankly, turned into something a little terrifying—she lurked in hallways, timing her entrances so that she could bump into him; during the field trip to see Vocal Adrenaline, she baited him into discussing the sordid details of his foundering marriage; she used her unrequited crush as an excuse to reject Ken Tanaka's overtures, politely informing him that she had feelings for someone else. Though she pretended to be aware that he was taken, her actions—and even her words, as she had no problem confirming her intentions to Terri in "Vitamin D"—very clearly spoke otherwise.

I'm the first to defend a woman against the notion that as the mistress she is solely culpable for the demise of a marriage. Of course, *of course* the real culprit is the individual who made the decision to break his or her vows and end his or her relationship. It takes two or three people to weave such a tangled web of deception and disappointment. It's an anti-feminist fallacy to think that a marriage has ended due to the actions of one person alone, and certainly, some of the world's greatest love stories came from the messiest of breakups. The end of a marriage, like life, is full of plenty of gray.

With this in mind, I'm reluctant to cast Emma in the role of homewrecker... except that that's precisely what she aspired to be. It's one thing to harbor a crush on a married man, but quite another to act on it, repeatedly and inappropriately, and did I mention repeatedly? Furthermore, it's doubtful that anyone would deny that if actively pursuing a married man is inadvisable, actively pursuing a married man with a pregnant wife at home is... well, there doesn't seem to be a pejorative strong enough, does there?

Even her momentary glimmers of clear judgment were not her own—when she begged off a second night helping Will play janitor, it was only because Ken Tanaka icily confronted her with the knowledge that she was chasing after a married man.

Worse, Emma proved through her halfhearted engagement to Ken Tanaka that she was capable of unspeakable cruelty. Agreeing to marry a man she didn't like, much less love, out of a misguided hope that it would force the hand of the man she truly *does* love was Machiavellian at best, gut-wrenchingly heartbreaking at worst. And this was before she allowed Will to sexily serenade her with "Thong Song" while she pranced around in a wedding dress, mere weeks before her nuptials. And though they never went through with those nuptials, it was Ken, not Emma, who pulled the plug on their relationship, recognizing Emma's commitment to Will after she postponed their wedding to attend Sectionals. Good job, Ken. Dodged a bullet with that one.

But that's not all.

From her affection for perfectly coordinated outfits accessorized down to the button to her habit of wiping down each grape individually before eating, Emma embodies obsessive-compulsive personality disorder. While at first her OCD is used as a way to make her seem endearing and quirky, it quickly becomes clear that Emma's issues run far deeper, like needing gloves in the lunchroom and an inability to tolerate any sort of touching without extensive preparation. Her OCD even leads to interactions with students that border on unethical—in "Showmance" (1-2), when she caught Rachel attempting to throw up in the bathroom, she could barely contain her horror. Instead of focusing on the true issue at hand, she offered the simple idea that bulimia is a "very messy disease" and furiously pumped hand sanitizer with the urgency of Lady Macbeth. Rachel, fortunately, was not bulimic, but I shudder to think of the consequences of Emma's reaction if she were.

We are later given a glimpse into the true extent of her disease, when in "Hell-O" (1-14), after seemingly getting what she wanted from Will, she was unable to let him kiss her before running frantically out of the room, full-body sanitary kit in hand. (We won't even begin to discuss Will's poor judgment in attempting to kiss her on school grounds, in her glass-walled office... right?) And later, she admitted she was a virgin due to the fear that someone might reject her because of her problems, including, one would imagine, fear of the mess inherent in most kinds of sex. These are not small obstacles in pursuing a relationship, or taking full advantage of all that life has to offer.

Fortunately or unfortunately, depending on what team you're on, the second half of the season finally showed Emma getting it together—and ultimately, it was her relationship with Will that pushed her to finally take care of herself. After all, it's hard to consummate your relationship with the man of your dreams when you can't even stand for him to touch you. And yes, it was Will who urged her to go to counseling, which was a bold, rare move of romantic kindness—though I could make a strong case for the fact that it was, quite literally, for no other reason than that he wanted to get in her pants.

As her therapy progressed, so did her skills in the counselor's office; she showed genuine care, warmth, and expertise when she coached Artie through the realization that his dreams of walking were likely never going to come to fruition. And though her bizarre confrontation with Will in the lunchroom was unprofessional, inappropriate, and more than a little *Jerry Springer*–esque, it was hard not to applaud her for finally standing up to Will, and not behaving like a meeker rendition of Adrian Balboa, the whispering wind beneath the wings of this great man. Even though she's still flawed—she reminded us that the only reason she went to therapy was for Will, when it should have been for *herself*—at least her flaws are housed in a body that has a backbone. I'm no Emma fan, but it was hard not to stand up and give her the old slow clap for that little outburst.

The applause got even louder when, after Will brought Emma flowers by way of apology, she harshly rebuked him, snidely informing him that she knew she was supposed to moon over him and be impressed by "how in touch he is with his feelings," but she just couldn't. It was precisely what Will deserved in that moment, and his reaction—focusing on his own feelings and how she perceived him—reinforced the fact that she'd done the right thing. Come *on*, Will. You've been caught red-handed, and instead of paying attention to how *she's* feeling, you're disappointed that she doesn't still think you're God reborn in the body of Brad Pitt?

Though Emma may be on the road to recovery from her special brand of crazy, it remains clear: it's unlikely that Will will ever see her as his equal. After all, he's the one who saved her, and if he has his way, he'll be the first to go where no man has gone before. And is during recovery from a debilitating disease really the time to strike up a new relationship, especially one built on a foundation of inequality?

Ironically, in Emma's case, Will is right: she is too fragile. Take, for example, the hallway kiss in the season finale, where Will (finally?) declared his love for her, albeit through some seriously shaky dialogue. Three words, one kiss, and Emma's eyes are stars, her pupils huge as saucers. Oh, Will, you may get the chance to love Emma for what you really want, after all: the way she looks at you. What a strong foundation for a healthy, fulfilling relationship!

Sometimes people are brought into our lives—or, in this case, onto a show—for a reason. Emma and Will have been good for each other in many ways. He's shown her how to seek help and become stronger, and she's given him the gift of self-reflection. Ironically, however, these traits only appear when they're apart; together, Will comfortably falls into the role of hero to Emma's weak, needy, bottomless well.

Take your winnings, cut your losses, and hit the road, friends. This relationship is a bad idea.

Terri Schuester: Calculating Bitch or Long-Suffering Wife?

It's hard to admit that I'm a fan of Terri, because, frankly, there's not much to like. Colossal acts of cruelty aside, she's not a particularly pleasant person: from the first moment we meet her, she's ungrateful to Will, rude to customers, and unkind to her fellow employees. Rooting for her sometimes feels a little like hoping the *Lost* smoke monster destroys humanity.

And yes, as I mentioned, most of her truly egregious actions are beyond disgraceful. It's impossible to conjure a viable excuse for faking a pregnancy and taking advantage of a young high school student, I realize. And I can't even begin to cover her brief stint as a school nurse, which quickly devolved into Terri Schuester as drug pusher, cheerfully dispensing Sudafed in large quantities to students en masse.

She's deplorable. I get it. But how did she get here? Even Terri has a few redeeming qualities, and if you look hard enough, it's not difficult to see a damaged, broken-down woman desperate to hold on to the man she loves—a man who, by all accounts, has given her every reason to be terrified that he's got one foot out the door, despite his insistence to the contrary.

The thing is, Terri loves him. That much is blatantly obvious. She was happy to see him when he visited her at work, and she made an effort to spend time with him in her own way. Yes, it's true, "puzzle night" isn't exactly Will's idea of a creative outlet, but she was clearly trying to help him the only way she knows how. Once he got his hands on the glee club, he began pulling further away from her—first through the simple fact that it took his time, and later, as Terri astutely noted, as he began to lose sight of himself, and his commitment to his family, by trying to recreate the (small-time) fame and notoriety of his high school days. (Really, Will? You want to make your first song for the club "Le Freak" because you won Nationals with it? Is this your gig, or theirs?) Her assertion that they both need to move past their high school identities was not entirely off base, and was, in fact, confirmed with the reemergence of his high school nemesis Bryan Ryan in "Dream On" (1-19), where the two rivals duked it out in stellar performances for a coveted role in local community theater. Terri has her sights set on a life beyond their adolescence, however tacky and nouveau riche that life may be, whereas Will is hell-bent on recapturing it.

Even still, she had moments of unselfish affection. In "Acafellas" (1-3), she was clearly proud of him, praising his performance and apologizing for her lack of support. That interaction, though brief, was genuine, and offered a glimpse into the couple who fell in love all those many years ago.

Further, if you look more closely at two of her biggest contraventions, they began innocently enough. The pregnancy ruse, though carried too far and for far too long, was unintentional and obviously driven by despair and desperation. Until Will spilled the beans to his parents—without Terri's permission, I hasten to add—it seemed like she was merely waiting for the right time to admit that she'd lied under duress. The mere fact that she had a hysterical pregnancy at all is indicative of a person under an extreme amount of stress, likely borne of a desire to save her marriage. A panicked lie, though unethical, is almost understandable under the circumstances. Well, provided you 'fess up to the truth later, that is, which yes, I know, Terri failed to do in any sort of reasonable, timely, or appropriate fashion.

Even her brief stint as McKinley High's soft-core drug dealer didn't begin as nefariously as it ended. Though her actions were thoughtless and incredibly damaging, they came from an organic place—the blue meanies were how Terri herself survived the rigors of secondary education, and though stupid, dispensing them to the students was not a malicious act. Besides, she only took the job after Sue Sylvester made it clear that she had a formidable romantic adversary in Emma Pillsbury and that to intervene would be in the best interest of her marriage.

Sue's warnings were never more warranted than when Terri surprised Will on her first day at work, and, instead of being welcomed, she was treated like an interloper, interrupting a private moment between Will and Emma. *Emma*! Why, it's enough to send even the most rational of spouses straight to the recipe for boiled bunny.

And worse, throughout Terri's first appearance at school, Will was sitting with Emma looking bereft, and, yes, painfully guilty. With good reason, too: though Terri was rude to Emma (licking her thumb and then wiping the lip of her coffee cup), instead of focusing on his wife's feelings, Will used the time to gauge *Emma's* reaction to Terri, and further, Emma's reaction to *him*. Concern for or interest in how his wife felt in that awkward moment didn't even cross his mind.

And consider this: the same action he later condoned with Emma (kissing on school grounds), he wouldn't deign to consider doing with his wife, who swooped in to affectionately remove a spot of mustard on his lip. It's no wonder Terri was caught up in a constant show of bald desperation. Add Terri's conniving sister Kendra to the mixing bowl of misery (she pressured Terri into keeping the pregnancy a secret by exploiting her worst fears about Will), and Terri's moral foundation is wobbling like a bowl of Jell-O. How can she possibly know which way is up anymore? And worse, Will reinforced this by constantly putting Terri's value as a wife on her position as the mother of his child—as though from the moment she conceived, she ceased to exist. ("You're carrying my baby. I have no right to expect anything else from you," he crooned in "Throwdown" 1-7.)

When it all came to a head (in an incredible performance by both actors, I hasten to add), Terri's admission that Will's lack of self-esteem was the key to their relationship's success was a bald, sad statement of her own insecurity. For her, the only way to feel worthy of Will was to ensure that he never felt worthy of her—in a twisted way, it was the only way she knew how to keep him. Though most of that is on her, Will has to accept a small bit of responsibility for his open affection (or lack thereof) for his wife. Did he do anything to make her feel valued? Did he see her for who she really was? Or, yet again, did he merely see the consequences of her actions as they impacted him?

It must have been hard for her to feel loved when Will felt free, on a relatively consistent basis, to tear her down publicly. When Will and Terri were confronted by Figgins for her (yes, awful, I know) drug pushing, Will took the opportunity to not only berate her for what she'd done at the school, but to turn it into a condemnation of her future parenting skills. What's worse, he did it in front of Figgins. At this point, if you take away Terri's part in this train wreck,

I almost wonder what in the Sam Hill she sees in *him*, and why she didn't pack her bags and head to Vegas years ago.

Terri's real redemption came later, however, long after Will confronted her with the truth about her pregnancy. In their first post-pregnancy meeting, she revealed that she'd been seeing a counselor. And although it's doubtless that she has a long road ahead, she clearly made the decision on her own, without the hope or expectation that Will would return to her. Her reasons for seeking professional help (okay, yes, fine, at the community center, I know) were entirely her own. And as anyone who's ever known anyone in need of help is aware, counseling is only effective if the patient is willing take responsibility for her actions and take a hard look at herself, for her own reasons—not for a relationship, not to appease a family member, not for anyone else but herself.

Though her reappearance in the finale was filled with Terri's quintessential biting comments and a touch of cruelty, she demonstrated growth by helping Finn with his glee club assignment. It's small growth, yes, but she's getting there.

No matter what happens with Will, Terri will survive.

I maintain, however, that the two are better together than apart, provided that they—*both* of them—can move beyond their personal issues. Will is clearly looking for love (yes, in all the wrong places), and though he's got his eyes on a potential doormat in Emma, that's the exact opposite of what he needs. He didn't really examine himself, or his motivations, until Emma stood up for herself and demanded an explanation for his actions. He is at his best when he's challenged—something Terri can provide in spades. But make no mistake—for all of her failings, Terri sees, loves, and accepts Will for exactly who he is, down to every last imperfection. Will doesn't have to meet a standard of impeccable excellence with Terri; he needs only to be himself, exactly as he is.

Ironically, the opposite is true for Terri. Stubborn, hard-headed, and at times lacking emotional maturity, Terri yields to almost no one—except for Will. She's at her softest, her most vulnerable, her most *human*, when she's near him. Though a dash of tough love is required to rein in her outlandish behavior, what she really needs is a gentle, attentive touch. What better outlet for Will's savior complex than a woman who can be saved with little more than his trademark assets: kindness and love?

With a little effort and a lot of forgiveness on both sides, these two have the potential to bring out the best in each other.

So, What Now?

If the back nine episodes showed us anything, it's that Will has a lot of soul searching to do. No matter what the impetus is behind the ending of his marriage, a breakup of any kind shakes one's sense of self to the very core, and it's obvious that Will is struggling to figure out who he is. By first declaring himself ready to commit to Emma, then throwing himself into a compromising position in Shelby's arms, and then, later, spooning with April Rhodes and singing about their mutual sense of profound loneliness while gazing at photos of Terri...oh dear. The man is crumbling to bits before our very eyes.

Among the overwhelming list of things he needs to examine, a major one is why he's so willing to help Emma—a woman he, when it comes right down to it, hardly knows one whit—to obtain counseling for her (many) problems so that they can be together. In itself, this is a noble act, until you consider that it was mere weeks ago that his wife and childhood sweetheart was seeking counseling for the betterment of herself and her marriage, and he coldly rejected her, hitting the road before the co-pay check cleared.

If he truly loved Terri as he claimed he did, he owes it to himself—and her—to examine their relationship and accept responsibility for his part in its dissolution. The termination of their marriage is a tangled mess of loose ends in need of closure, without throwing the complexities of another person into the mix.

Further, he needs to look at what he sees in Emma—she worships him, that much is true, and he's clearly distressed when his indiscretions come to light and shatter her Christ-like image of him. But while worship feels good, it's a terribly uneven way to maintain a relationship. Fresh out of therapy, Emma is fragile and in need of support. Should Emma's opinion of him ever change, I fear that he'd drop her and head for more ego-stroking pastures, like a drug addict desperate for his next high. Worse, he'd be unwittingly casting Emma into the same role he complained about during his marriage to Terri, with him on a pedestal and Emma left to languish in his shadow.

It's a little suspicious that Will's renewed love for Emma blossomed after he learned she'd been seeing her dentist. And before he made his move, he made sure to ascertain that the door was still briefly open for him to become her first. What better way to seal his power over her than to take her coveted virginity?

Meanwhile, there's still Terri, who deserves a second chance—in fact, Will *needs* to give her one, even if it ultimately fails. There was real regret at the divorce proceedings, from both parties, and to abandon her at her most broken is to abandon himself. If we are to assume that Will is at his most authentic when he's coaching glee club, then we can assume we're dealing with a generous spirit—after all, this is the same man who forgave Rachel for the "Push It" disaster and displayed a remarkable amount of empathy for what Quinn has endured since becoming pregnant. And if one of the glee students had pulled what Terri did, Will would have been the first to look closely at the reasons why—or, rather, he'd have deduced them already, as he did with Quinn and the Glist.

Terri is wildly imperfect. But she is, perhaps, the only person outside of glee club to know and love Will for precisely who he is at heart. Better yet, I imagine that no amount of counseling can take away Terri's urge to tell it like it is, and that includes informing Will precisely what she thinks of him, and her own transgressions have, perhaps, put them on equal enough footing that Will will be emboldened to stand up to her similarly.

The truth is, Will might not love her anymore. Puzzle night may have lost its luster, and they might truly find that they are at an impassable crossroad—but let those things be discovered separate from the cloud of Terri's recent actions. And at the very least, even if they decide to part ways, mutual forgiveness will give them both the closure they need to properly move on.

And for God's sake, Will, whatever you do, stay far away from Emma. Let the poor woman buy her coordinated cardigan-necklace-shoe combinations and date dentists in peace. And please, *please* don't sleep with Sue Sylvester. No amount of revenge is worth *that*.

• • •

JONNA RUBIN can't carry a tune to save her life, but that's never stopped her from belting out Britney Spears into a hairbrush in front of the bathroom mirror. When not downloading the entire *Glee* music catalog and petitioning for an all-Peter Gabriel episode, she spends her days writing, child-wrangling, and worshipping her coffee maker. A contributor to *A Taste of True Blood: The Fangbanger's Guide*, she ekes out a living writing and blogging about motherhood, pop culture, and life in New England at www. jonniker.com.

How *Glee* Helped Me Defy Gravity

Throughout most of my life, I never knew who I was. However, when I discovered *Glee* and began to participate in my school's theater department, my life changed for the better. I finally knew who I was meant to be, and that no one and nothing else would ever bring me down.

By the time the episode "Wheels" (1-9) was approaching its air date, I and my fellow Gleeks (at least those who had knowledge of the Broadway musical *Wicked*) knew the show-stopping number "Defying Gravity" would be a featured subplot in the episode. After hearing about this storyline with Kurt and Rachel, I decided that it was time to finally show my peers who I was.

I'd been made fun of in previous years for my way of living and my interests, and I needed to prove all of those people wrong. I was comfortable with ignoring their comments because *I* personally knew who I was and *they* didn't. A few weeks before the episode debuted, our school had auditions for our annual talent show. I walked on the stage and sang a male version of "Defying Gravity" and eventually made the cut.

The day of the talent show, a week after the episode aired, we had two shows: one in the daytime for a paying audience of students, and another in the evening for parents, relatives, etc. I was going to perform at both shows, wearing my *Wicked* shirt and singing my heart out...at least, that's what I hoped. During the first show, I suddenly felt my heart race as I was told my act was approaching. I walked into the wings and heard the applause for the previous act. It was time for me to go on.

I walked toward the apron of the stage, and the auditorium's grand drape closed behind me. As the spotlight hit my face, everyone who knew me (or knew *of* me) applauded, ready to see what I was going to do. As the intro played, a group of ne'er-do-well students in the corner of the house started to moan and groan. They suspected that this song was going to suck and I was going to bore them to death. These were the people I was trying to face; I was ready. I sang the song, and on the line "and you won't bring me down," I pointed toward them and garnered much applause from the other audience members. I smiled and continued with the song.

As I approached the song's coda, where the famous belt is, I glanced around the auditorium. I suddenly felt how Kurt felt during the "diva-off": these people, the audience, were ready to see the big finale, and in my mind, I knew it had to be perfection. At the signaling note, I belted my butt off. After the first five seconds of belting, the audience was on their feet. I went on, just as Elphaba, or even Kurt, would have. I finished the song, and the audience roared with approval, still standing. Even those pesky students who'd moaned at the beginning stood for me. In the end, I walked off, leaving the audience stunned and amazed at what I could do.

Because of *Glee* and theater, I've found my niche and my reason for being. This is what I want to do. As Rachel says, "Being a part of something special makes

Continued next page

you special." I want to hear that audience approval every night. I want everyone to appreciate my gifts. That's why I'm an actor in high school now and want to pursue it in college and as a career. No one knows how thankful I am for a TV show that encourages everyone to pursue their dreams and, as Emma Pillsbury says, "live the life you are truly passionate about."

JACOB E. SANCHEZ
Fort Worth, Texas

GABI STEVENS

At the Heart of Sue Sylvester

I N THE INTEREST OF FULL DISCLOSURE, I have to tell you that I'm a romance author. I'm also a sap; I freely admit it. I'm always looking for a happy ending. *Glee* is one of those wonderful visceral shows that allows someone like me to laugh and cry, often in the same episode. I sobbed when Kurt came out to his father. I forced my husband to watch the football team dancing to Beyoncé's "Single Ladies." Will and Emma's romance breaks my heart every week as it encounters those familiar obstacles found in all romance novels. If the show finishes like one of my books, Rachel will triumph over her own self-centeredness and win Finn, with a few missteps along the way; Finn will recover from Quinn's deceit, and Quinn will find her own happiness. Yet in spite of my cheering for the good guys, my desire for the triumph of good over evil, my natural proclivities to look for the emotionally satisfying endings, none of the *Glee* characters fascinates me as much as the villain of the series, Sue Sylvester.

Let's face it: Sue is successful, strong, and has the best lines in the show. She never tempers her brutality, her caustic wit generates fear in everyone from Principal Figgins to the students, and she probably deserves to be arrested for some of her actions, like when she pushed the school nurse down the stairs. Nevertheless, I adore her. I have no desire to emulate her (although I completely admire Jane Lynch, the inimitable actress who portrays Sue; we all know the difference between reality and fantasy, right?), but without Sue *Glee* would be flat. A good story deserves a good villain, a character who works tirelessly against the protagonists, one who keeps the heroes from achieving their goals, one who keeps the happy ending from coming too easily. Sue completes the atmosphere and tone of the show. While the kids and Will Schuester deal with their own demons, she adds bonus turmoil in their lives. She creates the external conflict for the glee club that compels them to bond and find strength together.

So what makes a villain a good villain? A flat, two-dimensional villain would have little more driving his or her actions than a desire to be bad. The stereotypical mustache-twirling bad guy becomes little more than a character from the comics. A villain is far more interesting if we see glimpses of a real individual beneath the surface, perhaps a vulnerability or weakness. For much of the season, Sue appeared as little more than that mustache-twirling bad guy, figuratively speaking. But a great villain not only provides external conflict for the protagonists, she shows signs of her own inner conflict, her own turmoil. By the end of the season, the cracks in her façade exposed the person beneath that harsh surface. Events in the story arc revealed Sue's insecurities and the root cause of her actions. They showed her heart. Deep down, Sue is looking for love.

Maybe that's too strong. Love and Sue seem not to mix. Love, by definition (at least by my definition), requires, if not placing others before oneself, at least delighting in thinking of others. Sue thinks of Sue—her position, her accomplishments, her rewards. Consideration of others doesn't feature in her plans. But Sue craves accolades, and she equates recognition with love. To Sue's thinking, attention of any kind is positive. As she said in "Preggers" (1-4), "There's not much of a difference between a stadium full of cheering fans and an angry crowd screaming abuse at you. They're both just making a lot of noise. How you take it is up to you."

Sue revels in being the top dog, the alpha female. As any parent can tell you, if a child can't get positive attention, he or she will settle for negative attention. Sue intimidates the entire school, and so the entire school fears her. That such tactics are not admirable is irrelevant to Sue. She'll disregard their complaints about her. As she said, if people can't love her, she'll settle for the loud noise they create about her. Either way, no one can ignore her, and she chooses to take their awareness as proof of her importance. It's all in her attitude. And the key to getting noticed is power.

For Sue, the search for actual love is fraught with risk. Much safer to let herself believe that power equals love than to expose herself to a vulnerable situation. Power brings her the adulation she can pretend is caring. Sue understands she's settling, but it's a conscious decision. In "Mash-up" (1-8) and "Funk" (1-21), she took a chance at the real emotion, and both times she was devastated: "I'm alone, William. I don't even like you, and I was willing to jump at the chance to be with you. And you know, for a second I saw a flash of something. I pictured myself living a normal life, having someone to come home to every night. And though I completely loathe you, you'd make a great trophy husband."

She won't risk her emotions again. So power will be her substitute for love. Sue understands power and can control it.

Sue holds the supreme position at McKinley High. She is the coach of the national-champion cheerleading squad, the Cheerios. Anyone familiar with the world of high school knows that sports teams, especially ones that win championships, bring in much-needed funds for a school. Sue's efforts with the Cheerios have brought fame and money to William McKinley High, which is why Principal Figgins allows her such freedom. Sue's success is the school's success. In order to maintain that success, Sue believes she must have complete and unquestioned power. And success and power have another perk that Sue thrives on: she is the celebrity of the school. Everyone knows her, everyone is in awe of her, everyone acknowledges her worth. Power is Sue's way of focusing attention on herself.

We are a society of celebrity. An examination of our daily newspapers shows just how obsessed with celebrity we are. *Glee* takes this idea to its absurd and satirical level. In the reality of the show, Sue's celebrity allows her to get away with her outrageous behavior and even be rewarded for it. What is her segment for the local news, "Sue's Corner," but a pandering to Sue's fame? Principal Figgins loathes her behavior, but can only make a halfhearted effort to censure her. She provides too much good press for the school. And while the students fear her, they willingly allow themselves to be bullied. Why? Her Cheerios are the elite of the school; all students envy them and, in turn, respect Sue. They tolerate her behavior because in high school, being among the elite is a cherished goal. The students all know how the system works; as Quinn said, "Status is like currency. When your bank account is full, you can get away with doing just about anything" ("Mash-Up"). This idea could be the school motto. The glee club kids wanted to appear in a commercial in part because no one throws slushies at stars. They wanted to win Sectionals because then the kids at school would respect them. They want to make deposits into their "status accounts," to boost their standing in the school, to be more like Sue. Sue understands this concept and manipulates it. Her status account is full. She can do anything.

And the squad itself? Well, they rule the school, but their popularity could crumble at a whim (witness Puck's fall from grace when he shaves his Mohawk), and they know it. Their precarious position lies wholly in Sue's control. Sue's power is absolute. And she guards and controls her girls with rigid, draconian rules. A quiver in the knee of her star cheerleader sends chills into Sue's heart. A teen pregnancy arouses no compassion in Sue's soul. Because if the Cheerios aren't the best thing about McKinley High, then who is she? She can only be important if she is a champion. She can only garner attention if she has power.

Therein lies her issue with Will Schuester. Glee club is a threat to her status in the school. If another school team is successful, her power will be diminished. And that is the crux of her relentless pursuit of the glee club's downfall. In every underhanded way she can conceive, she wants to get rid of the one other club that has a chance to achieve acclaim for the school. Remember, McKinley has fostered winning glee clubs in the past.

Will threatens her position in another way as well. He controls his students with humor, caring, and compassion. They can come to him—and they do—with their problems, and he neither mocks them nor dismisses them. The kids love Will easily. They work hard for him because he is as much a *member* of the glee club as the teacher. He sacrifices for them, financially and emotionally. He pours his heart and soul into the club, weakening his marriage but strengthening his position at the school. Because of his sensitivity, he is the one character who can see through Sue's façade. Will provides an interesting foil to Sue. Where she manipulates, he asks; where she intimidates, he leads. Will won't let himself use Sue or sink to her level. He fights for the glee club kids and stands up to Sue. He doesn't fall for or submit to her nastiness (although the dark side does beckon him, as we'll see later). In "Throwdown" (1-7), Sue splintered the club by claiming that Will was prejudiced and then gained control over the majority of the glee club students. But instead of defending himself, Will stood up to her. He recognized her weaknesses and fears and confronted her with them: "You spend every waking moment of your life figuring out ways to terrify children to try to make you feel better about yourself and the fact that you're probably going to spend the rest of your life alone." His insight stunned her and made her lose control. She stepped down as co-chair of the glee club.

Sue realized that Will's success could undermine her control of her students. She rules her squad not with love and kindness, but with sarcasm, criticism, and ridicule. But because she achieves success not only for herself but also her students, they tolerate her behavior and in fact willingly submit to her meanness. Sue is neither a friend nor a mentor to the Cheerios, but the girls do look to her for approval. She instills loyalty in them not through love but through intimidation. The Cheerios are the top of the school, and the girls know that Sue's demands for perfection bring them their championships. And being a champion is intoxicating. They would rather suffer Sue's temper than be failures. If Will shows the students that greatness can be achieved without fear and terror, Sue's power will diminish.

Sue's world is based on her success. She not only runs the school in every way but name, she has a national reputation, owns a condo in Boca, and can demand first-class treatment, like European dry cleaning, because of her fame. *Splits* magazine named her Cheerleading Coach of the Decade. People like her, if only because she's famous. She relishes her celebrity because it's the only love she receives. Power masks Sue's vulnerability. No one would guess that below her gruff exterior lies a woman who craves acceptance and love.

So by the time we got to the "Mash-Up" episode, we believed we had Sue figured out. We laughed at this tough, sarcastic woman with the biting, scathing tongue, and we looked forward to her next great line. But then the first few chinks appeared in that armored exterior. She shocked us by showing a softer side when she fell for anchorman Rod Remington. Here was a real live man whom Sue did not have to intimidate into liking her. In fact, he said, "I need a gal with a little backbone, and I think you might be that gal." He accepted her for herself and didn't want her to change. Sue became almost human. Yes, she still had her quirks, but she was (gasp!) actually nice. Someone loved her, and it altered her entire outlook. Her radical personality change proved that to love and be loved is her heart's desire.

Sue no longer had to wear her power like a mask. She could afford to be vulnerable. At the same time, this episode revealed her emotional immaturity. Look how easily she fell in love with Rod: one date, a few simple compliments, and Sue exposed her soft side. She and Will even danced together. Okay, so she required lessons for a swing dance competition, and they danced at her request, but she laughed and smiled and didn't insult him. The old Sue was a distant memory.

Of course, the new Sue vanished when Rod proved that he was a man-whore. (And honestly, did you really think that the show would get rid of its villain? Where would the best conflicts come from then?) When Sue caught Rod with another woman, she let that mask of power snap back over her demeanor and retreated into the world she could rule.

Now, here I have to give Sue props. As a romance writer, I applaud her reaction to Rod's cheating. She knows her self-worth and stands up for herself. (Contrary to popular belief, romance novels do not advocate turning women into dishrags just because they are in love.) She values herself too highly to be just one of Rod's many women. She would rather be alone than with a cheating skunk. No man will use Sue Sylvester, nor will she compromise her standards just to have a man. In this episode Sue earned my admiration along with my laughter.

Little by little, Sue's grasp of power slipped in the second half of the first season. Her failure with Rod was but the first of many humanizing events in Sue's life. In "Mattress" (1-12), Quinn Fabray realized that she didn't have to take Sue's bullying and exposed Sue's greatest nightmare—that people don't need her. Sue's mask was in place for the confrontation, but it still left her shaken. If the students realize they don't need her, where will she go? She has no one. Too soon thereafter, Will scored another victory over her when he resigned as the glee club sponsor but was able to find a substitute to take the club to Sectionals. The glee club thwarted her plans again when they won Sectionals. The final blow to Sue's composure came when Principal Figgins suspended her for leaking the set list to the other schools. When even the principal could stand up to her, her power was gone. She retreated to her condo in Boca to regroup, saying, "Get ready for the ride of your life, Will Schuester. You are about to board the Sue Sylvester Express. Destination? Horror" ("Sectionals," 1-13). Regaining her power was the only way she could once again get the attention she desires. Which, of course, led to blackmailing Figgins for her reinstatement.

Sue Sylvester returned with plans to dominate the school once again, but she didn't quite achieve that goal. More and more, people began to realize that they could stand up to Sue and survive. Her authority and power didn't have the force they once had. The school no longer feared her. Will not only challenged her role as winningest teacher, he also retaliated with his own insults. In "Home" (1-16), Quinn undermined Sue's authority with the Cheerios by telling Mercedes that she doesn't need to diet. Mercedes hijacked the assembly. In "Bad Reputation" (1-17), the students mocked Sue as she walked the halls. Sue's authority and power had crumbled. We could see her panic.

In the final blow before regaining her equilibrium, Sue once more exposed her desire to be truly loved. In "Funk," Will, in an effort to stop Sue's bullying once and for all, succumbed to the dark side and lowered himself to her level. Will seduced Sue and made her believe he cared for her. Once again showing her emotional immaturity, Sue fell for Will lightning fast, and when he dumped her, she took to her bed, abandoning even the next national championship for her Cheerios. In the revealing end scene, Sue admitted that she understood that power is a poor substitute for love, but Will pointed out the essential truth in her life:

> WILL: You're not alone, Sue. Your kids need you. So you do have love in your life.
> SUE: My kids don't love me. They fear me.
> WILL: But you love them, Sue.

Sue came out of this confrontation with a greater awareness of the love in her life, but still not trusting it. We sense that she is a changed person—her vote in the Regionals proved that—but she isn't giving up her manipulation just yet. She did the right thing offstage, where no one could witness her compassion. She told Will that the glee club has another year because she doesn't want to give up ridiculing his hair . . . and because she grudgingly admires what he's done for the kids. But she delivered the news in her signature scathing and mocking style.

Her soft side hidden, Sue is back in form, a force to be reckoned with. The illusion is enough for her. She will accept being admired and feared.

With the exception of one person.

I have purposely saved mentioning Sue's sister until the end of this essay. That storyline sheds the most light on Sue's character. In "Wheels" (1-9), we learned that Sue has an older sister with Down syndrome. Jean is the one person who *truly* loves Sue—no games, no manipulations needed. With Jean, we saw a side of Sue we never would have guessed existed. Earlier in the episode, Sue chose Becky Johnson, a girl with Down syndrome, as a replacement Cheerio. Will believed that Sue was using Becky for some nefarious purpose, especially after he witnessed Sue pushing Becky to jump rope better. Sue's line—"You think *this* is hard? Try auditioning for *Baywatch* and being told they're going in another direction. *That* was hard. Hit the showers"—sounded especially cruel, callous, and condescending after Becky's eager and enthusiastic attempt at keeping up with the Cheerios' routine. Sue appeared to have crossed the line—until we saw the last scene of the episode. That was when it struck us that Sue was actually being sincere when she said that line.

And Sue was also right.

Becky *will* have to work harder to succeed. That's a fact of her life. But just having Sue give her a chance and an opportunity to do that hard work was enough to show that *Glee*'s villain has a heart bigger than many regular people's.

I'm speaking from my own heart here. My youngest daughter has intellectual and developmental disabilities (IDD). She doesn't have Down, but she is clearly differently abled, or, as Sue put it, "handi-capable." And like Becky, my daughter is in high school, where most of the other students look past her or through her. She is judged by what she can't do, rather than being encouraged to show what she can.

People with IDD don't want pity, they just want to be given the chance to live and laugh, work and love. Becky's reaction to Sue's harsh-sounding words seemed to be a mockery of her own syndrome, but her reaction was genuine. That wide grin of joy wasn't because she didn't understand that her coach was disappointed in her; it was because she knew someone was treating her as a person, not merely someone with Down syndrome. (And didn't Lauren Potter do an incredible job in the role of Becky? I hope we see more of her in the series.)

That episode touched so many people because Sue showed her heart. She revealed that beneath the sarcasm, the acidity, and the ego, compassion and love flow. Sue realized just how strong Jean had had to be, and she apologized to her sister for not sticking up for her more often. Empathy and admiration are two emotions we never expected Sue to admit to, and when she did, it added a dimension to her character that shocked and surprised us. Although we aren't sure if we believe the little Sue has told us about her parents—we haven't got much reason to trust her words; she lies even in her journal—we can believe that she and her sister practically raised themselves and became a team. They truly respect each other. Sue unburdens herself to her sister and then follows her sister's advice in "Bad Reputation"—to great success. Sue is a star again, thanks to her sister. Sue is back on her game.

But I have to be honest. Sue was my favorite character long before "Wheels." As I said at the start, she has the best lines, the greatest comebacks, and the cleverest insults. Her strength would be admirable...if she wasn't quite so brutal with it.

So does this mellowing tendency—her vote in the Regionals, her fight for another year of glee club, relinquishing her blackmail—mean we'll see a change in Sue Sylvester? God, I hope not. And as shown in "Bad Reputation," Sue's idea of helping others differs from what we would consider normal. Her newfound humanity doesn't bode well for the rest of the cast. Her journal entries have her reflecting on whether her actions toward others have brought about a karmic justice, and whether she should change her behavior. However, once again, she eluded a true moral smackdown when her cringeworthy leaked video became a vehicle for her to work with Olivia Newton-John and rub her success in the faces of the faculty. Karma likes Sue Sylvester.

The complexity in Sue's character, while perhaps making us like her better, doesn't excuse her earlier behavior or her ruthlessness. If anything, it makes us wonder about her more and laugh at ourselves for falling under her spell. We're left with questions: Can we trust Sue? Can Sue change? But one thing is certain: Sue is more than a cookie-cutter character. She has depths—absurd depths to be sure, but depths that haven't yet been explored. Her outrageousness satirizes our society's worship of celebrity and sports, and her aggressiveness mocks our own obsession with success. How different is Rachel's desire for stardom from Sue's quest for success? Yet that one aspect of humanity that shines through Sue's character—the need to be loved—allows her to transcend the stereotype and become an adversary we enjoy watching. I wouldn't say anyone's rooting for her to win, but she sure gives *Glee* a whole new definition of competition.

• • •

GABI STEVENS was born in Southern California to Hungarian parents. After spending time in boarding school, college, and studying abroad, she's still in the classroom teaching eighth graders the joys of literature. An award-winning romance author, Gabi writes in New Mexico. She loves to play games, has a wicked addiction to reading, avoids housework and cooking, and doesn't travel nearly as much as she would like to. Her latest book and the first in a trilogy, *The Wish List*, is available from Tor Books. You can visit her at www.GabiStevens.com, or write to her at P.O. Box 20958, Albuquerque, NM 87154-0958.

JENNIFER CRUSIE

"You Think This Is Hard? Try Being an Antagonist, *That's* Hard"

Why Sue Sylvester Is Essential to *Glee*

SUE SYLVESTER is an iconic figure, ranking with Iago, Hannibal Lecter, and Voldemort in her dominance and shaping of the story she's in. Without her, *Glee* would just be a song list and Brittany and Santana discussing gay sharks. With Sue as antagonist, the stories rise to the level of Greek drama. Aristotle would have *loved* Sue Sylvester.

As Aristotle knew, the core of classic storytelling is the *agon*, or struggle; the main actors in the story are therefore agonists. The central or first character is the protagonist because his or her search for a goal begins the story and pushes it forward. In *Glee*, that's Will Schuester, a Spanish teacher at William McKinley High School in Lima, Ohio, who was once a member of the now-defunct glee club there. Will is lost, aimless, stuck in a marriage to a harpy, and half in love with the school guidance counselor but unwilling to admit it. His finest moments were when he was part of glee club; as he said in the pilot episode, "Being a part of that, I knew who I was in the world." Searching for meaning in his adult life, in a rare moment of decision, he went to the principal and began the arduous process of resurrecting the club by assembling a collection of talented losers in a group he called New Directions because they, like him, so desperately needed one.

But Will alone can't make a story. He needs somebody pushing back against him, somebody with a character equal to or stronger than his, an antagonist who will block him in such a distinctive way that she gives his story a new and surprising form. Will had miscellaneous problems along the way—an odd assortment of kids showed up, he had to fight for practice space, the principal told him he must win Regionals in order to keep the club after the first year—but he could have solved all of those easily if it weren't for the opponent in his *agon*, his antagonist, the formidable cheerleader adviser of WMHS, Sue C. Sylvester.

Beginning with her opening rant at the Cheerios in the pilot episode ("You think this is hard? Try waterboarding, *that's* hard!"), Sue is riveting, not only because she's a fascinating character in her own right, but also because she embodies the Three Rules of Great Antagonists: (1) She is much stronger than the protagonist she sets out to destroy, (2) she will stop at nothing to achieve her goal, and (3) despite all that strength and implacability, she's a vulnerable human being, not a cartoon.

The first rule, strength, can be shown in intelligence, skill, quickness of reaction, and individuality, that sense that the character is not only thinking outside the box, she doesn't even know the box is there. Sue is smart: she outwits Will at every turn, stunning him, for example, when she got herself appointed as his glee club co-advisor, took the half of the group who could be considered minorities ("gay kid, Asian, other Asian" ["Throwdown," 1-7]), and then created dissension by paying attention to them while Will concentrated on his lead singers. She's so skilled that she's nationally known as the country's greatest cheerleader adviser (six national titles). But mostly Sue is off-the-wall different. Her threat to Will of what would happen if he was one minute late giving her the club's playlist became an instant classic: "I will go to the animal shelter and get you a kitty cat, I will let you fall in love with that kitty cat, and then on some dark cold night, I will steal away into your house and punch you in the face" ("Mash-Up," 1-8). A lesser antagonist would have just told him she was going to do something awful to the cat. An even lesser antagonist would merely have threatened to punch him. Diabolical Sue feints with the kitty and then punches Will when he's off-guard, leaving him speechless, verbally unconscious. That ability to blindside an opponent, to constantly confound expectation, combined with her supreme indifference to everything but her own goals, gives her character all it needs to achieve antagonist greatness. The only other antagonist on television who has even approached Sue's megalomaniac brilliance was the Mayor in *Buffy the Vampire Slayer*, and he was an insane demon. Sue's neither crazy nor demonic, but she is almost otherworldly in her intelligence and her skill at bringing down her enemies.

All that intelligence and skill is backed by absolute implacability: Sue's goal is so important to her that she will stop at nothing—*nothing*—to achieve it. She's ruthless enough to send her Cheerios to spy on the club, to lie to Will's wife that he's cheating on her, to blackmail the principal (twice), and to put the elderly school nurse in a coma; as Sue C's it: "Never let anything distract you from winning. Ever" ("Hairography," 1-11). She is without boundaries in her defense and promotion of the Cheerios, and her assaults often leave Will speechless in disbelief. Sue, however, is never speechless. Even at the end of the first half of the season when Will had gotten her suspended and saved glee club, she could still one-up him, telling him that although she'd underestimated him, she was going to get herself back into fighting shape and return: "Prepare to be crushed" ("Sectionals," 1-13).

But Sue is not just supernaturally skilled at the evil nemesis game; she's also a fully dimensional human being. In the beginning of the season, Sue veered close to cartoonish with her need to dominate everyone around her, but in later episodes, having established her über-antagonist cred, the writers made her vulnerable and therefore human. She has, as *Buffy*'s Cordelia Chase once claimed for herself, *layers*. And those layers were most on display in Sue's interactions with her sister and Becky Johnson, in her short-lived relationship with promiscuous newscaster Rod Remington, and in her broken heart when Will seduced and abandoned her in order to destroy her. When she was forced to hold open auditions for the Cheerios, she chose Becky, who has Down syndrome, and then proceeded to harass her the same way she'd harassed every other miserable student on her team. When Will objected, Sue said, "You're asking me to treat this girl differently because she has a disability, when it seems to me she just wants to be treated like everybody else" ("Wheels," 1-9). Sue was absolutely right, and just as we viewers were wondering when Sue had gotten sensitivity training, she went to see her sister, who also has Down syndrome, and treated her with such immense love and kindness that she instantly morphed from Sue the Merciless into a vulnerable, caring woman. When she fell for shallow newscaster Remington and changed into a warm, delighted, dancing lover, viewers were as pained for her when he cheated as we were for Will when he discovered his wife's big lie. In fact, Sue is *more* vulnerable than Will when it comes to her heart, which is why his seduction and betrayal in the second half of the first season was so harsh. Sue deserves almost anything he can throw at her, but not that. She is, after all, not a cartoon; she's a human being. A deadly, devious, ruthless human being, but still a woman with a warm and loving—if well-hidden—heart, somebody viewers care about.

Not content with making Sue an icon of antagonism, the writers of *Glee* have given her even more resonance in the story by using the Doppelgänger Effect; that is, they have made Sue and Will essentially the same person, with the same fears, the same flaws, and the same strengths. Doppelgängers are shadow selves, literally "double walkers," often the bright and dark sides of the same persona (think Jekyll and Hyde). In *Glee*, Sue and Will's doppelgänger personalities, goals, and motivations make their fight even more vicious because they recognize themselves in each other, however subconsciously. Sue confronted Will with their mirror images when she told him in the second episode, "Face it, you want to be me" ("Showmance"). Will denied it, but it's true. He wants New Dimensions to be the choral

Cheerios, wants to empower his kids as cheerleading empowers the Cheerios, and to do so, he became as driven as Sue, repeatedly trying shady moves like bringing back an adult who'd never graduated to replace their missing star ("The Rhodes Not Taken," 1-5). Sue blackmailed Principal Figgins into giving her anything she wanted, much as Will framed Finn Hudson, the school football hero, with a drug charge to force him to sing with New Directions in the first episode. In their mimed fight in "Throwdown" Sue and Will were practically mirror images, to the point that Will said, "I'm so ashamed of myself; she's turned me into her." But Sue hadn't turned Will into her; he always was her. Her opposition just forced him to reveal himself as he truly is, something that's essential both to his growth as a protagonist and to the success of the club and the students he loves. Will had to learn to cowboy up if he was ever going to be a hero, and Sue's constant testing is what got him there.

The doppelgänger effect is also reflected in a similar vulnerability: their connections to the leaders of their groups. Sue sees herself in head cheerleader Quinn Fabray the same way Will sees himself in lead male singer Finn. It began with the last shot of the pilot episode, when Will and Finn beamed at each other, happy in their new club, while Sue and Quinn looked down at them from above in the darkened auditorium, eyes narrowed, identical determination on each face. Later, both Will and Sue acknowledged the connection: Will told Finn in "Mash-Up" that "Of all the students I've ever had, you remind me the most of me." Sue told Quinn in "Showmance," "I'm reminded of a young Sue Sylvester, although you don't have my bone structure," and then in "Mattress" (1-12), "You know, I'd forgotten how ruthless you really are. You're like a young Sue Sylvester." The fact that Finn has the survival skills of a lemming while gimlet-eyed Quinn can take on and defeat Sue may tell the viewer more about how Sue and Will see themselves than anything else. And the importance of those heirs was made manifest in the look of defeat on Will's face when Finn told him he was giving up glee for football because of Sue's manipulations, and on Sue's when Quinn turned her back on the Cheerios for glee and Will's support. Those were moments of truth for both adults: They need the kids more than the kids need them, and that need fires their battle to a new intensity. They're not just fighting for the clubs that define them; they're fighting for their own future selves.

And that battle between Will and Sue as good and evil twins led to the satisfying conclusion at the end of season one. At the end of the last episode, "Journey," Sue did something that seemed out of character: she gave glee club a second chance and a second year. But it was really part and parcel of her excellence as an antagonist. Sue is strong: she's not afraid to battle Will for another year, and confident she'll win again. She's implacable: she gave up her blackmail card with Figgins to get glee another year; whatever it takes, she'll do it. But, most of all, she's vulnerable, a feeling human being: she'd have to have a heart of stone to listen to the glee kids sing "To Sir With Love" and not be moved by their love and respect for Will and the club. As she told him, "I've proven that I can wipe you and your glee club off the face of this earth. But what kind of a world would that be, Will? A world where I couldn't constantly ridicule your hair, a world where I couldn't make fun of you for tearing up more than Michael Landon in a sweeps week episode of *Little House on the Prairie*? Sue Sylvester's not sure she wants to live in that world." Then she added the kicker: "You're a good teacher, and I don't like you much, but I admire the work you're doing with your kids. I really do." Sue knows that just as she shapes and shoves her Cheerios toward a better future, Will does the same for the kids in glee. And she also knows that she's a better person—stronger, sharper, more successful—because Will and his glee club are there to push back: the doppelgänger effect at its antagonistic best.

Sue Sylvester is a multi-layered, multi-faceted, multi-motivated juggernaut of ego and need. In a cast of weird and wonderful players, she is the weirdest and most wonderful, the salt in *Glee*'s chocolate soufflé, the rocket engine that makes the show go, the architect of its form and friction. And because of that, she is one of the great antagonists of our time.

• • •

JENNIFER CRUSIE was researching her dissertation on the differences in the way men and women tell stories when she got sidetracked into writing romance novels. Her first book was published in 1993 and her twenty-first in 2010, all of which she considers a minor miracle, especially since she is also a *New York Times*, *USA Today*, and *Publisher's Weekly* bestseller and a two-time Rita award winner. Her latest novel from St. Martin's Press is *Maybe This Time*, her homage to Henry James's *The Turn of the Screw*. She lives with two kids, two cats, and five dogs in southern Ohio, where she often stares at the ceiling and counts her blessings.

Every Girl Needs a Kurt

share your Glee

Every high school girl needs a Kurt. Rod was mine.

We met in sophomore English, fall of 1968, and soon gravitated together to the back of the class. When we studied *Romeo and Juliet*, Rod asked to read the part of Juliet. Miss M wouldn't let him. Of course, she also bragged about helping our principal expel Truman Capote from the high school. We shouldn't have been surprised by her decision, but I was proud of Rod for trying.

I focused on grades and student government and getting myself the heck out of that Connecticut town for college. Rod was the class thespian—president of the Dramatics Association who directed oodles of plays. Our senior show brought us back together for what turned out to be the highlight of my high school career, with Rod playing a starring role.

It was the school's first year out of the 1925 brick structure where the senior show had been called *Vaudeville* since, well, the Roaring Twenties. With a modern school building and theater, a new principal and a new decade, Rod and his co-directors defied tradition and christened the class of '71 show *SRO*, for Standing Room Only. I was in charge of ticket sales in addition to being part of the show, so I know there was indeed standing room only for every performance.

Managing tickets was my *SRO* job; singing and dancing were my joys. Thanks to Rod's leadership and love of all things theater, for two months that spring we were a show choir. My favorite number was "On the Good Ship Lollipop." Rod choreographed the tap dance for at least fifty of us, and damn, we were good! Perhaps I'm only imagining that we sang "Lollipop" or our opening number, "Swingin' on a Star," at graduation in June. I do know I gave Rod a huge hug that day.

I left town for college in California. Rod stayed; I heard he opened a flower shop that did a booming business with New York theaters. We failed to stay in touch, so it wasn't until I returned for a reunion that I heard from a fellow "Lollipop" dancer that, like so many gay men of our generation, Rod had died from complications of AIDS. So there I was, crying at my high school reunion, hoping Rod knew how much he'd meant to me.

My three daughters didn't wait till senior year of high school to become involved in theater. Through the years and all those shows, each has had her Rod, her Kurt—a boy who sings, dances, braids hair, trades fashion and shopping advice, and, most important, listens. A Kurt offers platonic love and tips on the male species during that crazy, confusing time in life when teens are figuring things out about the opposite sex and drama abounds. Girls can be themselves when they're around a Kurt. They may have crushes on the same guys, but they also like the same Broadway shows, movies, and (natch) *Glee*.

It's no wonder Kurt is my daughters' favorite *Glee* character. He's mine too.

DEBBIE DUNCAN
Stanford, California

CLAUDIA GRAY

"You're Having My Baby"

WAS THERE EVER ANY DOUBT I was going to be a *Glee* fan? That fate was sealed for me years and years before the show ever aired—back during my own time in high school, which I spent in taffeta and sequins, perfecting my jazz hands and learning show-choir dance routines to songs like Kool & the Gang's "Celebration."

But I have to tell you, *Glee* nearly lost me a couple months into the first season for one reason alone: the "pregnancy lie" storylines for Terri and Quinn.

I don't object to pregnancy stories as a general rule; as a die-hard soap opera fan, I'd have to say there are few things I like better than a good "who's the father?" mystery. And who lies more often than characters in soap operas? But the way *Glee* initially handled this made me crazier with rage than Sue Sylvester watching Will Schuester put styling product in his hair.

One funny thing about *Glee*, though—the show often takes a story, pushes it past humor to a place that's borderline uncomfortable, and then finds its way to a graceful, meaningful conclusion. More than once, the series surpassed my expectations by turning an awkward moment or troubling character trait into a thing of beauty. And that's exactly what happened with the pregnancy storylines by the midpoint of the first season.

The Soap-Opera Beginning

When *Glee* began, we had Will Schuester married to his high school sweetheart, Terri—very unhappily. He was committed to a simple life of teaching Spanish and starting the glee club; she was binge-shopping at home décor stores and dreaming of more. They came back together when it turned out that Terri was pregnant...

Except, of course, that she wasn't.

Terri's first trip to the obstetrician revealed that she was only suffering from a hysterical pregnancy. She wanted her life to change so badly—wanted an emotional connection so desperately—that her subconscious tricked her body into creating the same symptoms she'd have had if she were expecting.

The show really made this psychologically convincing. Terri and Will got together when they were very young, and it seems clear there was never another serious love interest for either of them before that. Their relationship as husband and wife seemed severely lacking—but possibly neither of them had ever fully realized that, because they didn't have any other romantic relationships to compare this one to. As badly as they fit together, Will was an essential part of Terri's entire adult life. She may have nagged him and wished he shared her interest in material comforts, but she was also genuinely attracted to him and deeply understood his personality.

Also, it was clear from the get-go that Terri was extremely uncertain about this lie. Once she'd had a little while to think about it, it seemed possible that she might come clean—but Will jumped the gun, revealing the pregnancy to his parents before they'd said they would. Once Terri's humiliating error was compounded, she could only have found it harder to confess. Her deception wasn't totally calculating; it was a blunder, the piling on of mistake after mistake until she was in a place that was difficult to back down from. We all understand how that feels. Although this was a whopper of a lie, *Glee* at least rooted Terri's motivation for it in her love for Will.

Of course, this lie was also a long shot. What were the odds that she'd be able to find a newborn to adopt, one due around the same time that she would supposedly be giving birth?

Well, this is television, which means the odds were actually pretty good—which brings us to Quinn.

When *Glee* began, head Cheerio Quinn Fabray was not only the most popular girl in school and the girlfriend of popular jock Finn; she was also the leader of the celibacy club. And yet the show had hardly gotten started when Quinn revealed that she was pregnant. Was she just a hypocrite? At first it looked that way, especially when we learned that Finn wasn't even the father.

However, even here, Quinn's decisions were made credible. We came to realize that her involvement in the celibacy club wasn't hypocritical as much as it was forced upon her by her overbearing parents. If those beliefs weren't genuinely hers to start with, is it any wonder that she didn't always follow them?

Cheating on Finn became more understandable, too. Finn's the boyfriend she tells her parents about, the one she walks down the school hallways with, the one she made join the chastity club with her. As far as Quinn's concerned, he's part of her image—the accessory that completes the false impression she has to show the world. So she pretended with him as much as she did with anyone else. She could only explore her sexuality with someone whom she was with out of the public eye. Someone who would keep her secrets. And that was Puck.

Maybe it's a slightly longer stretch to say that Finn would ever believe he'd gotten Quinn pregnant when they'd never had sex. But I suspect that this (along with Quinn and Puck's failure to use birth control) is the show's commentary on the misinformation that some less-effective abstinence programs for teens dole out in a misguided effort to prevent teenage sex through scare tactics rather than sincere conviction. If so, it's sly and almost sneaky—and extremely well done.

The Messy Middle

So, here we had two characters lying about their pregnancies: Quinn, who was lying about the father of her baby, and Terri, who was lying about being pregnant at all. But the *Glee* writers fully established why each of these women would make the choices she'd made. What, then, was the problem?

Well, the single biggest problem with Terri's lie is this: It only works if Will Schuester is a *total idiot*.

Maybe a pregnancy pad worn beneath her shirts could deceive Terri's coworkers and casual acquaintances. But seriously, how could she think that she could spend nine whole months living in the same house with Will, sharing the same bathroom and bed, and never be found out? Wouldn't Will, like most expectant fathers, want to put his hand on her belly sometimes to feel the baby kick? Even if she swore off sex for the entire "pregnancy"—which is pretty rare to start with—wouldn't she and Will even cuddle occasionally, so that he would feel the fakeness of the pad? Is he never going to walk into the bathroom while she's in the shower, to see her supposed baby bump hanging on the bar with the towels? The basic intimacy of a husband and wife (heck, even of the average roommates) makes her lie extremely unlikely to work.

Of course, we always hear stories in the news of women who did manage to pull off these kinds of lies, so I guess it's not impossible. But when you hear these stories, don't you think, on some level, *How stupid did that husband have to be?* Yeah, we all do.

This plan just doesn't work, basically. But Terri acted as if she believed she could pull it off. Quinn stood a better chance of managing her part in the lie, but didn't she wonder whether Mr. Schue might, you know, *notice* that his newborn looked a whole lot like her? Or, worse, like Puck? Were these women idiots, or convinced that Will and Finn were idiots? Either way, nobody comes out of this looking good.

Not to mention, there's just something off-putting about having two "lying woman" storylines going on in the same TV series at the same time. One such story *might* play out without being offensive, but two at once gets uncomfortable. It starts reminding us of sexist stereotypes of women as liars and manipulators. How could it not, when two of the female leads are primarily concerned with lying about the most important issues in their lives, to the most important people in their lives?

This stereotype got even stronger because of the way *Glee* portrayed the men involved. Will and Finn may each have been way too slow to catch on, and neither of them is perfect, but there's no question that they're each shown to be decent, good-natured guys. And yet, during the "pregnancy lie" storylines, both Will and Finn had other love interests. Will went back and forth between cheerfully preparing for the birth of his child and confiding in besotted guidance counselor Emma Pillsbury. Finn stuck by Quinn, but he was drawn more and more to Rachel Berry. In both cases, the secondary romances were the ones that we, the viewers, were invited to invest in.

So is it implausible to suppose that, in some ways, the lies about the pregnancies were supposed to excuse Will and Finn's behavior? That way, the audience could root for Will and Emma, even though Will was married to someone else, and for Finn and Rachel, even though Finn was committed to someone else. We didn't have to feel bad about cheering on potential cheating, because we knew Will and Finn's existing relationships were doomed the second the truth inevitably came out.[2] This snarl in the plot thread didn't just let the guys off the hook; it let the audience off the hook, too.

But even if it excused us, the viewers, it actually didn't excuse Will and Finn at all. If they believed they were about to become fathers with the women they were attached to—and they did—then

---

[2] And we knew the truth would come out eventually because *this is* TV.

the kind of flirting they were doing was, frankly, pretty scummy. And we were supposed to be rooting for these people?

When Sue Sylvester starts to look like a model of straightforward honesty, you know you've got trouble.

How *Glee* Turned It Around

Just when this all looked unsalvageable, though, *Glee* got back on the right track. In the fall finale, and the episodes leading into it, the truth about Terri and Quinn came out—and in such a way that everyone involved kept as much of their dignity intact as possible.

The fallout began when Will *finally* found a pregnancy pad lying around the house. He made the correct deduction immediately—reaffirming our faith in his intelligence, right about the time we could've been forgiven for assuming he had none. Although he was understandably angry when he confronted Terri, he didn't stoop to insulting her at length, declaring that he had never loved her, or going to any other melodramatic extreme. Will got the facts, made his anger known, and got out. Their break was sudden, but as realistic and underplayed as such a hugely emotional situation could ever be.

As for Terri, she responded as well as anyone in that situation could. Once she'd been outed, she felt real shame—and no small measure of relief. In the fall finale, she went into therapy to find out why she'd sunk so deeply into the pregnancy lie and to accept responsibility for her actions. This wasn't enough to save her marriage, or even to make us like her, but it was enough to make her a three-dimensional character instead of a cartoon.

Then *Glee* went one better. As the show neared the end of the first season, the Schuesters' marriage was finally legally ended. This was where I expected the show to forget that Terri ever existed, but instead, the writers found a way to weave her back into the drama. When Finn had to pay for his anti-Vocal Adrenaline vandalism in

"Funk" (1-21), he got a job at Sheets-N-Things, where Terri works. Instead of mining this for easy, spiteful humor, the show used the situation to show Terri's better side. She took Finn under her wing, sensing a chance to be a friend to someone who needed it—someone who reminded her of a young Will. It wasn't the same as making it up to her ex-husband, but it was as close as she's ever likely to get. Is it any wonder that "Funk" was also the first episode in which Terri sang? Her character was no longer merely an obstacle or a joke; she was a human being, and she got to join in the music.

Quinn's later story arc was even more surprising—and even better. By the finale, her storyline had gone from being my least favorite element of the show to being perhaps the best part of the entire year. How did we get there? Well...

One element of Quinn's lie about Finn never made much sense in the earlier episodes of the show: she always said that she had the right to choose someone who would provide for and take care of her. Finn is that kind of guy. Puck has his moments, but let's face it, he's not Mr. Reliable.[3]

But we had to ask: Why did it matter whether the father of her baby was a good provider? Although she might need prenatal vitamins and that kind of thing, Quinn was planning to give her child up for adoption. Her financial needs were short-term and not that substantial.

However, in "Ballad" (1-10), we finally found out something that might explain why she felt that way. When Finn had dinner with her family, they came clean about Quinn's pregnancy—and we learned what had been driving her for so long. Her parents are so rigid in their thinking, and so self-righteous, that they were incapable of responding to their weeping daughter with anything besides anger and scorn. And so Finn did what Puck almost certainly couldn't have done: he courageously stood up for her. When her parents commit-

---

[3] Puck got a lot better toward the end of season one, but at the beginning of it—e.g., when Quinn made her decision to lie about her baby's paternity—he still had a long way to go, and nobody could have blamed Quinn for not believing how far he could come.

ted the ultimate parenting fail by throwing her out of their house, Finn and his mother took her in.

The worst part of it all: Quinn had to have known this was coming. Knowing her parents as she does—having joined the celibacy club no doubt at their insistence—she'd gone through her entire pregnancy not only freaking out about having a baby she must give up for adoption, but also dreading the moment when her mother and father would reject her for it.

No wonder she lied. Quinn knew she was going to be thrown out on her own, completely vulnerable. She knew she needed someone who would come through for her, and Finn did.[4]

Then, when the show reached "Sectionals" (1-13), Quinn's storyline *really* got interesting.

In true soap-opera fashion, pretty much everyone else on the show figured out that Finn wasn't the baby's father before Finn did. As the glee club was getting ready for Sectionals, Rachel became the latest to put two and two together and get Puck. Her reaction—that Finn must be told the truth at once for his own good—was the one we would naturally expect ourselves to have, and the one we'd therefore expect the show to portray as the right thing to do.

But where I expected *Glee* to zig, it zagged. When Rachel confronted the glee club with her suspicions, everyone confirmed that Puck was the real father—but none of them supported telling Finn the truth. There was an element of selfishness there, of course, because nobody wanted to rock the glee club boat as they were heading into one of their biggest competitions of the year, and yet there was so much more to it—the club defended Quinn's decision to keep the secret. Mercedes even went so far as to say that Quinn had the right to provide for herself and her child as she saw fit—even if that meant lying to Finn.

Do I agree with this? I don't think so; I believe Finn had the right to know the truth. But I think Mercedes' take on events was a valid reminder that Quinn's lie wasn't nearly as evil as the condemnation

---

[4] Ultimately, Puck did take her in when he was revealed to be the baby's father, but again, I can see how Quinn might originally have doubted he'd come through.

and abandonment she was up against. Most of those "in the know" were women, and having Mercedes act as their voice and defend Quinn's decision to lie for her own protection and that of her child came across as a daring sign of female solidarity in morally murky circumstances.

Of course, Rachel didn't agree with Mercedes either, and she told Finn the truth right before Sectionals. But the show didn't play it as her doing the right thing by Finn; instead, we saw it as her putting her own feelings before Quinn's and before the good of the glee club.

Maybe it's unfortunate that Quinn didn't have the bravery to reveal the truth to Finn herself, which would have been an amazing, redemptive moment. But for me, the show's writers more than made up for that with the conversation Quinn and Rachel shared after the big reveal. Rachel apologized, and Quinn—once the chief mean girl of McKinley High—refused to condemn her. In fact, she accepted responsibility for her part in the situation. Instead of pitting the women against each other, *Glee* made it clear that the real darkness in the situation was neither Quinn's lie nor Rachel's revelation; it was the plight Quinn found herself in because of her parents' abandonment.

Later That Year

After the fall break, the show initially, mysteriously back-burnered Quinn's pregnancy. What had been one of the driving stories in *Glee* suddenly became almost invisible.[5] It took weeks or even months to resolve basic questions about her situation, such as, "Where is Quinn living now?" However, the show was once again working its way through an awkward period toward something great.

The awkward period for Quinn was pretty much summed up in "Hell-O" (1-14). Mercedes struggled with her body image after

---

[5] Nearly as invisible as Quinn's baby bump itself in the "The Power of Madonna" (1-15). Did anyone else spend all of "Express Yourself" wondering how that girl could fit into a corset by her sixth month?

joining the Cheerios, and Quinn proclaimed that she'd learned to look at food and health differently since being pregnant, achieving a more holistic outlook, telling Mercedes that her body and spirit were truly beautiful. While watching this, I could only think, "That blonde girl is really nice and very thoughtful. What has she done with Quinn?" I wondered if *Glee* was going in a bold new direction—maybe science fiction, complete with bodysnatchers.

But the show was building toward something with Quinn and Mercedes, something that finally broke out in the penultimate episode of the year, "Funk." Although Puck had finally come through for Quinn, and she was now living with him, neither she nor Puck's mother were thrilled. The audience saw that, while Puck's house provided shelter, what Quinn didn't have was a fully supportive home.

But in "Funk," Quinn finally burst out in song: in what may have been the single most bizarre musical number *Glee* offered all year, she brought other pregnant teenagers into class to sing a cover of James Brown's "It's a Man's Man's Man's World." With Lamaze breathing as backup! If you could watch that without your eyes bugging out, you're hard to shock. Harder to shock than I am, anyway.

After thinking about it, though, I decided I liked the number, mostly because it showed Quinn finally speaking out about the injustice of her situation. Yes, Puck was financially supporting her—providing what she thought she needed most of all—but it wasn't enough. She needed acceptance, and that came from Mercedes, who put her money where her mouth was earlier in the season by stepping up and offering to take Quinn into her home instead. This was undoubtedly the unlikeliest friendship of the year, but as of right now, it's the single thing I want to see explored most in season two. Now that Mercedes and Quinn are on the same team, I'm betting there's nothing they can't do.

Finally, in the season finale, "Journey," Quinn went into labor and delivered her daughter, Beth. Despite her evident love for her daughter and Puck's wholehearted support, Quinn knew she wasn't ready for motherhood. So just as she'd originally planned, she gave up her baby for adoption.[6] It was an act of courage, and of self-sacrifice. Over the course of the season, Quinn went from looking like a villain (by cheating on and then lying to Finn) to being portrayed as a hero.

Now, *that's* what I call a storyline save.

If I had to pick one favorite moment involving Quinn in the second half of the season, though, I'd choose her final scene in "Bad Reputation" (1-17). It wasn't exactly Quinn's proudest hour; we discovered that she was the author of the infamous Glist, which lists glee club members by suspected level of sexual promiscuity.[7] The publication of the Glist had put the club's existence in jeopardy, so when Will Schuester realized that Quinn was the one who'd written it, we expected him to come down on her hard.

Instead, he responded to her with sympathy and real understanding. I might've rolled my eyes a little bit when Will claimed he'd been in the exact same situation, just because he'd been publicly called out by Emma—yeah, that was awkward, but on the Suck-O-Meter, it doesn't compare to being teenage, pregnant, and homeless. And yet, that was the moment when I remembered that Quinn hadn't just lied to Finn about the baby; she'd lied to Will, too. She played a big part in a deception that wrecked his life as he'd known it.

And Will never said a word to her about it. Despite the depth of the lie, despite the ways in which it hurt him, Will never cast any blame on Quinn for her role in it. Instead, he kept being her teacher and providing her with what guidance and support he could. I don't think I ever liked Will Schuester more than in that moment, when we saw that he knew Quinn was just a scared kid doing the best she could.

That's when I knew Will got it...and that *Glee* did, too.

---

[6] Interestingly, Quinn's baby was adopted by Shelby Corcoran, the director of Vocal Adrenaline and Rachel's birth mother. *Glee* says some interesting, positive things about adoption in its first season...but that's another essay.

[7] Quinn put herself at the top of the list, too. Maybe it was just a way of avoiding blame, but there could be more to it than that. An act of defiance or of self-loathing? I think either possibility could be true.

• • •

CLAUDIA GRAY is the Chicago-based author of the *New York Times* bestselling Evernight series. She was an alto in her high-school show choir, Attaché, and therefore knows the correct way to perform a starburst, a box step, and jazz hands. You can learn more about her work at www.claudiagray.com.

GREGORY STEVENSON

Glee's Most Versatile Character
The Many Faces of *Glee* Club

I DO NOT SING or, God forbid, dance. My preferred method of moving my body to music is to stand ramrod straight and sway gently in the breeze, much like a pine tree. My high school in Effingham, Illinois, did not have a glee club, which may have been for the best, because I would have been tempted to join despite my abundant lack of musical talent. This is because there's something almost magical about belonging to a club. Joining together with like-minded people around a shared interest is a unique experience. To be in a club is to be in a relationship, not just with the individual members, but with the club itself.

The clubs that I gravitated toward in high school were athletic. Football and basketball were my teams of choice. My relationship with them was like that of best friends. I craved time with them and took immense enjoyment from being in their presence. We understood each other. In the spring, however, when football and basketball ended, I found myself grieving the loss of those relationships. It was like my best friends had gone out of town on an extended family vacation, and I was left behind to fill the void. So I joined the track team. The track team, for me, became the friend you call when you have no other options. It was the kid next door whom you hang out with only because he happens to be there when you're bored. It was a provisional friendship, designed to pass the time while I waited for my true friends to get back into town.

A club, though made up of individuals, has its own unique persona that transcends any one person. I do not particularly miss any specific members of my high school football team, but I do greatly miss being on the team. My relationship with the "club" ran much deeper than my relationship with any individual person on it.

At William McKinley High School in Lima, Ohio, individuals join or interact with the glee club for a variety of reasons, but one thing remains consistent—they all have entered into a relationship with the club that will leave an indelible mark upon them. For each person, the glee club serves as the relationship partner they require most. Will Schuester joined the club in order to fill a void in his life, and the club provided him with precisely what he sought. Quinn Fabray and Rachel Berry both joined the club to acquire a desired object, only to end up discovering something unexpected. Even Sue Sylvester found herself in a relationship with the club, and it's a relationship that she may need more than any of the others.

Will Schuester and the Surrogate Child

When we first met Will, he was driving a rusty utility car with a dragging muffler—an apt metaphor for his life. He was not enjoying a sports car existence, full of speed, bright colors, and excitement. No, he was stuck in a struggling marriage and living a rusty car kind of life. As he stared longingly at the inscription on the 1993 Show Choir Championship Trophy—"Glee is about opening yourself up to joy" ("Pilot")—we were introduced to a man trying to fill a very large void in his life. Although Will claimed that the reason he wanted to take over the glee club was because there was no joy in the kids, it was actually the lack of joy within himself that he hoped to remedy. Will's malaise resulted from the absence of a special relationship that he craved.

When Will's wife, Terri, informed him that she was pregnant, the joy on his face was unmistakable. The tangible link between Will's elation about this news and the glee club became apparent when Emma said she had never seen Will happier than in the video of him performing at the 1993 Nationals. In reply, he declared the Nationals the greatest moment of his life, the moment at which he understood his place in the world, and stated, "The only time I felt that way since then was when Terri told me I was gonna be a father" ("Pilot"). Of course, that child proved to be a phantom, the fiction of a faked pregnancy. Will's joy was real; the baby was not. Yet it exposed the real void in his soul—that the relationship Will craved most was that of a father to a child. Will's desire for this relationship was so strong that he adopted the glee club as a surrogate child, even before learning that the promise of a flesh-and-blood child had been a lie.

Despite the overabundance of advice books populating bookstore shelves, fatherhood does not come with a manual. And as with any new father, Will had to learn on the job. His relationship to the glee club is not a "father knows best" scenario where Dad always does what's right and remains a fount of wisdom and guidance. Instead, Will seems intent on running through virtually every classic parenting mistake.

Mistake #1: Using a child to relive your own glory days. Whether it was forcing the club to sing the same song he won with at Nationals or bringing in a ringer (April) because he didn't trust the club's collective talent, Will revealed himself as a father trying to make his own high school dream come true through his child ("Showmance," 1-2; "The Rhodes Not Taken," 1-5).

Mistake #2: Failure to pay attention. Will learned what it was like to be the clueless father who suddenly realizes he doesn't know his kids as well as he thought he did when he found out that the club members had taken a drug and he had to confess to the "authorities" that he knew nothing about it ("Vitamin-D," 1-6).

Mistake #3: Arguing in front of the children. When Sue temporarily joined the glee club as co-director, the constant bickering between her and Will played out as a marital spat that threw the children's lives into confusion. Finn chastised them both by saying that the members of the club could just go home "if we wanted to hear Mom and Dad fight" ("Throwdown," 1-7).

Mistake #4: Being overprotective. Will responds to any threat against his club the same way that a father does to threats against his children—he reacts immediately to protect them. Such a response is admirable, but as anyone who has ever attended a child's sporting event will attest, a father's perception that his child is being treated unfairly can cause previously hidden wells of immaturity to bubble to the surface. So, too, Will often reacts to unjust treatment of his club from Sue by responding with the same level of irresponsible behavior, such as when he retaliated for her co-opting of all of the minority students in his club by failing all of her Cheerios in his class ("Throwdown").

Mistake #5: Do as I say, not as I do. Will preaches compassion, kindness, and respect for others to his kids. Yet at the same time, because Sue had once again attempted to ruin the club's chance at Regionals, he sabotaged her shot at Nationals by treating her in the same uncompassionate, unkind, and disrespectful manner with which Jessie had treated Rachel ("Funk," 1-21). In doing so, he resembled every father who at one time or another finds it difficult to reconcile his advice with his actions.

However, these mistakes do not diminish the fact that when it truly counts, Will gets it right—even if sometimes he is the beneficiary of parenting by accident, as when the kids learned from him a valuable lesson about self-expression, despite the fact that he hadn't planned it that way ("Theatricality," 1-20). As a "father" to this club, Will instilled values in the members by teaching them compassion and respect for others ("Wheels," 1-9; "The Power of Madonna," 1-15). At other times, he acted appropriately as disciplinarian, often by refusing to give in to Rachel's childish demands despite her frequent refrain, well-known to any parent, that by refusing her desires he was "ruining my life" ("Preggers", 1-4; "Wheels"). He also demonstrates a willingness to sacrifice his own well-being for the sake of his "kids," such as when he gave up his own dream of starring in *Les Miserables* so that they would have a shot at achieving their dreams ("Dream On," 1-19).

Of all the relationships with the glee club explored in this essay, Will's is the one that most closely mirrors his relationship with the members themselves, as Finn made clear in the season finale when he identified Will as the father figure he'd never had ("Journey," 1-22). Yet Will's relationship to the club transcends those individual ones. Members of the club will come and go, but the club will remain, continuing to fill the child-shaped void in his life. Even so, Will's responsibility as a father is to prepare his child to stand on his or her own. Will recognized this when he told the glee club, "If you can't win without me there, then I haven't done my job" ("Mattress," 1-12). But a job well done is a source of joy to any parent. Thus, when his kids rose to the challenge on their own and won Sectionals without him, we were treated to a shot of Will beaming like a proud papa ("Sectionals," 1-13).

Quinn Fabray and the Accomplice

When we first met Quinn, she, like her mentor Sue, was committed to the proper order of things—popular kids rule, while the "losers" deserve every slushie facial they receive. From atop her throne as the queen of popularity, she looked down on the lowly glee club members and joyfully mocked them. But Quinn was not just an icon of popularity; she was also a schemer, one who would use anyone and anything to get her way. So when she noticed her boyfriend Finn becoming a bit too close with Rachel, Quinn joined the glee club in order to keep a hold on him, thus enlisting the club as an accomplice in her scheme ("Showmance"). That wasn't the only time Quinn employed the glee club in her schemes, whether it was using club members as a diversion for Finn so she could gauge Puck's worthiness as a father ("Hairography," 1-11), or creating the Glist (a list ranking the hotness quotient of glee club members) as a way to reclaim some of her lost popularity ("Bad Reputation," 1-17).

Having an accomplice in a scheme is a dangerous thing. Such accomplices are by nature schemers themselves, and they will likely turn on you at the most inopportune time. Quinn joined forces with the glee club in order to get what she wanted, but the glee club double-crossed her by instead giving her what she *needed*. Above all, Quinn craved acceptance, and she equated acceptance with popularity. By aligning with the glee club, she intended to cement her popularity by holding on to her quarterback boyfriend. Yet instead, her carefully crafted world crumbled: her popularity vanished, she was kicked off the Cheerios, and she lost her boyfriend. As one guy told her, "Welcome to the new world order" ("Mash-Up," 1-8). Quinn now ranked among the losers and the invisibles.

Rather than help Quinn fulfill her selfish schemes, the glee club instead showed her a new path. After watching the glee club refuse to give in to the berating of a hired choreographer, the same Quinn who had joyfully mocked others before now told a berating Sue, "When you really believe in yourself, you don't have to bring other people down" ("Acafellas," 1-3). This new awareness contradicted Quinn's previous mode of operation, in which acceptance was defined by appearances and by conformity to an established pattern of behavior that exalted oneself while reminding the "losers" of their place. Quinn acknowledged this when, having received an unexpected kindness from Rachel, she confessed, "I would have tortured you if the roles were reversed, you know" ("Vitamin-D"). What was so shocking to Quinn was that she suddenly found herself in the position of all those she had formerly mocked. Her newly minted "loser" status opened her eyes to a new definition of acceptance. When Quinn was kicked out of the Cheerios, the glee club still embraced her. After she realized that receiving slushie facials would continue to be a part of her life, Will informed her that she now had eleven friends to help clean her up ("Mash-Up"). When she was kicked out of her home, she walked into the music room, where the entire club serenaded her with "Lean on Me" ("Ballad," 1-10).

The critical moment for Quinn came when she had the opportunity to rejoin the Cheerios. The choice was between her old path, with its appearance of acceptance, and her new path, with the real thing. For the new Quinn, the choice was clear: "I don't want to be on a team where I only appear to belong. I'd rather be a part of a club that's glad to have me. Like glee club" ("Mattress").

Quinn joined the glee club for one simple reason—to use it as an accomplice in holding on to her boyfriend. Once she lost her boyfriend, though, she never quit the club—because she had discovered something unexpected: acceptance is not defined by popularity, but by the people who care about you. Never was anyone so fortunate to be betrayed by an accomplice.

Rachel Berry and the Business Partner

Rachel desperately wants to be someone special and, for her, specialness is defined solely by fame. She is a whirling dervish of self-promotion whose star-in-the-making drive is fueled by her ticking fame clock. Her lust for the spotlight would put any reality television show contestant to shame. So when Rachel joined the glee club, she did so with a single-minded purpose. From her vantage point, it was a business relationship, complete with contractual obligations. She would temporarily loan her prodigious talent to the glee club, and in return the glee club would help her achieve the next step on her quest for stardom. She made her demands clear from the outset. If the glee club could not provide her the necessary stepping stones to reach the heights to which she was entitled, then it was a waste of her time ("Pilot"). For Rachel, everything gets filtered through the lens of her individual career, so that even a yearbook photo became not a precious memory preserved for the future but merely practice for the paparazzi ("Mattress").

The glee club, however, had a different understanding of their relationship. Sometimes two people enter into a relationship with very different agendas. One person sees a relationship as romantic while the other sees it as platonic, or one views it as a relationship of convenience while the other takes it to be a lasting commitment. The glee club regularly refused to bow to Rachel's contractual demands, an action that typically provoked a patented Rachel storm-out. The first time Will gave a solo to someone else and informed Rachel that she would not always be the star, the look of sheer disbelief on her face was that of someone stunned that her partner would so brazenly violate the terms of their agreement ("Showmance"). This perceived violation stemmed from the fact that the glee club had a different agenda. Whereas Rachel viewed the club as a business partner whose contractual role was to put her on center stage, the glee club viewed her as a teammate whose voice worked best in concert with others. Thus the stage was set for a battle of wills. As Rachel continually tried to use the glee club to advance her personal goals, the glee club continually challenged Rachel to look beyond herself and to elevate the goals of the team above her own.

This does not come easy. It's like watching a chess match. For every move Rachel made to advance her personal career at the expense of the team, the glee club made a countermove that opened her eyes to the value of teamwork. In "Acafellas," Rachel declared that since glee club was her one shot at stardom, winning was the only thing that mattered, and that she was therefore going to hire an outside choreographer even if it hurt the team by causing Finn to quit (again). Yet when half the team threatened to quit due to the choreographer's abusive manner, it was Rachel who sent him packing by announcing to the club that they only needed each other. Later, although Rachel claimed to be a "team player," she quit the glee club when a solo was again given to someone else, and she joined the school musical as a way to better "showcase my talents" ("Preggers"). But the glee club had a brilliant countermove in store in the form of April Rhodes. Playing on Rachel's jealousy, the glee club showed her how well they could perform with April as her substitute. Humbled, Rachel returned and declared that "being a star didn't make me feel as special as being your friend." The glee club then underscored the value of teamwork by helping Rachel out with the dance steps she had not yet learned ("The Rhodes Not Taken"). Through these actions, the glee club taught her that standing on a stage as one member of a team was more special than standing alone in the spotlight.

A relationship in which those involved have differing conceptions of the terms can be quite confusing. Rachel thus found herself torn between her personal desires and the needs of her teammates. She told Mercedes how important it was for the whole team to come together, only to then disrupt the team herself by breaking up Quinn and Finn ("Sectionals"). Finn later informed Rachel that the team was more important than her relationship with a rival competitor, Jesse. Rachel, however, pursued this illicit relationship anyway, justifying her personal desire with the audacious claim that breaking up with Jesse to reunite with Finn would be bad for the "team" ("Hell-O," 1-14).

Even as Rachel slowly came to recognize herself as part of a team, she continued to struggle with what that meant. Will, the glee club's voice of authority, instructed her that a glee club is about "a myriad of voices coming together as one." Rachel's response to this bit of wisdom was to stand before the group and sing a song that is "about overcoming obstacles and beating the odds. In my case, the obstacle is you, my lackluster teammates who refuse to carry their own weight." However, having lost her own voice to laryngitis, Rachel suddenly realized that she was unable to carry *her* own weight. Her plaintive query—"Who am I without my voice?"—was answered by the glee club as Finn's actions taught her that what defines her is not her voice alone, but how her voice joins with the voices around her in harmony. The episode concluded with Rachel leading the group in singing "One," U2's stirring anthem to unity ("Laryngitis," 1-18).

Rachel's relationship with the glee club began as a simple business arrangement designed to further her fledgling career. The glee club thought differently, however, and before she knew it, Rachel had discovered that the terms of her contract had been changed. Even more surprising? She eventually didn't seem to mind.

Sue Sylvester and the Supervillain

Sue Sylvester is a superhero...in her own mind. Any viewer of *Glee* might protest that Sue is clearly the villain of the piece. Yes, but only for those who have some grounding in reality. If you were to don protective clothing and enter briefly into Sue's mind, you would discover that she inhabits a topsy-turvy world. How else to explain someone who could refer to individual students as "Asian" and "other Asian" while vowing that her "rainbow tent" would protect them from Will's racism ("Throwdown")? Who could proudly trumpet her "moral integrity" while concurrently bribing the principal ("Hell-O")? In Sue's world, reality is as she perceives it, and she perceives herself as a superhero. Every superhero needs a supervillain, and Sue's is the glee club.

Sue's self-appointed job as superhero is to protect the status quo. The natural order of things is that there are winners and losers, and Sue's divinely ordained task is to maintain that balance. Sue's world is very neatly ordered, as she herself explained nicely in the pilot:

> SUE: High school is a caste system. Kids fall into certain slots. Your jocks and your popular kids? Up in the penthouse. The invisibles and the kids playing live-action druids and trolls out in the forest? Bottom floor.
> WILL: And where do the glee kids lie?
> SUE: Sub-basement.

What makes the glee club a proper supervillain is that it refuses to conform to the established order. When members of Sue's Cheerios joined glee club, Sue accused Will of "blurring the lines" between the winners and losers, a move that she, as a "winner," found treasonous ("Pilot"). Once Sue realized that the glee club possessed the talent to move out of its sub-basement, that potential for upward mobility became a threat. They were rising above their station, challenging her place at the top of the heap, and thus becoming a societal force for disorder and chaos that needed to be stamped out.

By my unofficial count, Sue, the Great Defender of the Natural Order, launched at least fifteen attacks on the glee club during the first season. These attacks included highlighting rule violations, handling internal spies, sowing group dissension, taking down the leader (a move Sue learned "in Special Forces"), leaking set lists to the competition, encouraging Rachel's narcissistic tendencies, and even bribing the principal to ship the glee club kids to New York with only thirty-five dollars in their pockets. Yet Sue's every attack ultimately failed. The glee club proved to be not just a normal bad guy, but one of those iconic supervillains that just won't die. Sue revealed her own perception of the glee club's enduring villainous status when she lamented, "Every time I try to destroy that clutch of scab-eating mouth-breathers, it only comes back stronger, like some sexually ambiguous horror movie villain" ("Vitamin-D").

In fact, the glee club not only keeps coming back, but it counter-attacks. The club frequently throws punches that puncture Sue's perceived reality, leaving her with moments of all-too-brief clarity. The glee club's efforts to raise money for wheelchair-bound Artie ultimately prompted Sue to write a check for wheelchair ramps in the school. Despite having a mentally challenged sister of her own, it was only the involvement of the glee club that led to Sue including a mentally challenged student on her Cheerios squad ("Wheels"). Furthermore, the involvement of the glee club in one of Sue's Cheerios performances forced her to face her own prejudiced attitude ("Home," 1-16), while the glee club's posting of a video of Sue on YouTube resulted in her temporary acknowledgment that she needed to start playing nice ("Bad Reputation"). Like all superheroes, Sue has an Achilles' heel, a vulnerable spot. In her case it's not her heel, but her heart. Somewhere deep beneath that hardened outer shell of nearly impenetrable armor beats the heart of someone who occasionally cares. Once when Will attacked her weak point by targeting her heart, she confessed, "I felt something below the neck" ("Funk"). It was this very same weakness that led her to vote for the glee club at Regionals despite her better judgment ("Journey"). Of course, these moments were fleeting. Sue's mission to restore the natural order of things is far too important to be sidetracked by compassion; yet, these moments are a reminder that the glee club is a worthy adversary.

The relationship between a superhero and a supervillain is not merely a relationship of attempted mutual destruction; it is also a relationship of mutual self-definition. Batman has the Joker, Superman has Lex Luthor, and neither would be what they are without the other. Consequently, Sue *needs* the glee club. It gives her life purpose. Without an enemy to fight, a superhero is nothing more than a glorified hall monitor. It's the villain that makes the hero. It's Sue's battle against the glee club that allows her to define herself as a hero fighting on the side of right. When members of the glee club overstepped their place in the caste system by using the Cheerios' copier, Sue's demand that they be "hobbled" was rebuffed. After losing this battle over the copier, Sue proclaimed, "Lady Justice wept today" ("Showmance"). During a shouting match with Will, Sue identified herself in her own mind as "Ajax, mighty Greek warrior." In Sue's mind, even the divine is on her side, as she told Will that her quest to destroy the glee club was akin to a religious calling ("Throwdown"). Sue is able to align herself with Lady Justice, mighty Greek warriors, and a divine calling because she has a worthy villain to define herself against.

Occasionally, though, in any superhero narrative, the villain gets the best of the hero, prompting the hero to regroup and dig deep to find new reserves of strength. Sue found herself in this situation after being suspended for one of her attacks on the glee club. Speaking to her archenemy in "Sectionals," she announced:

> SUE: Well-played, sir. I underestimated you. Well, here's what happens now. I'm gonna head on down to my condo in Boca...Get myself back into fighting shape, and then I'm gonna return to this school even more hell-bent on your destruction...
>
> WILL: I look forward to it, Sue.
>
> SUE: You know you just woke a sleeping giant. Prepare to be crushed.

Sue is a self-proclaimed "winner," and winners, by definition, need competition. Without a worthy opponent, there can be no satisfying victory. Consequently, Sue learned that to lose her adversary would be to lose a part of herself. In the final episode of the first season, glee club was dead, and it was Sue who'd singlehandedly brought about its resurrection. She confessed to Will, "I've proven that I can wipe you and your glee club off the face of this Earth. But what kind of a world would that be, Will? Sue Sylvester's not sure she wants to live in that kind of world." With her parting words to Will in "Journey"—"I relish the thought of another full year [of] constantly besting you"—Sue revealed that, as much as it pains her to admit it, she needs this club, even though it has proven to be an impediment to her (very superheroic) desire for a "hovercraft" ("Vitamin-D").

New Directions

McKinley High's glee club is appropriately named New Directions because the relationships that individuals have with the club take them in new directions. Moving in a new direction, though, is often a slow and painful process. Progress must be measured incrementally. The glee club wears different faces depending on the needs of each relationship partner, yet those needs are deep-seated and not easily resolved. Will occasionally acts more like a child than a parent. Quinn is still not above the occasional scheme. Rachel confessed that she still requires "applause to live" ("Laryngitis"). Sue, despite her best efforts, occasionally manages to learn something along the way. Relationships are dynamic, not static. They change and evolve over time. The relationships that these characters have with the club will no doubt evolve too as the story continues to unfold, yet one thing will likely remain the same—the glee club will continue to provide them not with the relationship they want, but with the relationship they need.

• • •

GREGORY STEVENSON is a Professor of Religion at Rochester College in Michigan. He is the author of *Televised Morality and Power and Place*, and has contributed to other Smart Pop collections *Coffee at Luke's* and *In the Hunt*. He confesses that the *Glee* character he relates to the most is Will Schuester (minus the duplicitous wife, singing talent, and nice hair), but that sometimes when besieged by relentless students, he wishes he could be more like Sue Sylvester.

Gleeful

In "Dream On" (1-19), former show choir superstar Bryan Ryan wanted to shut down the glee club because he thought it was setting kids up for disappointment. Do high school arts and entertainment "careers" lead to disillusionment later in life, when the big leagues get bigger and the spotlight narrows down to a select few? Maybe. A solo in high school show choir isn't exactly a one-way ticket to the Great White Way. The thing is, we can't define success as making it in the finicky world of show business.

The value of the arts in schools doesn't lie in a measurable future, but in the present. High school art, theater, band, and chorus clubs give losers and outcasts a safe haven. Forget the library; the green room is where it's at. Just look at the Burger King Kids Club–level of diversity on *Glee*. It seems like a cliché, but those of us who were outsiders in high school nod along with every heartbreak and laugh.

Modern kids connect through Facebook and rapid-fire text messages. Rumors travel faster than ever. Parents struggle to keep up with issues like cyber-bullying. In the digital age, it's more important than ever to give kids a chance to engage face-to-face. The arts drag socially awkward kids away from the comforting glow of a computer screen and into the sometimes-painful heat of the spotlight.

I love that *Glee* presents a reality just a little skewed from our own. Instead of burrowing in online games or turning to destructive behaviors, the *Glee* kids cling to show choir and to each other. Their lives aren't ideal, but the situation is. Will Schuester's glee program models the type of outlet every high school student needs access to. Whether it means scrawling angst-filled poetry on notebook paper or learning to shoot and edit movies, kids need to create. They need to say, "I made this!" They need validation and pride once their accomplishments are no longer taped to the fridge at home.

The arts don't focus on the individual but the output. Music, fashion, and theater bring like-minded individuals together regardless of upbringing, creed, or sexuality. Instead of being marginalized or ridiculed for differences, kids in arts programs celebrate the quirks and talents that make them unique. It's a concept even Sue Sylvester can't deny. For every bitter Bryan Ryan, there's an adult who never stopped believing in the raw power of creativity.

After a brief high school thespian career, I never stepped foot onstage again. But I carry with me the joyful show-tune-laden soundtrack of my teenage years. I rarely meet up with my old theater buddies, but I know each one of us remembers dancing around a swimming pool at three in the morning bellowing "La Vie Boheme" from *Rent*.

Do you download the songs after each episode of *Glee* has aired? You can do more. Whether you're personally involved in the arts or not, make a point of supporting your local arts community. Attend a gallery opening. Take in an opera. Hit an avant-garde fashion show. Buy tickets to a museum event.

Give kids the chance to be weird, to be different. Supports the arts. Some dorky high school kid like me will thank you.

MARIA MORA
St. Petersburg, Florida

Tips for Creating Your Own Vocal Performance Group

Jamie Chambers

Are you inspired to perform? Do you sing in the shower or the car and yearn for an audience? Perhaps you have the dedication, talent, and musical ability to start a vocal performance group of your own.

"We're all here for the same reason:
because we wanna be good at something."
—*Finn Hudson, "Pilot"*

WILL SCHUESTER is a well-liked Spanish teacher who fondly remembers his younger days as a star performer in the William McKinley High School glee club. He jumped at the opportunity to launch New Directions, so that he could share his passion and offer the same chance to a new generation.

If you find yourself inspired by *Glee* and would like to be part of a performance group of your own, we can help you get started. Perhaps you have fond memories of show choir in high school or college, performed in musicals as part of a drama program or community theater, or once enjoyed singing in a church choir or other musical organization. Maybe you have a great voice and some musical ability but never had the nerve to sing anything other than margarita-fueled karaoke at a local bar. Or it could be that you may not possess a lick of talent on your own, but have a passion for ensemble music and a knack for organizing and motivating others. Whatever the case, with work and some good people involved, you can be a part of something truly special.

First you'll need to decide whether you want to find an existing group or create something from scratch. If you want to create your own group, you'll need to decide just how it will be structured, who will be in charge, and who will pay the costs involved. A group needs a director, musical accompaniment, choreography, and people to actually do the singing and dancing. You'll need to build a repertoire, decide on costumes, schedule rehearsals, and book performances. Sound like a lot of work? It is—but it's also really fun and incredibly rewarding.

Create or Join?

Before you begin the sizeable task of creating a show choir from scratch, you might want to think about joining up with an existing group in your school or local community. Such groups are often looking for strong vocalists, and if you've got the chops, you might only be an audition away.

There are a ton of resources to find what you need. Check the classifieds in your local papers, especially small-town publications. Ask the directors of local school-based groups, or talk to the managers of the venues where such groups perform, as these folks are often plugged in to the performance-music subculture and may know about people and resources you don't. And the modern world of websites, online classifieds, and social networking could make some of the information you need just a few clicks away.

If you're musically trained and an active singer, you may not need a lot work to prepare yourself for an audition. But remember: your voice is both an instrument and a living thing; it needs both exercise and rest to stay in top shape. You don't need to put Rachel-level obsession into honing your talent, but you can work at it to achieve greater range and tone. Rehearse the different disciplines of singing solos versus working with an ensemble. You probably won't be doing a full dance number in an audition, but remember that most show choir–style performance groups have dancing or at least some movement as part of the performance, so make sure your solo work isn't static and uninteresting to watch.

If an existing group is not available or does not match the vision you have in mind, then you might consider assembling a group of performers and starting something entirely new.

New Directions

If you've decided that you're going to form a group from the ground up, you've got a lot on your plate. It's rewarding, to be sure, but go ahead and remind yourself that there will be plenty of sweat and tears before you get to the standing ovations.

First you need a plan, and then you need some people. If you're young or don't know where to begin (beyond these pages), reach out and get help. The culture of music is one filled with kind and generous people who do what they do out of love for it. Most won't mind mentoring someone or passing along what they've learned on their own journey.

Goals

You're doing this for love and the joy of performance and to offer something to your community. But you need to figure out just how high a bar you want to set for your group, so it's time to ask some important questions. The good news is that you can always revisit some of these decisions later, if things aren't working. It might be good to start with things that are achievable before you expand, grow, and take over the world! Remember, New Directions started with five singers and only one strong number. Every group has to begin somewhere.

Type of group. Are you going for a men's ensemble, women's group, or mixed? What is the age range you're looking for, or is that even a factor? Each of these decisions offer an advantage or disadvantage.

Openness will make it easier to find the talent your group needs, whereas specializing might help you find a niche that other groups haven't already filled or give your ensemble a sound that others lack. Figure out what else is out there, and then decide what you're going to do in order to stand out. If you're starting a school-based group, you'll need to check the regulations for student organizations and make sure you're recruiting by the rules. Also remember that you shouldn't look for reasons to reject anyone. Male groups can sometimes include a woman that sings tenor, while even groups that include dancing might have a handicapped performer like Artie.

Performance style. Decide just what you want your audience to see and hear when your group puts on a show. Is this going to be chamber choir–style singing, showcasing vocal talent alone? Are you going to incorporate some body movement or some individual dance routines? Or are you going to go the full *Glee*-style show-choir route, with fully choreographed numbers and costumes? Figure out if you're planning to unify the performances by tying the music to a particular theme or genre. These kinds of decisions will give your group its own personality.

Where might you perform? It may seem premature to worry about this, but figuring it out early makes sense, because this choice will inform many of your other decisions. A school-based group can schedule its own performances and offer to enhance other events, and of course must stay within the tastes and restrictions of the school's principal and faculty. If your group is performing in a church, you need to make sure you have music appropriate for that audience. Community fairs might be looking for traditional, family-friendly songs, while younger audiences will enjoy more contemporary fare. The answer might well be "all of the above," but you should figure out where you're looking to start as you build up a repertoire.

Who's paying for this? We'll go ahead and assume that all the performers are going to volunteer their time, but there are plenty of other things that cost money, so it's important to figure out how this will be paid for as you bootstrap your new group to success. Further down the road, you might be able to perform for donations or even charge a fee, but you'll have to pay your dues first— and paying dues may be exactly the way you want to go. Consider treating it as a club and asking all those involved to chip in a small amount each week or month to cover the basic operating costs. You can also organize booster events and fundraisers, like car washes, bake sales, or something more creative. Having a starting fund will let the organizers make budget decisions down the line. Resist the urge to borrow money (if you're old enough), since the future is always uncertain for a new group. School-based groups can usually find support from faculty and parents, and should ask an active adult to formally organize a booster club to help promote the group.

People

Once you've got those first ideas set down, you're going to need people in key positions to get the wheels turning. So figure out which roles should be established and get to recruiting! Note that while all of these positions can be filled by performers in the group—which may be necessary, depending on your resources—it's usually a good idea to have those in the support positions stay out of the spotlight and focus on their jobs. But they can and should be acknowledged for their hard work!

Director. This is the Will Schuester of the group, the guy or gal who brings the individual voices together and makes them into music. The director can be one of the performers if necessary, though it's really a big job all unto itself. Ideally, this person will be the most trained musically, have experience leading rehearsals and coaching others with their vocals, and be able to act as leader to inspire and motivate the whole group. The director chooses the music, assigns the parts and solos within a song, and thinks on his feet to adjust when something goes wrong. Whoever steps into this role must be prepared for dedication and hard work. While the performers must learn their parts and moves, the director has to handle the big-picture thinking and figure out how it's all going to come together.

A co-director or assistant director is often needed to help manage a larger group, to act as backup and handle particular duties. A performer might fill this role, or one might also be assigned as a backup director in case of illness or emergencies. Remember that, as with all live entertainment, things can and will go wrong! You can't be ready for everything, but try to have a backup plan in place for the big stuff.

Accompaniment. If you've decided on a purely a cappella group, you've got this one covered. Or if, as in *Glee*, you've got a pianist or band that magically appears when needed, you're all set. Otherwise you'll need to figure out the music that will accompany your performers. This might be licensed performance tracks you purchase online or at music stores, it may be one person tickling the ivories, or if you're blessed with an honest-to-gosh band ready to back the vocals, then go for it! When just starting out, it might be easier to go with the path of least resistance, because piano or band accompaniment can't be easily replaced at the last minute if something were to happen to your musicians. It's also easier to provide practice tracks to your performers if they're pre-recorded. But live music is undeniably more impressive to an audience, so decide how you want to start when it comes to your vocal accompaniment, as well as where you hope to progress to. You might have vocal performers who can play instruments, but it's an incredible challenge for anyone to do both at once.

Choreographer. If you're going for vocals-only or just really simple movement, this isn't something your group will need as you start out. But if you want to give the full show-choir experience to your audience, there's gonna be some dancing, so you'll need to recruit someone to put together routines for the group. Dance in show-choir performances is often less about extreme movement between individuals or pairs, but rather features the coordinated simple movement of a large number of people. Seeing a group singing and dancing in costume is undeniably impressive. If you've got a Rachel within your group, make use of her. Otherwise, talk to folks who run the local community theater or ask around in dance studios, as they may know just the person to pitch in and come up with dance moves to go with your music. A good choreographer is going to cost some money, but if you're going this route, it is money well spent.

If you can't find someone to put together impressive dance routines, or if you just want to focus on the vocals, that's okay. Just remember that lack of dancing doesn't mean the performance should be static, with unmoving singers standing like statues. Live musical performance is a visual experience, too, so figure out ways to keep it interesting. Alternating the position and pose of your singers, and the use of simple props or parts of costuming (hats or canes, for example), can go a long way to improving the entertainment value of a bunch of folks standing around singing! Make sure not to ignore posture and facial expressions as part of the performance.

Performers. These guys and gals are the ones who get up in front of the audience and sing their hearts out. The group is only as good as the combination of talent and dedication of your singers. You'll need to decide at what size your group will start out. While you may hope to eventually have a full-size group of thirty or more performers, you might want to recruit a small base group and slowly grow from there.

Unless you're doing this just for fun, you'll need to have your director host auditions and set the standard for vocal quality and musical ability. Make sure you understand the level of musical training each singer has, along with his or her experience performing in ensembles. Those who can't read music may require extra help to learn their parts. If dancing is part of the planned performances, you'll need to see how each person can move. You should also take the time to get to know each performer and find out what else he or she can bring to the party, like experience in costuming or prop work, great ideas for routines, or family members who might offer connections to potential rehearsal space or performance venues.

When selecting performers for your group, you'll need to make sure you have good coverage in all the different vocal parts. For a mixed group (male and female), you're looking at at least four parts—highest to lowest, the first two usually being the female parts, that's soprano, alto, tenor, and bass. If you're creating a large group and are looking at music with more complex arrangements, you might also include some mezzo-sopranos (between soprano and alto) and baritones (between tenor and bass). Some of your singers are going to have a wide range, so you'll want to place them where their vocal quality is at its peak. Practice and vocal coaching will be able to improve your singers' range and overall sound.

Preparing

You've got the plan and the people needed to pull it off. Now begins the work of putting together a show. First your group needs music, costumes, and a place and time for regular rehearsals. When starting from scratch with a completely new group, it'll take some time for everything to gel, but eventually there will be a magical moment during a rehearsal when it all comes together—inspiring smiles, hugs, and high fives. It just takes time and effort to get there!

Repertoire. You need music. The decisions made earlier by the director or the group as a whole will now come into play. The group can only learn so many songs in a limited time, so it's better to start small, with the set planned for that first performance, and grow from there. You want a strong debut that reflects the message and style of your group, so pick songs that are going to highlight the talent of the performers and will knock the audience's socks clean off.

You'll be able to find a wealth of material at music stores and online—both in terms of sheet music and accompaniment tracks if necessary. Most songs will be ready to go, though a director may tweak or modify things here or there based on the specific voices in your group. Be sure that you obey all the applicable copyright laws regarding the use and performance of your chosen songs. (Searching "performing rights" on Wikipedia or another online resource will get you started on the right track.)

Put some thought into the mix of music you choose for a particular set. You should include a strong opening number designed to wow the audience and set the tone for the remainder of the performance. After that, mix it up! Some of the songs should be energetic and fast-paced, and some show choirs enjoy putting in at least one that incorporates humor to get a laugh from the audience. Intersperse these with ballads—slower songs that emphasize the vocals and have little or no movement. You might consider including one song that is completely a cappella, even if you use accompaniment for the rest of the set. Some songs may be full choral mixes, while others should highlight solos by the strongest singers in the group. Mixing these different styles keeps the audience interested throughout the performance. Think about the set New Directions performed at Regionals—tied together by Journey, starting with a ballad ("Faithfully"), then a fun, energetic middle ("Any Way You Want It," "Lovin', Touchin', Squeezin'"), and a show-stopping finish ("Don't Stop Believin'").

Musical genre is up to the group and the vision of the director. Show tunes old and new are typical show-choir fodder, but pop music and jazz adapted to the format make great choices as well. The music has to be enjoyable for the performers, because if they're not having any fun, it's not likely the audience will either.

Costuming. The word "costume" is extremely flexible in the show-choir format. Tuxes and gowns are traditional when performing at formal events, though not a must. Contemporary groups may go with simple matching jeans and T-shirts (think of the costumes worn when the *Glee* cast sang "Don't Stop Believin'" for the first time). If you're going with theme music or singing songs from a specific period, and if you have someone who can put together costumes, you can have the stage dress be a direct reflection of the music. Just be practical! Don't choose costumes that will restrict movement if there's dancing, and be sure not to require heavy costumes if you're doing outdoor performances in south Florida. Heat stroke is no fun!

If you're going to perform onstage, you also need to consider makeup. Yes, boys, this means you, too. Stage lights wash out faces, so even if it looks funny from a few feet away, the group will look great for the audience. This isn't something you need to worry about if you're performing in natural lighting—though whatever makeup the girls wear should match and complement the costumes. Jewelry should be avoided, unless it's something thought out across the entire group.

Rehearsals. Scheduling practice sessions for your fledgling group is going to be a balancing act. You have to understand that everyone has their own busy lives and hectic schedules, but everyone needs to be willing to dedicate enough time to make sure the group is ready to perform. Ideally a group will meet at least once or twice a week, but if your performance goals are more modest, you might be able to make due with a few times over the course of a month—especially once everyone has the basics down.

Make the most of rehearsal time—usually a couple of hours—for it to be effective. Everyone needs to learn their parts before rehearsal and come fully prepared. Each member of the group should have the sheet music and, ideally, a CD or tape for easy practice at home. Rehearsal time should be used to balance the voices, fine tune, and solidify the other elements. Everyone has to pull his or her own weight and make sure they are not wasting anyone else's time.

If your show choir is only using simple movements, you can work that practice into the normal rehearsals. But if you're incorporating real dance, you'll want to hold a few dance workshops to learn the steps separate from the vocal rehearsals. It's likely that your choreographer, if you've hired one, will have limited availability, so make use of that time wisely. The first dance rehearsal should be spent learning the routines, and at the next, practice incorporating the singing and dancing together. A full dress rehearsal is always a great idea shortly before a performance, so the group can get comfortable working with all the elements combined.

Try to find a good location to rehearse. If someone has a big enough space in their home, that'll do in a pinch, but if you can borrow space in a school choir room or auditorium, or at a church, community center, or similar space, that will be even better. Good acoustics will help practice the sound the group is trying to achieve. Once you know where you'll be performing, it's always a good idea to scout the location and make sure that the rehearsals leading up to it make use of the same amount of space. A dress rehearsal *at* the venue is ideal, though not always possible.

Vocal performance is a lot of hard work, so maintaining morale and camaraderie among the group is critical. A few minutes to socialize at the beginning of each rehearsal before getting down to business is fine, and a get-together or party to celebrate everyone's hard work will go a long way to keep spirits lifted. Once the group's repertoire has grown, you can throw in a few "just for fun" songs that you may not use anytime soon, such as some group favorites that everyone's been wanting to try. And you never know when you'll need to mix up a set with something different, or pinch-hit with something you've always used as a backup.

Performing

All that hard work and preparation are done for a reason: to perform in front of an audience. While all the other work is going on, the director (working with anyone else in the group helping in this area) should also be securing gigs.

A strong school or community show choir is a welcome addition to many events. Churches love music performances appropriate to their faith. Club and lodge meetings will be receptive to entertainment, as will school events, local festivals, and local business functions. In the beginning, the group will probably perform for donations only, though if you build a great reputation you might eventually be able to get paid for your shows. The need to appoint a treasurer to manage the group's funds is a great problem to have.

Depending on the style of music and the venues you choose, you'll need to figure out what sort of sound equipment you can and should be using for a performance. Ideally, everyone would have multi-thousand-dollar wireless microphones all managed and balanced by a dedicated sound person. But in the real world, you may have to make do with a handful of decent standing mics, a few speakers, and a small performer-facing monitor so the group can hear the music and themselves. If you can't get someone to be the "roadie" of the group and manage the equipment, the director might be dealing with it with the help of a few performers. Just work to get the best sound using the gear that's available. Over time, the group might be able to earn enough money to buy a better sound system.

Once you're all ready to perform, it's time to get the word out. Local and community papers are a good place to advertise, as are bulletin boards in community centers and office buildings. Jump online and post on local blogs, create online classified ads, and find forums and chatrooms. Get creative and spread the word! Record performances, take photographs, and get a tech-savvy member or friend to build a website to showcase the group's talent.

It's worth saying this one more time in regard to performance: HAVE FUN! Music is a joyful thing, and the hard work your group has done to put it all together will have a huge payoff when you get to perform in front of a live, appreciative audience. There will be moments of pure magic, when everyone present gets goose bumps and infectious smiles, followed by thunderous applause and standing ovations. It is a huge rush that will make everything else worth it, and it'll inspire you to work even harder the next time.

Get Out There and Sing!

This article barely scratches the surface of running a successful show choir or vocal ensemble. Even an encyclopedia-thick book could only teach so much, because, like any form of live entertainment, you learn the most by doing it. You gain direct knowledge from more experienced mentors, and the rest comes by trial-and-error. You'll get irritated and frustrated. Things can and will go wrong! But if you love music and want to share it with the world, it'll be a *Glee*ful experience for you and those lucky enough to hear you sing.

I'd like to thank Christi Whitney and Susan Hannah for offering their ideas and insight, and also for inspiring me to get in front of people to sing once again!

• • •

In 1992, **JAMIE CHAMBERS** co-founded a men's quartet as an unofficial addition to the Sequoyah High School chorus program in Canton, Georgia. In three years, the Sequoyah Men's Ensemble had over thirty-five performers and was added to the curriculum as an available music class that continues to this day. Jamie writes stories and designs games in his hometown of Woodstock, Georgia, and invites you to check out his antics on the web at www.jamiechambers.net.

GLEE EPISODE GUIDE

Pilot (1-1)

Original Air Date	Tuesday, May 19, 2009
Written by	Ryan Murphy, Brad Falchuk, and Ian Brennan
Directed by	Ryan Murphy
Glee Club Assignment	Join the club!

Inappropriate behavior by glee club director Sandy Ryerson toward a male student creates a golden opportunity for Spanish teacher Will Shuester: lead McKinley High's glee club! Starting from scratch and renaming the club New Directions, he holds auditions. Five students come aboard, including three divas-in-training—Rachel Berry, Mercedes Jones, and Kurt Hummel—as well as a shy goth girl with a stutter named Tina Cohen-Chang and a guitar-playing paraplegic with a killer voice named Artie Abrams. The cheerleading coach, Sue Sylvester, who is the most successful coach at the school—if not the state, nation, world, and universe (just ask her)—mocks his efforts, but Will moves forward optimistically.

The club has its foundation but is still short on members. Where to find more talent? Will presents the idea to the football team; they don't exactly jump at the idea. But when Will overhears quarterback Finn Hudson singing in the locker room shower, he knows that he has found some raw, natural talent, so he resorts to blackmail to recruit him. Now with six students in the club, they and guidance counselor Emma Pillsbury take a field trip to see their main competition: Vocal Adrenaline. Blown away, they realize that they have a long, long, long way to go.

But wait! Will's wife Terri is less than thrilled about the idea of Will coaching the kids. She has more important things for him to pay attention to—mainly, her. She has needs, and those needs have needs: money. She wants Will to become an accountant so that she can have the life she'd like to become accustomed to, without working more than the oh-so-stressful part-time retail work she already does.

Then Terri delivers the big news: she's pregnant. Will decides that, in order to create a better life for his family, not only must he leave the glee club, he also needs to leave his much-loved but low-paying teaching job. Meanwhile, Finn, ridiculed by his teammates for joining glee club, decides to quit as well; but when he saves Artie from a messy Porta-Potty fate, he reconsiders.

Emma, deciding to guide like a guidance counselor often does (and absolutely not in *any way* impacted by her crush on Will), reminds Will of his high school glee club glory days. He loved his experiences with the club back then, and she tells him that his love for glee can and should be shared with the kids today. Between that and the newly formed club's version of "Don't Stop Believin'," Will is convinced to stay at McKinley High.

Will is about to become a father; any nascent feelings for Emma are swept aside.

Quinn is Finn's girlfriend and the most popular girl in school, but a bond with Rachel has begun to form.

Quotes

"You think this is hard? Try waterboarding, that's hard!"
—Sue

"I won my first dance competition when I was three months old."
—Rachel

"I'm not afraid of being called a loser, because that's what I am."
—Finn

Music List

Where Is Love? (from the musical Oliver!)

PERFORMED IN *GLEE* BY:	Sandy Ryerson (Stephen Tobolowsky) and Hank Saunders (Ben Bledsoe)
WRITTEN BY:	Lionel Bart
ORIGINALLY PERFORMED ON STAGE BY:	Keith Hamshere (1960)
ORIGINALLY PERFORMED ON SCREEN BY:	Mark Lester with vocals performed by Kathe Green (1968)

Respect

PERFORMED IN *GLEE* BY:	Mercedes Jones (Amber Riley)
WRITTEN BY:	Otis Redding
ORIGINALLY PERFORMED BY:	Otis Redding (1965)
ALSO PERFORMED BY (PARTIAL LIST):	Aretha Franklin (1967), Janis Joplin (1968), Ike & Tina Turner (1971)

Mr. Cellophane (from the musical Chicago)

PERFORMED IN *GLEE* BY:	Kurt Hummel (Chris Colfer)
WRITTEN BY:	John Kander (music) and Fred Ebb (lyrics)
ORIGINALLY PERFORMED ON STAGE BY:	Barney Martin (1975)
ORIGINALLY PERFORMED ON SCREEN BY:	John C. Reilly (2002)

I Kissed a Girl

PERFORMED IN *GLEE* BY:	Tina Cohen-Chang (Jenna Ushkowitz)
WRITTEN BY:	Cathy Dennis, Lukasz "Dr. Luke" Gottwald, Max Martin, and Katy Perry,
ORIGINALLY PERFORMED BY:	Katy Perry (2008)

On My Own (from the musical Les Misérables)

PERFORMED IN *GLEE* BY:	Rachel Berry (Lea Michele)
WRITTEN BY:	Claude-Michel Schönberg (music) and Herbert Kretzmer (lyrics)
ORIGINALLY PERFORMED ON STAGE BY:	Frances Ruffelle (1985)
ALSO PERFORMED ON STAGE BY (PARTIAL LIST):	Lea Salonga (1995), Celia Keenan-Bolger (2006), Lea Michele (2008)

Sit Down, You're Rockin' the Boat (from the musical Guys and Dolls)

PERFORMED IN *GLEE* BY:	Artie Abrams (Kevin McHale), Rachel Berry (Lea Michele), Tina Cohen-Chang (Jenna Ushkowitz), Kurt Hummel (Chris Colfer), and Mercedes Jones (Amber Riley)
WRITTEN BY:	Frank Loesser
ORIGINALLY PERFORMED ON STAGE BY:	Stubby Kaye (1950)
ORIGINALLY PERFORMED ON SCREEN BY:	Stubby Kaye (1955)

Can't Fight This Feeling

PERFORMED IN *GLEE* BY:	Finn Hudson (Cory Monteith)
WRITTEN BY:	Kevin Cronin
ORIGINALLY PERFORMED BY:	REO Speedwagon (1984)

You're the One That I Want (from the musical Grease)

PERFORMED IN *GLEE* BY:	Rachel Berry (Lea Michele) and Finn Hudson (Cory Monteith)
WRITTEN BY:	Jim Farrar
ORIGINALLY PERFORMED ON SCREEN BY:	Olivia Newton-John and John Travolta (1978)

Rehab

PERFORMED IN *GLEE* BY:	Vocal Adrenaline
WRITTEN BY:	Amy Winehouse
ORIGINALLY PERFORMED BY:	Amy Winehouse (2006)

Leaving on a Jet Plane

PERFORMED IN *GLEE* BY:	Will Schuester (Matthew Morrison)
WRITTEN BY:	John Denver
ORIGINALLY PERFORMED BY:	Chad Mitchell Trio (1967)
ALSO PERFORMED BY (PARTIAL LIST):	Peter, Paul and Mary (1967, released as a single in 1969), John Denver (1969), Liza Minnelli (1969), Frank Sinatra (1971), Me First and the Gimme Gimmes (1997), Chantal Kreviazuk (1998)

That's the Way (I Like It)

PERFORMED IN *GLEE* BY:	The 1993 McKinley High School Glee Club
WRITTEN BY:	Harry Wayne "K.C." Casey and Richard Finch
ORIGINALLY PERFORMED BY:	KC and the Sunshine Band (1975)

Don't Stop Believin'

PERFORMED IN *GLEE* BY:	Artie Abrams (Kevin McHale), Rachel Berry (Lea Michele), Tina Cohen-Chang (Jenna Ushkowitz), Finn Hudson (Cory Monteith), Kurt Hummel (Chris Colfer), and Mercedes Jones (Amber Riley)
WRITTEN BY:	Jonathan Cain, Steve Perry, and Neal Schon
ORIGINALLY PERFORMED BY:	Journey (1981)

Showmance (1-2)

Original Air Date	Wednesday, September 9, 2009
Written by	Ryan Murphy, Brad Falchuk, and Ian Brennan
Directed by	Ryan Murphy
Glee Club Assignment	Perform at a school assembly in hopes of recruiting new members

New Directions has formed and they're starting to gel, but they don't have enough people to compete at Sectionals. How will they swell their ranks? With a performance at the school assembly! Will's bright idea is to perform a disco number, but to the kids of New Directions, disco is dead. To avoid lifelong shame, they take matters into their own hands. *Any* fate is better than singing "Le Freak."

Rachel suffers yet another indignity this week (other than disco) when she temporarily joins the celibacy club. Why? Because Finn is a member, and she wants to get closer to him. Inconveniently, Finn's girlfriend Quinn Fabray is the president of the club. She's also head cheerleader. With that much popularity going for her, she can mock the club's newest member unmercifully. Unfazed, Rachel sees that the club is really a joke and says so. Finn is impressed.

At the assembly, New Directions switches the assigned disco song with "Push It." Will and Sue are shocked and the principal is aghast, but the students erupt in cheers. Their performance high is short-lived—Figgins gives New Directions a list of "approved" songs for the future (which they promptly ignore for the rest of the season).

Glee club gets three new recruits for their efforts: Quinn and her Cheerios cohorts Santana and Brittany. Will gives one of Rachel's solos to Quinn to teach Rachel a lesson, and worse, all is not above board with their newest members: Sue has tasked them with destroying the club from within.

Will has problems at home as well as at school. Now that she's pregnant, Terri wants a new house (used ones aren't clean, didn't you know that?) near her sister. A big one. With a grand foyer and a sun nook. To come anywhere close to affording such a place before their baby is born, Will will need a second job. One magically appears before him: school janitor. Emma sees him working after hours and, while "helping" him by cleaning a single pencil sharpener, they have a bit of a moment. Football coach Ken Tanaka sees this and warns Emma away, so she accepts a date with him to distract herself from Will. After all, he has a baby on the way, right?

Well, not so much. Terri learns that she isn't actually pregnant—not that she shares that information with her husband. Worried that her marriage is hanging by a thread, she perpetuates the pregnancy myth and offers her craft room as a nursery for the baby so they won't need to move. Pacified, Will is back down to one job.

Finn and Rachel have a moment themselves while they rehearse. They kiss, but Finn gets, um, a bit overwhelmed. He heads for the hills and back to Quinn, leaving Rachel sad and confused.

Will is still dedicated to his wife, but Emma's willingness to help him draws them a bit closer.

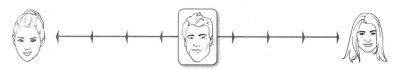

Rachel's gumption in standing up to the Celibacy Club makes an impression on Finn.

Quotes

"They're gonna throw fruit at us. And I just had a facial."
—Kurt

"My father always said you'd become a man when you bought your first house. I'm not sure what he meant, though, because he burned ours down during a drunken fight with Mom."
—Will

"That was the most offensive thing I've seen in twenty years of teaching. And that includes an elementary school production of Hair."
—Sue

Music List

Le Freak

Performed in *Glee* by:	Artie Abrams (Kevin McHale), Rachel Berry (Lea Michele), Finn Hudson (Cory Monteith), Kurt Hummel (Chris Colfer), and Mercedes Jones (Amber Riley)
Written by:	Bernard Edwards and Nile Rodgers
Originally performed by:	Chic (1978)

Gold Digger

Performed in *Glee* by:	Will Schuester (Matthew Morrison) and New Directions
Written by:	Renald Richard and Kanye West, with samples by Ray Charles
Originally performed by:	Kanye West featuring Jamie Foxx (2004)

All by Myself

Performed in *Glee* by:	Emma Pillsbury (Jayma Mays)
Written by:	Eric Carmen and Sergei Rachmaninoff
Originally performed by:	Eric Carmen (1975)
Also performed by (partial list):	Frank Sinatra (1976), Hank Williams Jr. (1977) Shirley Bassey (1982), Eartha Kitt (1989), Sheryl Crow (1994), Céline Dion (1996), Il Divo (2005), John Barrowman (2007)

Push It

Performed in *Glee* by:	Artie Abrams (Kevin McHale), Rachel Berry (Lea Michele), Finn Hudson (Cory Monteith), Kurt Hummel (Chris Colfer), and Mercedes Jones (Amber Riley)
Written by:	Hurby "Love Bug" Azor
Originally performed by:	Salt-n-Pepa (1987)

I Say a Little Prayer

Performed in *Glee* by:	Brittany (Heather Morris), Quinn Fabray (Dianna Agron), and Santana Lopez (Naya Rivera)
Written by:	Burt Bacharach and Hal David
Originally performed by:	Dionne Warwick (1967)

Take a Bow

Performed in *Glee* by:	Rachel Berry (Lea Michele)
Written by:	M. S. Eriksen, T. E. Hermansen, and Ne-Yo
Originally performed by:	Rihanna (2008)

Acafellas (1-3)

Original Air Date	Wednesday, September 16, 2009
Written by	Ryan Murphy
Directed by	John Scott
Glee Club Assignment	Hire a new choreographer while the director is distracted by a new hobby

Will Shuester is many things, including (he thinks) a soon-to-be father, whose own dad doubts himself and the job he did with Will. However, an award-winning show choir choreographer he is not. Rachel, egged on by Quinn and Santana, decides they need to up their game when it comes to dance, and that bruises Will's ego. Of all things, it's a rousing chorus of "For He's a Jolly Good Fellow" for Henri, the newly thumbless shop teacher, that provides inspiration for Will. He forms an all-early-R&B a capella group, the Acafellas, teaming up with the thumbless Henri, Ken, and Terri's lackey from Sheets-N-Things, Howard.

With Will distracted, the Cheerleading Trio of Imminent Glee Club Doom begins a two-pronged assault. Phase One is to cheer on Rachel's idea to hire a choreographer. Not just any choreographer will do; at the Cheerios' suggestion, Rachel decides she wants Dakota Stanley, known tyrant of the dance floor. If he can drive a few members away, the club's chances of survival are slim.

Phase Two involves Mercedes, whose presence and voice is too much of a benefit for the club to ignore. Seeing a budding connection between her and Kurt, Quinn and Santana convince Mercedes that the Fabulous One has feeling for her, knowing full well that she's, well, not really his type.

As the cheerleaders help fundraise for Phase One with a car wash, Phase

Acafellas Everywhere

Several a cappella groups used the name "Acafellas" before *Glee* did, including:

o The Muhlenberg AcaFellas of Allentown, Pennsylvania

o The AcaFellas of Embry-Riddle Aeronautical University in Daytona Beach, Florida

o The Aca'fellas of Loyola University Chicago

o The Acafellas of Mendocino, California

Two comes to a head when Kurt has to let Mercedes know that his interests lie elsewhere (saying Rachel, meaning Finn). Furious, Mercedes smashes the windows of his dad-given car, then sings about it using a conveniently-named song. To the cheerleaders' disappointment, Kurt and Mercedes reaffirm their friendship when Kurt comes out to her, ruining Phase Two. Phase One also fails when Dakota Stanley arrives and tries to make the club into something it isn't; Rachel stands up to him and fires him. Looks like the cheerleaders wore their car wash bikini outfits for nothing.

Through all of this, Will continues singing with the Acafellas, mostly clueless about what his glee club is doing. The Acafellas' first performance is a smash success; their CDs sell out and the reviews are (mostly) stellar. But when thumbless Henri ODs on cough syrup and Howard drops out, the Acafellas are left shorthanded. Will recruits the dissatisfied-with-glee Finn, but what about a fourth? Enter Finn's best friend Puck, glad for the opportunity to MILF-hunt. And whaddaya know, the guy can sing! (Oh wait, it's *Glee*, everyone can.) Will gives both Finn and Puck a crash course to learn the choreography, and their quick success helps rebuild Will's confidence as a dance teacher.

Then the Acafellas reluctantly pick up a fifth member, Sandy, but only because he's arranged for superstar Josh Groban to be at their concert. The second show with the new version of the Acafellas goes just as swimmingly, cheered on by the entire PTA and Will's parents (after which we never see them again. Ah well, maybe next year . . .). Josh Groban becomes a fan, too, but he's really only there to ask Sandy to stop stalking him. Well, that, and to pick up older women if he gets the chance. Like, say, Will's mother.

His Acafellas experience was great and all, but Will realizes that his heart is with the glee club. The group is disbanded and Will, his confidence restored, refocuses on the kids.

Will thinks that his and Terri's sex life has improved due to the Acafellas; Terri is just hoping to make a non-pretend baby.

The Dakota Stanley situation doesn't sit well with Finn; he nearly quits the club.

"They say it takes more certainty than talent to be a star. Just look at John Stamos."
—Emma

"Throngs of screaming teenagers don't do it for Josh Groban."
—Josh Groban

"I'm going to ask you to smell your armpits. That's the smell of failure, and it's stinking up my office."
—Sue

Music List

This Is How We Do It

PERFORMED IN *GLEE* BY:	Acafellas (Kent Avenido, Ken Gallagher, Matthew Morrison, John Lloyd Young)
WRITTEN BY:	Montell Jordan, Oji Pierce, and Ricky Walters
ORIGINALLY PERFORMED BY:	Montell Jordan (1995)

Poison

PERFORMED IN *GLEE* BY:	Acafellas (Kent Avenido, Ken Gallagher, Matthew Morrison, John Lloyd Young)
WRITTEN BY:	Elliot Straite (a.k.a. Dr. Freeze)
ORIGINALLY PERFORMED BY:	Bell Biv DeVoe (1990)

Mercy

PERFORMED IN *GLEE* BY:	Vocal Adrenaline
WRITTEN BY:	Steve Booker and Aimée Ann Duffy (a.k.a. Duffy)
ORIGINALLY PERFORMED BY:	Duffy (2008)

Bust Your Windows

PERFORMED IN *GLEE* BY:	Mercedes Jones (Amber Riley)
WRITTEN BY:	Salaam Remi, Jazmine Sullivan, and DeAndre Way
ORIGINALLY PERFORMED BY:	Jazmine Sullivan (2008)

I Wanna Sex You Up

PERFORMED IN *GLEE* BY:	Acafellas (Ken Gallagher, Cory Montieth, Matthew Morrison, Mark Salling, Stephen Tobolowsky)
WRITTEN BY:	Elliot Straite (a.k.a. Dr. Freeze)
ORIGINALLY PERFORMED BY:	Color Me Badd (1991)

Preggers (1-4)

Original Air Date	Wednesday, September 23, 2009
Written by	Brad Falchuk
Directed by	Brad Falchuk
Glee Club Assignment	Break out of their boxes and shake things up

When Kurt's dad Burt sees him dancing to Beyoncé with Tina and Brittany, Kurt has to think fast for a valid-sounding excuse. Uh...football! That's it! He joined the team! Needing to turn this lie into reality, he goes to Finn, who brings him to Coach Tanaka for a tryout. With a little help from Beyoncé, Kurt makes the team.

Finn, however, is having a bad week. Quinn is pregnant—even though they've never actually had sex. According to her, a hot tub is to blame. Panicked, he looks for ways to improve his lot in life. One of those ways could be winning a football scholarship, but the problem is, the team sucks. He asks Will to coach the football team at dancing in the hopes that it will help.

The situation is worse than Finn knows. Not only is his girlfriend pregnant, but he isn't the actual father. Puck is. When the Mohawked One finds out, he confronts Quinn, but she rejects him as a loser; she'd rather have Finn standing by her. On the other pregnancy front, the not-actually-pregnant Terri tells her sister Kendra the truth. Rather than encouraging honesty, Kendra suggests going through with the deception by finding themselves a baby. Hmm, where could they possibly find one of those? I wonder.

But back to important things, like football. The team puts their dance training into a game situation by performing the "Single Ladies" choreography mid-game as a distraction. The other team is indeed distracted—enough that McKinley actually scores, and Kurt's extra-point kick gives them the victory. The crowd goes wild, and Kurt's dad (finally) couldn't be prouder. When Kurt comes out to him after the game, Burt tells him that he already knows he's gay, and has known it since Kurt was three. Burt isn't thrilled, but he loves his son for exactly who he is.

But wait! All is not football and teen pregnancy! Sue, newly hired as a local news commentator in "Sue's Corner," has another scheme to destroy the glee club. She blackmails Figgins into appointing Sandy (without his creepy dolls) as the new Arts Director, in order to put on *Cabaret* as the school musical, which is guaranteed to steal the New Directions lead singer. Rachel, angered when a *West Side Story* solo is awarded to Tina, auditions for and is given the role of Sally Bowles, then quits the glee club completely when the coveted solo isn't returned to her. Oh, the drama!

On the plus side, the club acquires three new members: Puck and fellow football players Mike (a.k.a. Other Asian) and Matt (a.k.a. wait, that character has a name?).

Status quo. Will doesn't know about Terri and Kendra's machinations.

Finn thinks he's going to be a daddy! Also, Rachel quit the club.

Puck may be the father, but Quinn would much rather stay with Finn.

Quotes

"Yes. We. Cane!"
—Sue

"Hi, I'm Kurt Hummel and I'll be auditioning for the role of kicker."
—Kurt

"The more times Rachel storms out of rehearsal, the less impact it has."
—Artie

Music List

Single Ladies (Put a Ring on It)

Danced in *Glee* by:	The McKinley High Football Team featuring Kurt Hummel (Chris Colfer)
	Also danced in *Glee* by Brittany (Heather Morris) and Tina Cohen-Chang (Jenna Ushkowitz)
Written by:	Thaddis "Kuk Harrel" Harrell, and Beyoncé Knowles, Terius "The-Dream" Nash, and Christopher "Tricky" Stewart
Originally performed (and danced) by:	Beyoncé (2008)

Taking Chances

Performed in *Glee* by:	Rachel Berry (Lea Michele)
Written by:	Kara DioGuardi and David A. Stewart
Originally performed by:	Kara DioGuardi and David A. Stewart (2007)
Also performed by:	Céline Dion (2007)

Tonight (from the musical West Side Story)

Performed in *Glee* by:	Tina Cohen-Chang (Jenna Ushkowitz)
Written by:	Leonard Bernstein (music) and Stephen Sondheim (lyrics)
Originally performed on stage by:	Carol Lawrence (1957)
Originally performed on screen by:	Natalie Wood with vocals performed by Marni Nixon (1961)

The Rhodes Not Taken (1-5)

Original Air Date	Wednesday, September 30, 2009
Written by	Ian Brennan
Directed by	John Scott
Glee Club Assignment	Perform at Invitationals, with or without Rachel

With Rachel in full Sally Bowles mode, New Directions needs another member, someone who can tackle the lead female vocal parts. And one happens to be available, albeit unexpectedly: April Rhodes, the star senior of the glee club during Will's freshman year, who conveniently never graduated from high school. But can April be the lead singer that Rachel was? Considering how she handles "Maybe This Time," yes, she most certainly can.

But April is now an alcoholic with a wreck of a life. Will sees joining New Directions as a new beginning for April, a chance for her to get back on her feet. He encourages her to become part of the team and bond with them, so she gets Kurt drunk, teaches Mercedes and Tina how to shoplift, and quite possibly sleeps with the entire football team. Emma sounds the warning bell, so Will goes to April, imploring her to change. She promises to try, and Will believes her.

Finn, still dealing with the revelations of the previous week, goes to Emma concerned for his future. She suggests that pursuing music is a better path than trying for a football scholarship. But for the club to do well, they need one missing ingredient: Rachel. Finn tries to coax her back, making her think that he wants to be with her. Between that and the horrible time she's having with the musical, Rachel relents...until she finds out that Finn is going to be a father. She quits again.

At Invitationals, April brings the house down, receiving the standing ovation she always dreamed of getting on Broadway. She realizes it's time for her to move on to Branson, Missouri. She departs, leaving the club short for the second half of their show. Rachel, missing her teammates, returns to the club and joins them in singing "Somebody to Love."

Emma is the voice of reason in this episode, which is just what Will needs sometimes...and he knows it.

Finn might pretend to like Rachel in this episode, but he's only doing it to try for a scholarship. Still, he's pretty good at it. Maybe a little too good?

Quotes

"I have no problem with nudity. Let me tell you about my planned production of Equus."
—Sandy

"We'll get you sobered up, find you some underwear. It's not too late for you."
—Will

"When I heard Sandy wanted to write himself into a scene as Queen Cleopatra, I was aroused. And then furious."
—Sue

Music List

Don't Stop Believin'

PERFORMED IN *GLEE* BY:	Quinn Fabray (Dianna Agron) and Finn Hudson (Cory Monteith)

Song information listed in "Pilot" (1-1)

Maybe This Time (from the musical *Cabaret*)

PERFORMED IN *GLEE* BY:	Rachel Berry (Lea Michele) and April Rhodes (Kristen Chenoweth)
WRITTEN BY:	John Kander (music) and Fred Ebb (lyrics)
ORIGINALLY PERFORMED ON SCREEN BY:	Liza Minelli (1972)
ORIGINALLY PERFORMED ON STAGE BY:	Natasha Richardson (1998 Broadway revival)

Alone

PERFORMED IN *GLEE* BY:	April Rhodes (Kristen Chenoweth) and Will Schuester (Matthew Morrison)
WRITTEN BY:	Tom Kelly and Billy Steinberg
ORIGINALLY PERFORMED BY:	i-Ten (1983)
ALSO PERFORMED BY:	Heart (1987), Céline Dion (2007)

Last Name

PERFORMED IN *GLEE* BY:	April Rhodes (Kristen Chenoweth) and New Directions
WRITTEN BY: Luke Laird,	Hillary Lindsey, and Carrie Underwood
ORIGINALLY PERFORMED BY:	Carrie Underwood (2008)

Somebody to Love

PERFORMED IN *GLEE* BY:	Rachel Berry (Lea Michele), Finn Hudson (Cory Monteith), and New Directions
WRITTEN BY:	Freddie Mercury
ORIGINALLY PERFORMED BY:	Queen (1976)

Vitamin D (1-6)

Original Air Date	Wednesday, October 7, 2009
Written by	Ryan Murphy
Directed by	Elodie Keene
Glee Club Assignment	Perform a mashup in teams of boys vs. girls

Sue has a problem: her head cheerleader is not performing up to snuff. Unable to tell Sue the truth, Quinn blames the glee club. Like Sue needed another reason to cause show choir destruction! But now that she has one, she tries a new tack: ruin Will's life. The chemistry between Will and Emma provides the perfect foothold, so Sue talks to Terri about the Emma situation.

Shortly thereafter, Terri appears in the faculty lounge. Surprise! She's not just there to visit her husband. Oh no, she's been hired as the new school nurse. (Just pretend that it's perfectly reasonable for a public school to hire a school nurse with zero experience and no training whatsoever. Got it? Good. Moving on.)

With Terri so near at hand at school, Emma has to consider the reality of her situation with Will. Then Ken surprises Emma with a marriage proposal. With Will unavailable (and with a "pregnant" wife), Emma accepts. It is better to be with someone you don't love than to be alone, she reasons.

Not all is adult drama. The kids have their own curveball thrown at them when Will challenges them to compete against each other, boys vs. girls. No complacency allowed in this club! The girls are confident, but the boys are stressed. How can they measure up to the powerhouses on the girls' side?

Through all this, Finn is tired. Really, really tired. So tired that he goes to the pseudo-nurse's office for a nap. Instead of naptime, Terri gives him a little pill-based boost. Hey, it's over-the-counter. Perfectly safe. Acting like a hamster on speed isn't a warning sign at all. Finn shares his newfound boosters with the glee club guys to give them an edge in the competition, and it does the trick. The boys kill it, and the girls worry that they may not win as easily as they thought.

Kurt admits to the girls that a secret ingredient enhanced their show, so they get their own doses and begin bouncing off walls just like the boys. Eventually they all fess up to their wrong-pill-doing, but the whole situation blows up, leading to Terri's rightful firing and the addition of a co-director for New Directions, Sue, to keep an eye on things that Will apparently can't.

Terri comes out of the situation with one thing to her advantage: a baby. Quinn promises to let her adopt her child, enabling Terri to continue her pregnancy deception.

Will is furious with Terri after she gives uppers to the students. But Emma's sudden engagement throws him for a bit of a loop.

Finn's tired, but he's still Quinn's.

Quotes

"We're planning on smacking them down like the hand of God."
—Artie

"It's cubic zirconia. I know how affected you were by Blood Diamond.*"*
—Ken

"We were just taking a lesson from Major League Baseball. It's not cheating if everyone does it."
—Rachel

Music List

MASHUP #1:

It's My Life

PERFORMED IN *GLEE* BY:	Artie Abrams (Kevin McHale), Mike Chang (Harry Shum Jr.), Finn Hudson (Cory Monteith), Kurt Hummel (Chris Colfer), Noah "Puck" Puckerman (Mark Salling), and Matt Rutherford (Dijon Talton)
WRITTEN BY:	Jon Bon Jovi, Max Martin, and Richie Sambora
ORIGINALLY PERFORMED BY:	Bon Jovi (2000)

Confessions Part II

PERFORMED IN *GLEE* BY:	Artie Abrams (Kevin McHale), Mike Chang (Harry Shum Jr.), Finn Hudson (Cory Monteith), Kurt Hummel (Chris Colfer), Noah "Puck" Puckerman (Mark Salling), and Matt Rutherford (Dijon Talton)

WRITTEN BY: Bryan Michael Cox, Jermaine Dupri, and Usher Raymond,

ORIGINALLY PERFORMED BY: Usher (2004)

MASHUP #2:

Halo

PERFORMED IN *GLEE* BY: Rachel Berry (Lea Michele), Brittany (Heather Morris), Tina Cohen-Chang (Jenna Ushkowitz), Quinn Fabray (Dianna Agron), Mercedes Jones (Amber Riley), and Santana Lopez (Naya Rivera)

WRITTEN BY: Evan Bogart, Beyoncé Knowles, and Ryan Tedder

ORIGINALLY PERFORMED BY: Beyoncé (2009)

Walking on Sunshine

PERFORMED IN *GLEE* BY: Rachel Berry (Lea Michele), Brittany (Heather Morris), Tina Cohen-Chang (Jenna Ushkowitz), Quinn Fabray (Dianna Agron), Mercedes Jones (Amber Riley), and Santana Lopez (Naya Rivera)

WRITTEN BY: Kimberley Rew

ORIGINALLY PERFORMED BY: Katrina and the Waves (1983, re-released in 1985)

Throwdown (1-7)

Original Air Date	Wednesday, October 14, 2009
Written by	Brad Falchuk
Directed by	Ryan Murphy
Glee Club Assignment	Perform while split into two groups, one directed by Will and one by Sue

It's on! Complete with super-slo-mo arguments and *Carmina Burana* background music! How did Will vs. Sue turn into a shouting match? Let's go back a few days and find out.

The battle's first stage begins when Sue asserts herself as co-director and splits the team in two: minority students of every sort vs. the few remaining kids who don't quite qualify as such. Sue takes the first group and works at turning them against Will. They only get to sing backup to Rachel and Finn! They aren't appreciated in their own right! How awful, right? Will fights back by failing all of the Cheerios in his Spanish class. Take that! Things fall apart pretty quickly from there.

Sue's efforts aren't very successful with most of the students, as the two sides still get together to sing in secret. However, Sue uses Puck and Brittany's respective Jewish and Nordic heritages to convince them to defect from Will's side of the battle, leaving him with only Rachel, Finn, and Quinn as their bitter backup singer.

Quinn also learns that she is carrying a little girl, who will most certainly *not* be named Drizzle. Will, already in a bad mood, insists on an OB/GYN appointment for Terri so he can see his baby, too. Kendra and Terri arrange for a fake baby viewing. It goes perfectly. Will is overcome by the sight of what he thinks is his daughter (not a son, as Terri had asserted previously), and Terri makes him promise to remember that feeling.

But back to Quinn, who bursts into "Keep Me Hanging On" for only vaguely apparent reasons in the middle of all this. Her situation is about to be made very public, thanks to that pesky Jacob and his journalistic persistence. Rachel goes so far as to offer her underwear for his silence, but when Sue finds out the truth, she orders him to run the story, underwear or no. The club sticks by Quinn, singing "Keep Holding On" to show her their support.

Seeing the sonogram of "his" daughter brings Will closer to Terri than ever.

It's now public knowledge that he and Quinn are having a baby, and he stands by her, although he's grateful for what Rachel did to try to help them.

Quotes

"I don't trust a man with curly hair. I can't help but picture little birds laying sulfurous eggs in there, and it disgusts me."
—Sue

"I empower my Cheerios to be champions. Do they go to college? I don't know. I don't care. Should they learn Spanish? Sure, if they want to become dishwashers and gardeners."
—Sue

"Fellow glee clubbers, it would be an honor to show you how a real storm-out is done. I encourage you to follow my lead."
—Rachel

Music List

Hate on Me

PERFORMED IN *GLEE* BY:	Sue's Kids (Chris Colfer, Kevin McHale, Amber Riley, Naya Rivera, Harry Shum Jr., Dijon Talton, and Jenna Ushkowitz)
WRITTEN BY:	Jill Scott
ORIGINALLY PERFORMED BY:	Jill Scott (2007)

Ride Wit Me

PERFORMED IN *GLEE* BY:	New Directions
WRITTEN BY:	El DeBarge, Randy DeBarge, Jason Epperson, and Nelly
ORIGINALLY PERFORMED BY:	Nelly featuring City Spud (2001)

No Air

PERFORMED IN *GLEE* BY:	Rachel Berry (Lea Michele), Brittany (Heather Morris), Quinn Fabray (Dianna Agron), Finn Hudson (Cory Monteith), and Noah "Puck" Puckerman (Mark Salling)
WRITTEN BY:	James Fauntleroy II, Eric "Blue Tooth" Griggs, Harvey Mason Jr., Steve Russell, Michael Scala, and Damon Thomas
ORIGINALLY PERFORMED BY:	Jordin Sparks and Chris Brown (2008)

You Keep Me Hangin' On

PERFORMED IN *GLEE* BY:	Quinn Fabray (Dianna Agron)
WRITTEN BY:	Lamont Dozier, Brian Holland, and Edward Holland Jr.
ORIGINALLY PERFORMED BY:	The Supremes (1967)
ALSO PERFORMED BY (PARTIAL LIST):	Kim Wilde (1986), Reba McEntire (1996)

Keep Holding On

PERFORMED IN *GLEE* BY:	Rachel Berry (Lea Michele), Finn Hudson (Cory Monteith), and New Directions
WRITTEN BY:	Lukasz "Dr. Luke" Gottwald and Avril Lavigne
ORIGINALLY PERFORMED BY:	Avril Lavigne (2006)

Mash-Up (1-8)

Original Air Date	Wednesday, October 21, 2009
Written by	Ian Brennan
Directed by	Elodie Keene
Glee Club Assignment	Combine two songs to create something new

This episode proves that two great tastes only taste great together sometimes.

In the case of Ken and Emma's wedding, the combination of their respective favorite songs should have been a big flashing sign that read: THIS WEDDING IS A BAD IDEA. But they move forward anyway, and they need Will's help to combine their songs into one wonderfully cohesive mashup. The songs are as far apart on the spectrum as they possibly could be: "Thong Song" and "I Could Have Danced All Night." Yeah, good luck with that.

Ken knows something isn't quite right. Even *he* can see that his fiancée has feelings for Will, and as their wedding nears, he's less and less happy about it. Feeling bitter, he schedules extra football practice on the same day as glee rehearsals, making his four singing players choose between the two extracurricular activities. After talking with Finn, Ken realizes punishing the kids isn't very helpful, and he changes the schedule back to how it was.

Romance may not be in the air for near-to-nuptials Ken, but it is for Puck and the unexpected target of his attention. Thanks to his mother and a dream that features a nightgown-clad Rachel at his window, Puck realizes that he should be dating a hot Jewish girl. Rachel qualifies. Surprised and not sold on the idea, Rachel figures that insisting on a man who can sing a solo will dissuade him, but he counters by singing "Sweet Caroline." And she's sold! Then again, so is Quinn, to a certain extent. But it doesn't last; Rachel likes Finn, Puck likes Quinn, and Puckleberry (isn't that what the kids call it?) can never be. For now, anyway.

Quinn and Finn, between glee club and the pregnancy, have lost a lot of their status in the school. To their dismay, they are now the slushie-ed rather than the slushie-ers. Even sunglasses don't restore their cool. Nor does threatening to slushie Kurt, who responds by taking one for the team. But Quinn's coach, inexplicably supportive of the situation, is distracted and can't help her when she falls for Rod Remington, cheesy news anchor. While feeling all gooey about Rod, Sue is even nice to Will. Weird. But Rod neglects to inform her that he doesn't see theirs as an exclusive relationship, so when

Sue catches him kissing Anchorwoman Andrea, she leaves him. Infuriated, she takes it out on poor Quinn, kicking her out of the Cheerios.

Will still has that mashup to do. And he tries. He goes with Emma while she shops for wedding dresses to work on it, although that turns out to be less than helpful. In the end, Will admits defeat. The two just don't work together.

The songs, he means. Yeah, that's it.

Seeing Emma in her Hepburn-esque wedding dress and spending time with her rekindles the feelings between them.

Rachel has a fling with Puck; Finn stays loyal to Quinn.

Quinn sees something in Puck during "Sweet Caroline" that makes her ponder the possibilities.

Quotes

"I will go to the animal shelter and get you a kitty cat. I will let you fall in love with that kitty cat. And then on some dark cold night, I will steal away into your home and punch you in the face."
—Sue

"Someone get me to a day spa, stat!"
—Kurt

"It was a message from God: Rachel was a hot Jew and the good lord wanted me to get into her pants."
—Puck

Music List

Bust a Move

PERFORMED IN *GLEE* BY:	Will Schuester (Matthew Morrison) and New Directions
WRITTEN BY:	Matt Dike, Michael Ross, and Marvin Young,
ORIGINALLY PERFORMED BY:	Young MC (1989)

Thong Song

PERFORMED IN *GLEE* BY:	Will Schuester (Matthew Morrison)
WRITTEN BY:	Mark Andrews, Desmond Child, Tim Kelley, Bob Robinson, Robi Rosa
ORIGINALLY PERFORMED BY:	Sisqó (1999)

What a Girl Wants

PERFORMED IN *GLEE* BY:	Rachel Berry (Lea Michele)
WRITTEN BY:	Shelly Peiken and Guy Roche
ORIGINALLY PERFORMED BY:	Christina Aguilera (1999)

Sweet Caroline

PERFORMED IN *GLEE* BY:	Noah "Puck" Puckerman (Mark Salling) and New Directions
WRITTEN BY:	Neil Diamond
ORIGINALLY PERFORMED BY:	Neil Diamond (1969)

Sing Sing Sing (With a Swing)

DANCED IN *GLEE* BY:	Will Schuester (Matthew Morrison) and Sue Sylvester (Jane Lynch)
WRITTEN BY:	Louis Prima
ORIGINALLY PERFORMED BY:	New Orleans Gang (1936)
ALSO PERFORMED BY:	Benny Goodman (1937)

I Could Have Danced All Night (from the musical My Fair Lady)

PERFORMED IN *GLEE* BY:	Emma Pillsbury (Jayma Mays)
WRITTEN BY:	Frederick Loewe (music) and Alan Jay Lerner (lyrics)
ORIGINALLY PERFORMED ON STAGE BY:	Julie Andrews (1956)
ORIGINALLY PERFORMED ON SCREEN BY:	Audrey Hepburn with vocals performed by Marni Nixon (1964)

Wheels (1-9)

Original Air Date	Wednesday, November 11, 2009
Written by	Ryan Murphy
Directed by	Paris Barclay
Glee Club Assignment	Spend three hours a day in a wheelchair, raise money for Artie's wheelchair-accessible bus with a bake sale, and do a wheelchair dance number. Also, choose who will sing "Defying Gravity." Busy week.

Will informs the glee club that the school won't pay for a special bus to allow Artie to travel with the rest of the team, and he tries to get them to raise money for it, but the team doesn't find the bus to be all that big of a deal. But to Artie, losing that experience with his teammates *is* a big deal, so Will makes the fundraising mandatory. Not only that, but the students have to spend a few hours every day in wheelchairs all week *and* learn to perform in them. The club is less than thrilled, but as the week goes on, they start to realize how different Artie's life truly is.

Will has more in store for the club; another new song! When "Defying Gravity" is automatically offered to Rachel, Mercedes objects, but she is mollified with the promise of a future song. Then Kurt *really* objects: it's in his range, he can sing it well, he loves the song, so why shouldn't he sing it? Will rejects this idea, so Kurt brings the situation to his dad. Burt takes the fight to Figgins, defending his son's right to sing like a girl. Once in front of the principal, Will agrees that the fair way to assign the song is to hold an audition. Soon after, Burt receives a rude crank call about his son.

Let the diva-off commence! Kurt and Rachel both sing well, but when Kurt gets to the high F, he flubs it and Rachel wins the solo. Later, Kurt admits to his father that he blew the note on purpose: had he won the audition, his father would have had to deal with more crank calls, and his dad means more to him than performing the song ever could.

Speaking of open auditions, Figgins orders the Cheerios to hold them to fill the slot formerly held by Quinn, much to Sue's chagrin. Will supervises and many try out, but the chosen one is Becky, a friend of Brittany's who has Down syndrome. Will becomes mighty suspicious. Why would Sue choose Becky to be a Cheerio?

Tina asks Artie about how he ended up in a wheelchair, and he explains about the car accident he was in when he was eight years old. He compares his disability with her stutter. They go on a date, during which Tina admits that her stutter is faked. Artie, who thought he had found a kindred spirit, gets angry and ends the date.

Meanwhile, in their wheelchairs, the glee club fails at selling baked goods. Also failing is Finn, since Quinn has medical bills piling up and needs him to handle them. Actual-baby-daddy Puck offers to help, but although Quinn softens to him a bit while "baking," she refuses him; she wants Finn to be the baby's one and only father. Puck and Finn get all macho and fight over Quinn, and both succeed at finding ways to take care of the bills in their own ways: Puck laces the bake-sale cupcakes with marijuana to increase sales and then steals the money, and Finn finds a job, with Rachel's help. Quinn chooses Finn, and they roll away in Finn's wheelchair.

Puck returns the "special cupcake" money to the club for Artie's bus, but Artie chooses to use the money for a ramp in the auditorium. Instead, Sue donates money for ramps at the school so the bake-sale funds can go to the bus. Why? Unbeknownst to Will and the glee kids, Sue's sister Jean has Down syndrome, and meeting Becky had opened a temporary soft spot in her. With Artie's special bus secured and a new understanding of their teammate, the club performs "Proud Mary" in wheelchairs. Rollin', indeed.

With the focus on the kids, things slide back toward status quo...for the time being.

Finn does his best to support Quinn and help her with bills, although it's Rachel who helps him find a job.

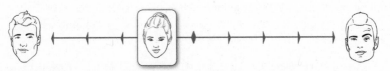

Puck gathers more funds to pay for the doctor bills than Finn does. (Of course, Finn does so with an actual job.)

Quotes

"Mr. Schue, kids are busier than when you went here. We've got homework and football, teen pregnancy, lunch..."
—Finn

"You're irritating. But don't take that personally."
—Artie (to Rachel)

"If I have a pregnant girl doing a handspring into a double layout, the judges aren't going to be admiring her impeccable form, they're going to be wondering if the centrifugal force is going to make the baby's head start crowning."
—Sue

Music List

Dancing With Myself

PERFORMED IN *GLEE* BY:	Artie Abrams (Kevin McHale)
WRITTEN BY:	Billy Idol and Tony James
ORIGINALLY PERFORMED BY:	Generation X (1981)
ALSO PERFORMED BY (PARTIAL LIST):	Billy Idol (1981), Blink-182 (1997), The Donnas (2004)

Defying Gravity (from the musical Wicked)

PERFORMED IN *GLEE* BY:	Rachel Berry (Lea Michele) and Kurt Hummel (Chris Colfer)
WRITTEN BY:	Stephen Schwartz
ORIGINALLY PERFORMED BY:	Idina Menzel (2003)

Proud Mary

PERFORMED IN *GLEE* BY:	Artie Abrams (Kevin McHale), Tina Cohen-Chang (Jenna Ushkowitz), Mercedes Jones (Amber Riley), and New Directions
WRITTEN BY:	John Fogerty
ORIGINALLY PERFORMED BY:	Creedence Clearwater Revival (1969)
ALSO PERFORMED BY (PARTIAL LIST):	Elvis Presley (1970), Ike & Tina Turner (1971), Tina Turner (1993)

Ballad (1-10)

Original Air Date	Wednesday, November 18, 2009
Written by	Brad Falchuk
Directed by	Brad Falchuk
Glee Club Assignment	Sing a ballad to your assigned partner

Will, young cute high school teacher that he is, tends to attract student crushes. Hey, these things happen! And this week, it happens again. Since Matt (you know, that football guy who isn't Other Asian) is absent, Will is forced to take his place and sing a ballad with Rachel. Bam! In the course of one eighties duet, she develops a crush on him. "Endless Love" is a dangerous song, it seems. Will knows the signs: gifts, knocks on the door, and puppy-dog-like following around. Here we go again.

Terri, who has been through all of this before, makes the situation (and Rachel herself) work for her. Student crush = instant housekeeper! Even Emma is little help when she sits in on Will's attempt at an educational mashup song to Rachel: they both miss the lyrics and focus on the pretty.

Enter Suzy Pepper, cautionary tale. She put herself in the hospital over her crush on Will. She understands Rachel in a way that Rachel doesn't yet understand herself. She knows that a crush on Will reveals Rachel's deep-seated self-esteem issues. Somewhere in her heart, Rachel doesn't feel like she deserves love. Rachel has a lot to think about thanks to Suzy, and she apologizes to Will for being crazy all week.

Other pairings cause their own issues. To Kurt's delight, he and his crush Finn are put together for the assignment. When Finn can't come up with an idea, Kurt suggests singing to his unborn daughter. Great! Emotional connection, beautiful moment...and a perfect way for his mom to find out about her future granddaughter when she sees him singing to the sonogram.

Finn moves forward with another bad idea from Kurt when he sings about Quinn's pregnancy in front of her ultra-conservative parents. Quinn's father throws her out of the house. She moves into Finn's house and his mom welcomes her. But Quinn's other secret starts to leak out when Puck tells Mercedes that he is the father of the baby. Even without that, Finn and Quinn have had a tough week. The rest of the club surprises them with "Lean on Me" at the end, hoping that the knowledge that the club is standing by them will help boost their morale.

Will isn't happy with Terri for taking advantage of Rachel, and Emma has more trouble than usual hiding her crush.

Finn takes Quinn in when her parents throw her out.

Quotes

"I've never noticed this before because he's always trying to destroy my career, but Mr. Schue has really pretty eyes."
—Rachel

"I've been dealing with these schoolgirl crushes for years. Why shouldn't I get something out of it?"
—Terri

"Love is hard for us. We look for boys we know we can never have. Mr. Schue is a perfect target for our self-esteem issues. He can never reciprocate our feelings, which only reinforces the conviction that we're not worthy of being loved."
—Suzy Pepper

Music List

Endless Love

PERFORMED IN *GLEE* BY:	Rachel Berry (Lea Michele) and Will Schuester (Matthew Morrison)
WRITTEN BY:	Lionel Ritchie
ORIGINALLY PERFORMED BY:	Lionel Richie and Diana Ross (1981)
ALSO PERFORMED BY:	Mariah Carey and Luther Vandross (1994)

I'll Stand by You

PERFORMED IN *GLEE* BY:	Finn Hudson (Cory Monteith)
WRITTEN BY:	Chrissie Hynde, Tom Kelly, and Billy Steinberg
ORIGINALLY PERFORMED BY:	The Pretenders (1994)

MASHUP:

Don't Stand So Close to Me

PERFORMED IN *GLEE* BY:	Will Schuester (Matthew Morrison)
WRITTEN BY:	Sting
ORIGINALLY PERFORMED BY:	The Police (1980)

Young Girl

PERFORMED IN *GLEE* BY:	Will Schuester (Matthew Morrison)
WRITTEN BY:	Jerry Fuller
ORIGINALLY PERFORMED BY:	Gary Puckett & The Union Gap (1968)

Crush

PERFORMED IN *GLEE* BY:	Rachel Berry (Lea Michele)
WRITTEN BY:	Kevin Clark, Berny Cosgrove, Andy Goldmark, and Mark Muller,
ORIGINALLY PERFORMED BY:	Jennifer Paige (1998)

(You're) Having My Baby

PERFORMED IN *GLEE* BY:	Finn Hudson (Cory Monteith)
WRITTEN BY:	Paul Anka
ORIGINALLY PERFORMED BY:	Paul Anka (1974)

Lean on Me

PERFORMED IN *GLEE* BY:	Artie Abrams (Kevin McHale) and Mercedes Jones (Amber Riley), and New Directions
WRITTEN BY:	Bill Withers
ORIGINALLY PERFORMED BY:	Bill Withers (1972)

Hairography (1-11)

Original Air Date	Wednesday, November 25, 2009
Written by	Ian Brennan
Directed by	Bill D'Elia
Glee Club Assignment	Meet the Jane Addams Academy and the Haverbrook School for the Deaf

Something's rotten in the state of Ohio. Will knows that Sue has been undermining the glee club, and all he needs is proof. He decides to visit one of the school's rivals at Sectionals to find that proof. Considering that the Jane Addams Academy is a school for female hooligans in training, they *must* be in on it, right?

Grace Hitchens, their show choir director, schools him on how much the club means to the girls and how it helps them. Chastened, Will invites her club to perform in their auditorium. The girls do, and they are awesome, so much so that Will, previously confident about his club's chances, worries that Jane Addams Academy could beat them.

All is not lost! Rachel explains that their secret to performing can be summed up in one word: "hairography." If you don't sing or dance well, toss your hair around and no one will notice. Brilliant! Will buys wigs for those without sufficient hair for tossing, and Brittany trains them in all things hairography. Now they're ready to face opponent #2: the Haverbrook School for the Deaf.

Their deaf-in-one-ear director, Dalton Rumba, insists on their own performance at McKinley High. New Directions shows off their new hairography, but Haverbrook counters with "Imagine." When New Directions joins them, Will realizes that the hairography experiment was a failure.

However, Will was right all along in his suspicions: Sue meets with Grace and Dalton and gives them songs from the New Directions set list.

Kurt, his crush on Finn still going strong, teams up with Quinn to discuss the Rachel situation. A plan is hatched. He offers Rachel a makeover, but turns her into exactly the type of girl Finn doesn't like. Finn's confusion leads to Rachel's realization that she was set up. Kurt admits to it. They both realize that, even though they both want Finn, they'll never take him away from Quinn.

But what if Quinn leaves Finn? She considers it, giving baby-daddy Puck a test-run during babysitting duty, a duty she does brilliantly in a near-impossible situation: taking care of Kendra's kids. Quinn even begins to consider keeping her baby rather than giving her up for adoption. But when she learns that Puck sexted Santana all night while they were babysitting, she drops the idea. Her daughter needs a better father than Puck is capable of being.

With the focus on the kids, things slide back toward status quo...for the time being.

Rachel's makeover doesn't exactly entice Finn. She and Kurt realize that, as long as Finn has Quinn, no one else stands a chance.

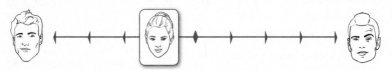

Puck and Quinn seem like natural childcare partners, although Puck's sexting ruins it.

Quotes

"Rachel manages to dress like a grandmother and a toddler at the same time"
—Kurt

"I'm gonna say this as nice as I can. But you look like a sad clown hooker."
—Finn

"I'm gonna be a good dad. But I'm not gonna stop being me to do it."
—Puck

Music List

Bootylicious

PERFORMED IN *GLEE* BY:	Jane Addams Academy
WRITTEN BY:	Rob Fusari, Beyoncé Knowles, Falonte Moore, Stevie Nicks, and Frank Tai
ORIGINALLY PERFORMED BY:	Destiny's Child (2001)

You're the One That I Want (from the musical Grease)

PERFORMED IN *GLEE* BY:	Rachel Berry (Lea Michele) and Finn Hudson (Cory Monteith)

Song information listed in "Pilot" (1-01)

Papa Don't Preach

PERFORMED IN *GLEE* BY:	Quinn Fabray (Dianna Agron)
WRITTEN BY:	Brian Elliot and Madonna
ORIGINALLY PERFORMED BY:	Madonna (1986)

MASHUP:

Crazy in Love

PERFORMED IN *GLEE* BY:	New Directions
WRITTEN BY:	Shawn Carter, Rich Harrison, Beyoncé Knowles, and Eugene Record
ORIGINALLY PERFORMED BY:	Beyoncé featuring Jay-Z (2003)

Hair (from the musical Hair)

PERFORMED IN *GLEE* BY:	New Directions
WRITTEN BY:	James Rado, Gerome Ragni, and Galt MacDermot
ORIGINALLY PERFORMED ON STAGE BY:	Walker Daniels, Gerome Ragni, and cast (1967)
ORIGINALLY PERFORMED ON SCREEN BY:	John Savage, Treat Williams, Dorsey Wright, and cast (1979)

Imagine

PERFORMED IN *GLEE* BY:	Haverbrook School for the Deaf and New Directions
WRITTEN BY:	John Lennon
ORIGINALLY PERFORMED BY:	John Lennon (1971)

True Colors

PERFORMED IN *GLEE* BY:	Tina Cohen-Chang (Jenna Ushkowitz) and New Directions
WRITTEN BY:	Tom Kelly and Billy Steinberg
ORIGINALLY PERFORMED BY:	Cyndi Lauper (1986)

Original Air Date	Wednesday, December 2, 2009
Written by	Ryan Murphy
Directed by	Elodie Keene
Glee Club Assignment	Yearbook photo

The glee club photo *will* be defaced; that's just how it is. Therefore, Figgins (with Sue's help) decides that there will be no glee club photo in the yearbook this year. And Quinn has her own yearbook woes: she believes that she should be included in the photos of the Cheerios, but Sue refuses.

Rachel, who joins clubs just for the yearbook photo opportunities, is crushed by the glee club yearbook situation. Everyone else is okay with it. Except for Will, that is. He buys yearbook space with his own money so that at least two members of New Directions will be represented. Rachel arrives ready for her close-up, but Finn, tapped by Rachel to join her, does not. He doesn't want his face defaced.

But in this there is a silver lining: their big break! The photographer also plans to shoot a commercial, and what could be a better way for New Directions to gain respect than that kind of local exposure? They film the commercial their way, bouncing on mattresses in their pajamas while singing Van Halen, and it's a huge success. The mattress store owner delivers a pile of mattresses to the school as a thank-you payment.

The kids may be having a great week, but Will gets hit with a double whammy. First, he learns that Ken and Emma's wedding will be the same day as Sectionals. Ouch. But that pales in comparison to the big secret of his recent life being revealed: Terri's faux pregnancy. When he finds the pregnancy pad while searching for his pocket square, her story begins to falls apart. Terri was never pregnant. Furious, he tears off her padding, confronts her, then leaves her, goes to the school, opens up one of the mattresses, and goes to sleep.

Which turns out to be a bad move (the mattress, not the leaving). Since the glee club received payment for the commercial, they lose their amateur status and can't compete at Sectionals. And since Will opened one of the mattresses, it can't be returned. Will takes full responsibility and loses his position as glee club director. New Directions must go to Sectionals without him.

Quinn can't solve that issue, but she can solve the yearbook issue.

Knowing about the perks the Cheerios receive that would make them just as ineligible for competition as the glee club almost was after the mattress fiasco, she blackmails Sue into giving the glee club one of their pages. Sue agrees, and the club gets their full yearbook photo, although they have to do it without Will. Impressed, Sue asks Quinn to rejoin the cheerleading team, but Quinn turns her down. That isn't the person she wants to be anymore. The club takes the photo without Will and, just like always, students deface it when the yearbooks come out.

Will learns the truth about Terri. Emma, however, is still engaged.

Rachel can't even convince Finn to be in a yearbook photo with her.

Quinn continues to stand by her story and Finn.

Quotes

"Ken has a lot of flaws. He has seventy-four flaws as of yesterday."
—Emma

"The guys said if I took the glee club photo, they'd make me choose between a Hitler mustache and buck teeth. And I can't rock either of those looks."
—Finn

"All I want is just one day a year when I'm not visually assaulted by uglies and fatties."
—Sue

Music List

Smile

PERFORMED IN *GLEE* BY:	Rachel Berry (Lea Michele)
WRITTEN BY:	Lily Allen, Iyiola Babalola, and Darren Lewis
ORIGINALLY PERFORMED BY:	Lily Allen (2006)

When You're Smiling

PERFORMED IN *GLEE* BY:	Rachel Berry (Lea Michele)
WRITTEN BY:	Mark Fisher, Joe Goodwin, and Larry Shay
ORIGINALLY PERFORMED BY:	Seger Ellis (1929)
ALSO PERFORMED BY (PARTIAL LIST):	Louis Armstrong (1929, 1932, 1956), Duke Ellington (1930), Cab Calloway (1936), Cliff Bruner (1939), Frank Sinatra (1952), Judy Garland (1961), Mel Tormé, (1995), Michael Bublé (2001)

Jump

PERFORMED IN *GLEE* BY:	New Directions
WRITTEN BY:	Michael Anthony, David Lee Roth, Alex Van Halen, and Eddie Van Halen
ORIGINALLY PERFORMED BY:	Van Halen (1984)

Smile

PERFORMED IN *GLEE* BY:	Rachel Berry (Lea Michele), Mercedes Jones (Amber Riley), and New Directions
WRITTEN BY:	Charlie Chaplin (music) and Geoffrey Parsons and John Turner (lyrics)
ORIGINALLY PERFORMED IN:	*Modern Times* (1936, instrumental)
ORIGINALLY SUNG BY:	Nat King Cole (1954)

Sectionals (1-13)

Original Air Date	Wednesday, December 9, 2009
Written by	Brad Falchuk
Directed by	Brad Falchuk
Glee Club Assignment	Win Sectionals!

On the eve of Sectionals, the truth about Puck's paternity leaks out. The club tries to keep this information from Finn. They also try to keep it from a suspicious Rachel, who they know is a "total trout-mouth" and will run straight to Finn with the info. Rachel figures it out anyway and spills the beans, so a very upset Finn quits the club. Now New Directions is without both their male lead and their director, since Will can't accompany New Directions to Sectionals after the mattress debacle.

Emma postpones her own wedding for a few hours so that she can take the club instead, although Ken sees this act as her choosing Will over him. For the club, that's one problem solved, but how do they go on without Finn? Not only are they without their male lead, they are short one person to qualify. They recruit Jacob as a warm body to fill the quota.

Things go from bad to worse when they discover that their competitors are performing all of the same songs that they'd prepared. They smell a rat, a rat who leaks set lists to rival show choirs, and that rat's name is Sue Sylvester. Emma desperately contacts Will, who goes to Finn to convince him to return to his teammates and help them out in their time of need. And help he does, rallying the troops and bringing a new number for them. After their performance, the director of Jane Addams Academy tries to come clean, but the judges (including Anchorman Rod, the fifth runner-up to Miss Ohio, and the state Vice Comptroller) have made their decision...

The winner is: NEW DIRECTIONS!

Meanwhile, Will leaves his wife for good and heads to Ken and Emma's wedding. It's been cancelled; Ken called it off after Emma delayed it for Sectionals...and more so for Will. She decides to quit her job and leave the school rather than deal with the fallout. Will's answer? Telling her that he just left his wife. Emma answers that yes, he *just* did. She realizes that it is too early for either of them to jump into a new relationship.

Back at school, Figgins suspends Sue for her evil acts and has Will reinstated as the glee club director. The kids perform for Will as part of their celebration, bringing back choreography from the entire semester.

But the half-season has to end with a kiss, and Will supplies that when he stops Emma from leaving the school.

Now both Will and Emma are free, although each has some healing to do.

Quinn's secret comes out, and Rachel is the one who tells Finn the truth.

Finn leaves Quinn, but when Puck offers to help her, she instead chooses to continue on her own.

Quotes

"I say we lock Rachel up until after Sectionals. I volunteer my basement."
—Kurt

"You'll be adding revenge to the long list of things you're no good at, right next to being married, running a high school glee club, and finding a hairstyle that doesn't look like a lesbian. Love ya like a sistah!"
—Sue

"Because sometimes being special . . . sucks."
—Will (to Finn)

Music List

And I Am Telling You I'm Not Going (from the musical Dreamgirls*)*

PERFORMED IN *GLEE* BY:	Mercedes Jones (Amber Riley)
Also PERFORMED IN *GLEE* BY:	Jane Adams Academy
WRITTEN BY:	Henry Krieger (music) and Tom Eyen (lyrics)
ORIGINALLY PERFORMED ON STAGE BY:	Jennifer Holliday (1981)
ORIGINALLY PERFORMED ON SCREEN BY:	Jennifer Hudson (2006)

Proud Mary

PERFORMED IN *GLEE* BY:	Jane Addams Academy

Song information listed in "Wheels" (1-9)

Don't Stop Believin'

PERFORMED IN *GLEE* BY:	Haverbrook School for the Deaf

Song information listed in "Pilot" (1-1)

Don't Rain on My Parade (from the musical Funny Girl*)*

PERFORMED IN *GLEE* BY:	Rachel Berry (Lea Michele)
WRITTEN BY:	Bob Merrill and Jule Styne
ORIGINALLY PERFORMED ON STAGE BY:	Barbra Streisand (1964)
ORIGINALLY PERFORMED ON SCREEN BY:	Barbra Streisand (1968)

You Can't Always Get What You Want

PERFORMED IN *GLEE* BY:	New Directions
WRITTEN BY:	Mick Jagger and Keith Richards
ORIGINALLY PERFORMED BY:	The Rolling Stones (1969)

My Life Would Suck Without You

PERFORMED IN *GLEE* BY:	New Directions
WRITTEN BY:	Lukasz "Dr. Luke" Gottwald, Claude Kelly, and Max Martin
ORIGINALLY PERFORMED BY:	Kelly Clarkson (2009)

Hell-O (1-14)

Original Air Date	Tuesday, April 13, 2010
Written by	Ian Brennan
Directed by	Brad Falchuk
Glee Club Assignment	Sing a song with "hello" in it

Now that New Directions has won Sectionals, all is well with the world. Rachel and Finn are together and happy! The glee club will be respected! Sue Sylvester is history!

Uh, no dice on any of that. Not much has actually changed for New Directions at McKinley High. Slushie facials continue, Sue is back thanks to falsified blackmail, and Rachel and Finn...are together, yes, but it isn't going swimmingly. Rachel commits fully to Team Finn, complete with schedule-keeping and t-shirt, but a depressed and confused Finn wonders if he should be with Rachel at all. He isn't quite over Quinn, and pretending to listen to Rachel is *hard*.

Winning Regionals will also be hard, very hard. Will asks the club to find a way to start fresh: a new "hello." And thus, the assignment of the week begins!

Sue berates Brittany and Santana for not ruining the glee club from the inside and assigns them to pursue Finn, with the goal of infuriating Rachel. Meanwhile, Finn and Will have a guy-talk about their respective Pregnancy Lie Situations. Will says that he had to find the new Will after his PLS, and so Finn needs to find the new Finn. But new, post-PLS Finn wants to be a rock star who is free, single, and trailed by a parade of cheerleaders.

Rachel's obliviousness to Finn's wandering eyes opens the door for Brittany and Santana and their Sue-contrived seduction plan. Of course, that's when Rachel asks Finn to be honest with her, so Finn dumps her. Rachel's response? A slight deviation from the "hello" assignment: "Gives You Hell."

With Rachel's heart freshly broken, enter Jesse St. James, lead vocalist of über–glee club Vocal Adrenaline. He criticizes Rachel's performance at Sectionals as flawed, and brags about his UCLA scholarship and concerts for the homeless. The brokenhearted Rachel becomes star-struck. Singing "Hello" with him completes the spell, and she agrees to a date with the competition. Between their date, the Santana/Brittany date with Finn, and an earlier-planned date for Emma and Will now that Terri is history, Friday turns out to be quite the date night.

Finn's date with Santana and Brittany isn't all he'd imagined. The duo debate his cute vs. hot status in front of him, don't allow him to talk, make him pay for dinner, and then ask him to wait in the car. Despite Brittany's lack of a bra, Finn takes off.

Over at the grownup date, Will moves a little too fast, and Emma admits that she hasn't been intimate with anyone. Ever. Their date ends uncomfortably.

Unlike the others, Rachel's date goes swimmingly, so when Finn tries to go back to her after his duo date debacle, she tells him that she's in love. He's too late.

Finn runs to Will about Rachel fraternizing with the enemy, so Will meets with Shelby Corcoran, the director of Vocal Adrenaline...and then makes out with her. That'll come back to haunt him. Things get intense, so Will calls a halt and they talk shop, then relationships. Shelby recommends that he take the time to reintroduce himself to himself.

Mercedes, Kurt, Tina, and Artie confront Rachel about her new boyfriend and threaten to quit if she doesn't break up with him. Sue, all in favor of the destruction it would cause, encourages Rachel to stick with Jesse by introducing her to the McKinley High Old Maids Club. The message? Walk away from this relationship and you'll be alone forever. Rachel goes to Carmel to confront Jesse under the glare of their high-powered spotlights, but he tells her that he's crazy about her, as a pleased Shelby looks on. What does *she* have up her sleeve?

Terri surprises Emma as she's making dinner for Will at his house. Emma starts out confident, but when she learns that her and Will's song is also Will and Terri's prom song, she starts to doubt him. Oops, bad move there, Will. When he sees the yearbook photo of his junior prom, he claims that he'd forgotten the song and has no feelings about that night, but Emma doesn't believe him, and says that he needs some time alone.

Rachel lies to Finn, telling him that she and Jesse broke up, and then turns him down when he asks her again to get back together. Finn says that he won't give up, leading to a very uncomfortable final song for them both.

Although starting out squarely on Team Finn, his rejection of her and the arrival of Jesse make things complicated for Rachel.

It's Terri and Will's prom song more than Terri herself, but it's enough to make Emma push Will away.

Quotes

"My personality, though exciting and full of surprises, isn't exactly low-maintenance."
—Rachel

"Are you gay? Because most of the show choir directors I make out with are gay."
—Shelby Corcoran

"Well, Rachel, if I weren't ignoring what these ladies were saying due to my deep revulsion, I would probably be hearing them encourage you to go for it with your Carmel High beau."
—Sue

Music List

Hello, I Love You

PERFORMED IN *GLEE* BY:	Finn Hudson (Cory Monteith)
WRITTEN BY:	John Densmore, Robby Krieger, Ray Manzarek, and Jim Morrison
ORIGINALLY PERFORMED BY:	The Doors (1968)

Gives You Hell

PERFORMED IN *GLEE* BY:	Rachel Berry (Lea Michele) and New Directions
WRITTEN BY:	Tyson Ritter and Nick Wheeler
ORIGINALLY PERFORMED BY:	The All-American Rejects (2008)

Highway to Hell

PERFORMED IN *GLEE* BY:	Jesse St. James (Jonathan Groff) and Vocal Adrenaline
WRITTEN BY:	Bon Scott, Angus Young, and Malcolm Young
ORIGINALLY PERFORMED BY:	AC/DC (1979)

Hello

PERFORMED IN *GLEE* BY:	Rachel Berry (Lea Michele) and Jesse St. James (Jonathan Groff)
WRITTEN BY:	Lionel Ritchie
ORIGINALLY PERFORMED BY:	Lionel Richie (1984)

Hello, Goodbye

PERFORMED IN *GLEE* BY:	Rachel Berry (Lea Michele), Finn Hudson (Cory Monteith), and New Directions
WRITTEN BY:	John Lennon and Paul McCartney
ORIGINALLY PERFORMED BY:	The Beatles (1967)

The Power of Madonna (1-15)

Original Air Date	Tuesday, April 20, 2010
Written by	Ryan Murphy
Directed by	Ryan Murphy
Glee Club Assignment	MADONNA

Madonna. Madonna Madonna Madonna.

Also, other stuff happens.

Sue looks up to Madonna more than any other person, concept, or deity. In voice-over worship, she decides to spread her devotion to all of McKinley High. Using her blackmail-enhanced influence, she institutes a new policy to blast Madonna songs over the P.A. system. She also encourages her Cheerios to be more Madonna-like, from dropping their last names to dating younger men.

Over at New Directions, before a rehearsal filled conveniently with just girls, Rachel asks their advice about an entirely hypothetical situation involving someone certainly not named Jesse, since she's absolutely not dating anyone. At all. No sir. But this hypothetical secret boyfriend got upset when she refused to sleep with him and lose her virginity in the process. Their responses are sympathetic; many of the girls admit to feeling pressure from boys, and Mr. Eavesdropping Schuester is surprised to hear it. Seeking advice, Rachel had spoken to Emma, but since this particular topic is a blind spot for her, she wasn't much help. Will and Emma talk, and they decide to come up with a way to help empower the girls.

Then the Cheerios dance to "Ray of Light." With stilts.

Moving on.

The stilt dance does accomplish one thing: it inspires Will to make this week's assignment Madonna, causing the school to become All Madonna, All The Time. Kurt and the girls are thrilled, but the remaining guys aren't, not understanding how Madonna is relevant to them. They try the excuse of Madonna ≠ show choir, but the girls show them how wrong they are with a performance of "Express Yourself," complete with the requisite monocles.

The Cheerios continue their own Madonna assignment by seeking out younger men. Brittany finds her intellectual equal in a seven-year-old, but Santana goes for slightly older fare: Finn. He's single, a virgin, and a bit younger than she is. Success with him could even win her Head Cheerleader. As she explains to Finn, it's a win-win situation...for her.

But Finn still cares for Rachel, and he confronts her about Jesse. She avoids the topic and suggests a double-Madonna combo of "Borderline" and "Open Your Heart," sung wandering the halls and library with a collection of various Madonna wannabes in the background. It goes, as Finn/Rachel romantic duets often do, a little too well.

By this point, Sue has had enough of the glee club infringing on her Madonna territory. Will holds his ground, and even gets in a few retaliatory hair insults. Sue, stunned, takes out her anger on innocent student passers-by. While that isn't unusual, her emotional response to Will's hair jabs is. Kurt and Mercedes notice and visit her office. Amid claims of Nazi-hunting parents, household napalm, and a slight age aberration, Sue admits to being jealous of Will's hair. That part of her story actually seems like truth, especially as her "handicapable" sister figures in it.

The Dynamic Bravo Duo are moved and decide to make Sue the star of their project of the week: VOGUE. But even after a successful transformation and faithfully reproduced video (a few lyric changes notwithstanding), it's Figgins who helps Sue realize that she is already a powerful woman and an original as she is, requiring no reinvention. Instead she decides to reinvent Mercedes and Kurt.

The Madonna-ness of the week starts to affect other people as well. Emma, even though Sue deemed her unworthy and made her office a Madge-free zone, decides to take control of her body by sleeping with Will. Rachel decides to do the same with Jesse, and Finn also accepts Santana's offer. The three couples each perform "Like a Virgin" as their evenings begin, but the results aren't what they planned: Emma runs; Rachel locks herself in the bathroom, admits that she's not ready, and then later lies to Finn; Finn goes through with it, but regrets it and denies it to Rachel afterward.

Will and Emma talk the following Monday, and Will apologizes that everything happened the way it did. He returns her shoes and they decide on a no-dating policy until his just-applied-for divorce is finalized.

If any week is a good week for a few shake-ups, Madonna Week would qualify, and New Directions gets two in quick succession: first, Jesse transfers to McKinley, claiming that it is all for Rachel. Then the Cheerios debut their two newest members: Kurt and Mercedes. In order to have more opportunities to "shine," Kurt and Mercedes have decided to be in both groups. The Cheerios and the marching band perform "4 Minutes," with Kurt and Mercedes as the stars.

The weekly assignments haven't been finished yet, so Will and the boys sing "What It Feels Like For a Girl," after which some of them get the message and apologize to the girls they've been disrespectful or rude to. New Directions wraps things up on stage with "Like a Prayer," complete with a gospel choir. Wait, McKinley High has one of those, too? Sure, why not?

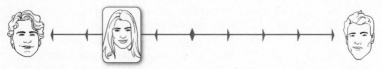

Rachel almost goes all the way with Jesse. Then she tells Finn that she did. Was she trying to make him jealous?

Quotes

"Mercedes is black, I'm gay: We make culture."
—Kurt

"When I pulled my hamstring, I went to a misogynist."
—Brittany

"Enough with the hair jokes. By the way, how's the Florence Henderson look working for you?"
—Will

Music List

Express Yourself

PERFORMED IN *GLEE* BY:	Rachel Berry (Lea Michele), Brittany (Heather Morris), Tina Cohen-Chang (Jenna Ushkowitz), Quinn Fabray (Dianna Agron), Mercedes Jones (Amber Riley), and Santana Lopez (Naya Rivera)
WRITTEN BY:	Stephen Bray and Madonna
ORIGINALLY PERFORMED BY:	Madonna (1989)

MASHUP:

Borderline

PERFORMED IN *GLEE* BY:	Rachel Berry (Lea Michele) and Finn Hudson (Cory Monteith)
WRITTEN BY:	Madonna
ORIGINALLY PERFORMED BY:	Madonna (1984)

Open Your Heart

PERFORMED IN *GLEE* BY:	Rachel Berry (Lea Michele) and Finn Hudson (Cory Monteith)
WRITTEN BY:	Gardner Cole, Madonna, and Peter Rafelson
ORIGINALLY PERFORMED BY:	Madonna (1986)

Vogue

PERFORMED IN *GLEE* BY:	Kurt Hummel (Chris Colfer), Mercedes Jones (Amber Riley), and Sue Sylvester (Jane Lynch)
WRITTEN BY:	Madonna, Shep Pettibone
ORIGINALLY PERFORMED BY:	Madonna (1990)

Like a Virgin

PERFORMED IN *GLEE* BY:	Rachel Berry (Lea Michele) and Jesse St. James (Jonathan Groff), Finn Hudson (Cory Monteith) and Santana Lopez (Naya Rivera), Emma Pillsbury (Jayma Mays) and Will Schuester (Matthew Morrison)
WRITTEN BY:	Tom Kelly and Billy Steinberg
ORIGINALLY PERFORMED BY:	Madonna (1984)

4 Minutes

PERFORMED IN *GLEE* BY:	Kurt Hummel (Chris Colfer) and Mercedes Jones (Amber Riley)
WRITTEN BY:	Nathaniel Hills, Madonna, Timbaland, and Justin Timberlake
ORIGINALLY PERFORMED BY:	Madonna featuring Justin Timberlake and Timbaland (2008)

What It Feels Like for a Girl

PERFORMED IN *GLEE* BY:	Artie Abrams (Kevin McHale), Mike Chang (Harry Shum Jr.), Finn Hudson (Cory Monteith), Kurt Hummel (Chris Colfer), Noah "Puck" Puckerman (Mark Salling), and Matt Rutherford (Dijon Talton)
WRITTEN BY:	Madonna, Guy Sigsworth, and David Torn
ORIGINALLY PERFORMED BY:	Madonna (2001)

Like a Prayer

PERFORMED IN *GLEE* BY:	Rachel Berry (Lea Michele), Finn Hudson (Cory Monteith), Kurt Hummel (Chris Colfer), Mercedes Jones (Amber Riley), and New Directions, with backup gospel choir
WRITTEN BY:	Patrick Leonard and Madonna
ORIGINALLY PERFORMED BY:	Madonna (1989)

ALSO HEARD IN THE EPISODE:

Ray of Light

WRITTEN BY:	Dave Curtiss, Christine Leach, Madonna, Clive Muldoon, and William Orbit
ORIGINALLY PERFORMED BY:	Madonna (1998)

Burning Up

WRITTEN BY:	Madonna
ORIGINALLY PERFORMED BY:	Madonna (1983)
BONUS TRACK ON *GLEE: THE MUSIC:*	*The Power of Madonna* performed by: Jonathan Groff

Justify My Love

WRITTEN BY:	Ingrid Chavez, Lenny Kravitz, and Madonna
ORIGINALLY PERFORMED BY:	Madonna (1990)

Frozen

WRITTEN BY:	Patrick Leonard and Madonna
ORIGINALLY PERFORMED BY:	Madonna (1998)

Home (1-16)

Original Air Date	Tuesday, April 27, 2010
Written by	Brad Falchuk
Directed by	Paris Barclay
Glee Club Assignment	Practice despite a lack of auditorium

New Cheerios Kurt and Mercedes kick off the week by getting called into Sue's office. Horror of horrors, Mercedes has been wearing pants, and not doing so in homage to Sue. Shocking! With a reporter from *Splits* magazine on the way, Mercedes is ordered to lose ten pounds and wear a "gender-appropriate" outfit or be kicked off the team. She tries, but instead of losing weight by the mid-week weigh-in, she gains two pounds.

Trying desperately to succeed and stay a Cheerio, Mercedes hallucinates Tina ice cream and Artie cake while they try to talk sense into her. The vision of Rachel the Cupcake with a side of Jessieburger is the final straw; she passes out.

Quinn meets Mercedes in the nurse's office. She gets what's going on. She's been there. And she doesn't want Mercedes to go through what she did. Mercedes was comfortable with herself the way she was, and being a Cheerio shouldn't change that. Mercedes agrees and sings "Beautiful" at the school assembly, inspiring the student body and mortifying her coach—until the magazine reporter tells Sue that, thanks to that performance and message, he'll write a positive article about Sue rather than exposing her for, well, herself. Sue takes all the credit.

Sue has more tricks up her sleeve (or, in this case, in her waistband): a sign-up sheet for auditorium use time filled completely with Cheerios practice, leaving room for nothing else. With Figgins still under Sue's blackmail-enhanced thumb, the glee club has to find a new practice space for the week.

Without anywhere else to go, Will stops by the local roller rink to see if it might be available. There, he finds none other than April Rhodes, now a cabaret roller rink boss and hostess. Her dream of Branson didn't pan out, since she stopped at a bar on her way out of town and didn't leave for months, instead becoming the mistress of a strip-mall tycoon.

April solves Will's problem when she offers the rink as a rehearsal space, but then creates a new one when she learns about Will's impending divorce and apartment availability. She shows up on Will's doorstep with her overnight bag, ready to give the place (and Will) a test run. Instead, they share their loneliness via song, during which Will gazes at a photo of him and Terri, then puts the photo away in a drawer. He and his houseguest fall asleep next to each other. Later, after a pep talk, April is inspired to live her own life. She tries to break up with her tycoon; he conveniently drops dead. With her new hush-money riches, April buys the auditorium for the glee club and then heads off to Broadway to produce the first all-white production of *The Wiz*.

Meanwhile, Finn's life starts to get weird. First, Kurt asks for Finn's help with decorating. And Finn's mom is selling their old furniture. Worse, she's changing: new clothes, new haircut, and new boyfriend. To Finn's shock, the new boyfriend is Burt Hummel, Kurt's dad. But then circumstances become clear: scheming a way to spend more time with his crush Finn, it was Kurt who set up his father with Finn's mother. After all, they both have dead spouses, right? What could be more perfect? But Finn hates the idea of his mother moving on and forgetting his father. Even his dad's chair is still an honored place.

Kurt realizes that his plan worked a little too well when Burt and Finn start to bond and spend guy-time together. Hurt, Kurt lashes out at his dad and wonders if he made a mistake by pushing the love connection. Kurt asks Finn to help break up their parents, and he agrees. But when Finn confronts his mom, she tries to convince him that what she and Burt have could be a good thing. However, it's Burt who really convinces him, telling him that he could never take his father's place, but that he'd try to be Carole's hero. As a peace offering, Finn offers Burt his dad's chair. Kurt looks on, hurt at the growing bond between his father and Finn, who he thinks is kind of son that Burt always wanted.

Hold on a second... Did we go an entire episode without a solo from Rachel? Weird.

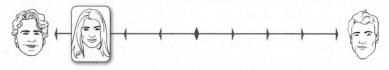

With Jesse now a student at McKinley, Rachel is free to be his girlfriend openly. Plus, Finn has other things on his mind.

"How do you two not have a show on Bravo?"
—Sue (to Kurt and Mercedes)

"I'm pretty sure my cat is reading my diary."
—Brittany

"Don't sweat that old chair. I have a lovely chaise picked out."
—Kurt

Music List

Fire

PERFORMED IN *GLEE* BY:	April Rhodes (Kristen Chenoweth) and Will Schuester (Matthew Morrison)
WRITTEN BY:	Bruce Springsteen (written for Elvis Presley)
ORIGINALLY PERFORMED BY:	Robert Gordon (1978)
ALSO PERFORMED BY (PARTIAL LIST):	The Pointer Sisters (1978), Bruce Springsteen (1986), Kenneth "Babyface" Edmonds and Des'ree (1998)

A House Is Not a Home

PERFORMED IN *GLEE* BY:	Kurt Hummel (Chris Colfer) and Finn Hudson (Cory Monteith)
WRITTEN BY:	Burt Bacharach and Hal David
ORIGINALLY PERFORMED BY:	Dionne Warwick (1964)
ALSO PERFORMED BY (PARTIAL LIST):	Luther Vandross (1981, this version was sampled by Kanye West for "Slow Jamz" in 2004), Aretha Franklin (2005)

> "A House Is Not a Home" was also performed by Kristen Chenoweth in the Broadway revival of *Promises, Promises* in 2010. It was added to the show specifically for her and hadn't been sung in prior productions.

MASHUP:

A House Is Not a Home

PERFORMED IN *GLEE* BY:	April Rhodes (Kristen Chenoweth) and Will Schuester (Matthew Morrison)

Song information listed above

One Less Bell to Answer

PERFORMED IN *GLEE* BY:	April Rhodes (Kristen Chenoweth) and Will Schuester (Matthew Morrison)

WRITTEN BY:	Burt Bacharach and Hal David
ORIGINALLY PERFORMED BY:	Keeley Smith (1970)
ALSO PERFORMED BY (PARTIAL LIST):	The 5th Dimension (1970), Shirley Bassey (1972), Dionne Warwick (1972)
	Medley of "A House Is Not a Home" and "One Less Bell to Answer" first performed by: Barbra Streisand (1971)

Beautiful

PERFORMED IN GLEE BY:	Mercedes Jones (Amber Riley)
WRITTEN BY:	Linda Perry
ORIGINALLY PERFORMED BY:	Christina Aguilera (2002)

Home (from the musical The Wiz)

PERFORMED IN GLEE BY:	April Rhodes (Kristen Chenoweth) and New Directions
Music and Lyrics by:	Charlie Smalls
ORIGINALLY PERFORMED ON STAGE BY:	Stephanie Mills (1975)
ORIGINALLY PERFORMED ON SCREEN BY:	Diana Ross (1978)

Bad Reputation (1-17)

Original Air Date	Tuesday, May 4, 2010
Written by	Ian Brennan
Directed by	Elodie Keene
Glee Club Assignment	Perform a song with a bad reputation and find the good in it

Sue Sylvester, YouTube star! Kurt happens across a video of Sue dancing to Olivia Newton-John's "Physical" and promptly uploads it for all of the internet to see. She who always mocks becomes the mocked, to the joy and slow-motion laughter of her fellow teachers, including new arrival Brenda Castle. But after a visit with her sister, Sue has the last laugh, slow-motion or otherwise. First, she wrecks Emma and Will's budding romance and spreads the word about the recent dalliances—innocent or not—that Will (a.k.a. "Man-Whore") had with Shelby and April. Then, Olivia Newton-John herself invites Sue to perform with her in an update of the "Physical" video after seeing Sue's version, making her a Top 700 recording artist.

New Directions' reputation also hang in the balance due to the dreaded Glist, a ranking of the glee clubbers based on both their hotness quotient and their sexual promiscuity at McKinley High. Sue shows the list to Figgins, who demands the Glister be found or the entire club will be expelled. Will is certain that the Glist maker is Puck, since it's such a Puck-ish thing to do, but he denies it. Everyone is questioned; no one fesses up.

Artie, Tina, Kurt, and Mercedes aren't even on the Glist, and they don't like it one bit. Along with a drugged-up Brittany (who didn't make the top three; horrors!), they plot ways to rectify this situation. And what better way to sour their reputations than... um, creating some Hammer Time in the school library? Perhaps not the best idea. Rather than becoming horrified, the librarian offers to have them perform at her church. Mission: nowhere close to accomplished.

And who is actually the Glist culprit? Quinn, the girl who lost everything, including her stellar reputation. Will doesn't turn her in and the matter is dropped. Another Figgins threat disappears.

Rachel completes her glee club assignment of the week by becoming "musically promiscuous," making a video of "Run, Joey, Run" with Jesse, Finn, and Puck (and Sandy) assisting her. Each of the boys has no idea about the involvement of the other two. All are angry, and Jesse takes off. Cue "Total Eclipse of the Heart."

When Rachel creates a video with three different guys playing her boyfriend—including actual-boyfriend Jesse and wannabe boyfriend Finn—her true feelings are questioned.

Quotes

"I might buy a small diaper for your chin because it looks like a baby's ass."
—Sue

"I like setting stuff on fire and beating up people I don't know. I own that. But I'm not a liar."
—Puck

"You had me at 'sex tape.' How can I help?"
—Artie

Music List

Ice Ice Baby

PERFORMED IN *GLEE* BY:	Will Schuester (Matthew Morrison) and New Directions
WRITTEN BY:	DJ Earthquake and Robert Van Winkle (a.k.a. Vanilla Ice)
ORIGINALLY PERFORMED BY:	Vanilla Ice (1990)

U Can't Touch This

PERFORMED IN *GLEE* BY:	Artie Abrams (Kevin McHale), Brittany (Heather Morris), Tina Cohen-Chang (Jenna Ushkowitz), Kurt Hummel (Chris Colfer), and Mercedes Jones (Amber Riley)
WRITTEN BY:	MC Hammer, Rick James, and Alonzo Miller
ORIGINALLY PERFORMED BY:	MC Hammer (1990)

Physical

PERFORMED IN *GLEE* BY:	Olivia Newton-John and Sue Sylvester (Jane Lynch)
WRITTEN BY:	Steve Kipner and Terry Shaddick
ORIGINALLY PERFORMED BY:	Olivia Newton-John (1981)

Run Joey Run

PERFORMED IN *GLEE* BY:	Rachel Berry (Lea Michele), Finn Hudson (Cory Monteith), Jesse St. James (Jonathan Groff), and Noah "Puck" Puckerman (Mark Salling)
WRITTEN BY:	Paul Vance
ORIGINALLY PERFORMED BY:	David Geddes (1975)

Total Eclipse of the Heart

PERFORMED IN *GLEE* BY:	Rachel Berry (Lea Michele), Finn Hudson (Cory Monteith), Jesse St. James (Jonathan Groff), and Noah "Puck" Puckerman (Mark Salling)
WRITTEN BY:	Jim Steinman (originally written for Meat Loaf)
ORIGINALLY PERFORMED BY:	Bonnie Tyler (1983)
ALSO PERFORMED BY (PARTIAL LIST):	Nicki French (1994), Tori Amos (2005)

Laryngitis (1-18)

Original Air Date	Tuesday, May 11, 2010
Written by	Ryan Murphy
Directed by	Alfonso Gomez-Rejon
Glee Club Assignment	Sing a song that best represents how you see yourself

Is Rachel nothing without her voice? She thinks so. At first angry that the other glee club members aren't pulling their weight, she pushes for everyone to work as hard as she does. But when her vocal chords fail her during a Miley Cyrus song (as good a time as any), her doctor informs her that she has tonsillitis. Fearing that surgery will ruin the only thing she thinks she has going for her, she panics and refuses to go under the knife. Finn gives her a hefty dose of reality when he takes her to visit his friend Sean the quadriplegic. Luckily for Rachel, she recovers without surgery anyway. Phew!

If Rachel's self-identity is in her voice, Puck's rests in his mohawk, which he has to shave due to his mother's freckle panic. When Jacob's Band of Nerds uses this lost-mojo opportunity to deposit Puck in the Dumpster, Puck schemes a way to regain what he's lost. His method? Date a popular chick. In this case, the newly popular Mercedes. Although she knows better, she temporarily accedes to their "Lady Is a Tramp" duet. She even battles with Santana (via song) over him. Mercedes soon realizes that Puck is still, well, Puck and breaks things off, quitting the Cheerios as well.

Kurt questions his own identity after his father continues his sports outings with Finn without including him. Sue confronts Kurt about who he (and she) thinks he is. He decides to turn himself into a mini-Burt, complete with plaid shirts and Mellencamp, inspiring Brittany to make out with him to keep up her perfect record of making out with everyone at the school, including the janitor. Burt gets confused and concerned, Will gets confused and concerned, the audience gets confused and...you get the drift. But the transformation doesn't last long. Kurt belts out some *Gypsy* (which suits him far better than John Cougar Mellencamp ever could), and Burt and Kurt have another one of their heartwarming father–son chats.

Finn's dilemma? He wants "Jessie's Girl." We should've seen that one coming.

While Jesse enjoys spring break in San Diego, Finn is the one who leads Rachel to her lesson of the week. But, as the song says, she's still Jesse's girl.

Quotes

"So you like show tunes! It doesn't mean you're gay. It just means you're awful."

—Sue

"You're pretty much the only guy in this school I haven't made out with, because I thought you were capital-G gay. But now that I know you're not, having a perfect record would mean a lot to me. Let me know if you wanna tap this."

—Brittany

"Get ready, black girl from glee club whose name I can't remember right now! The Puckster is about to make you his."

—Puck

Music List

The Climb

(Almost) Performed in *Glee* by:	Rachel Berry (Lea Michele)
Written by:	Jessi Alexander and Jon Mabe
Originally performed by:	Miley Cyrus (2009)

Jessie's Girl

Performed in *Glee* by:	Finn Hudson (Cory Monteith)
Written by:	Rick Springfield
Originally performed by:	Rick Springfield (1981)

The Lady Is a Tramp (from the musical Babes in Arms)

Performed in *Glee* by:	Mercedes Jones (Amber Riley) and Noah "Puck" Puckerman (Mark Salling)
Written by:	Richard Rodgers (music) and Lorenz Hart (lyrics)
Originally performed on stage by:	Mitzi Green (1937)

> The original *Babes in Arms* film version (1939) had "The Lady Is a Tramp" as an instrumental only.

ORIGINALLY PERFORMED ON SCREEN BY:	Lena Horne in *Words and Music* (1948)
ALSO PERFORMED BY (PARTIAL LIST):	Tommy Dorsey and His Orchestra (1937), Frank Sinatra (1956, in the film *Pal Joey*), The Supremes (1967).

> Sammy Davis Jr. sang "The Lady Is a Tramp" in live performances but never did a formal studio recording of it.

The Boy Is Mine

PERFORMED IN *GLEE* BY:	Mercedes Jones (Amber Riley) and Santana Lopez (Naya Rivera)
WRITTEN BY:	LaShawn Daniels, Fred Jerkins III, Rodney "Darkchild" Jerkins, and Brandy Norwood
ORIGINALLY PERFORMED BY:	Brandy and Monica (1998)

Pink Houses

PERFORMED IN *GLEE* BY:	Kurt Hummel (Chris Colfer)
WRITTEN BY:	John Cougar Mellencamp
ORIGINALLY PERFORMED BY:	John Cougar Mellencamp (1983)

Kurt's Turn, based on Rose's Turn (from the musical Gypsy: A Musical Fable)

PERFORMED IN *GLEE* BY:	Kurt Hummel (Chris Colfer)
Music by:	Julie Styne
Lyrics by:	Stephen Sondheim
ORIGINALLY PERFORMED ON STAGE BY:	Ethel Merman (1959)
ORIGINALLY PERFORMED ON SCREEN BY:	Rosalind Russell (*Gypsy*, 1962)

One

PERFORMED IN *GLEE* BY:	Rachel Berry (Lea Michele), Finn Hudson (Cory Monteith), and New Directions, with Sean Fretthold (Zack Weinstein)
WRITTEN BY:	U2
ORIGINALLY PERFORMED BY:	U2 (1991)

Dream On (1-19)

Original Air Date	Tuesday, May 18, 2010
Written by	Ryan Murphy
Directed by	Joss Whedon
Glee Club Assignment	Will forgets to give them one, so they decide to create a dance number. That, and accept Bryan Ryan's jean jackets.

Meet newest member of the school board and Will's high school rival: Bryan Ryan. Bryan Ryan now believes that dreams are silly things and that the show choir is a waste of time. He even runs a show choir conversion group. And, like every other Will nemesis, Bryan Ryan (how can one resist using both of his names?) wants to shut down the glee club. Because "show choir kills."

Bryan Ryan's message to the kids? Their dreams will never happen. Dreams are to be forgotten, shoved aside, because they are wastes of time. Least inspiring pep talk *ever*.

Artie's dream is to be a dancer. He knows that it isn't a realistic dream, but he still dreams about it. Tina suggests, since they don't have an assignment, that the two of them work on a dance number. Because, gee, that won't remind Artie of his unrealistic dreams at all. They rehearse, and the results are (unsurprisingly) not so great. Artie tries to "take it up a notch" and stand with crutches, but it's a disaster.

Speaking of dancing, Jesse and Rachel talk in the dance studio as she rehearses Laurie's dream sequence from *Oklahoma!*, since she knows she will eventually be cast in the role (that, *Evita*, and *Funny Girl*, if you're keeping track). Rachel's eventual stardom may be the dream everyone knows for her, but her true, secret dream is to find out who her mother is. Jesse promises to make her dreams come true, even if her mother is neither Patti LuPone or Bernadette Peters. They go through boxes of her baby stuff, giving Jesse the perfect opportunity to plant a mystery cassette tape. Rachel freaks out.

Who is behind this nefarious cassette tape scheme? Shelby Corcoran, who isn't allowed to confess that she's Rachel's mother. It's Jesse's assignment to get close to Rachel in order to pave the way for her to find Shelby. Jesse makes her listen to the tape of her still-unknown mother singing "I Dreamed a Dream" to her.

After Artie's walking attempt, Tina goes online (the repository of all medical knowledge) to give Artie some hope that his dream could come true. She also convinces him to buy tap shoes at the mall, then suggests post-purchase pretzels. But wait! Artie's been working on the exciting new internet-suggested exercises. And they work! He moves his foot! He stands up! He…dances? He starts a flash mob doing the Safety Dance? And a bunch of the other glee kids are there? Ah, got it, it's a dream sequence. Artie is still in his wheelchair when Tina returns with the pretzels.

But Tina's enthusiasm has sparked some real hope in him, and he starts looking at ways to make his transition to a walking person easier. Emma has the sad task to bringing his hopes back within realistic parameters. Chances are he won't ever dance. Or walk. He has to accept that some dreams can't come true.

Will takes Bryan Ryan out for a beer, hoping to convince him that the glee club is worth saving. As it turns out, Bryan Ryan is actually still chock full of dreams, still loves show tunes, and still dreams of being a star. He's a miserable shell of a man who is "living a lie." Will and "Piano Man" convince him to start following those dreams again. And boy does he! He and Will both audition for *Les Misérables*; inconveniently, both try for Jean Valjean. This results in an Aerosmith sing-off. Plus, Bryan Ryan buys the glee club sheet music and really frightening jean jackets! And has angry sex with Sue after a fight over the Cheerios budget!

Let's just forget that last part.

When Will wins the role of Jean Valjean, Bryan Ryan decides to cut the glee club out of spite anyway. Will negotiates a trade with Bryan Ryan: the lead in *Les Misérables* in return for the glee club. His dream of stardom rekindled, Bryan Ryan agrees. He gets his dream, Rachel is on her way to her dream, and Artie's dream stays a dream. Artie gives up his part in the dance routine, admitting that he'll never dance. Tina dances with Mike the Other Asian as Artie sings "Dream a Little Dream of Me."

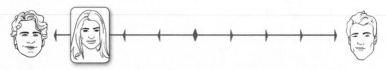

Jesse returns on Shelby's orders, leading Rachel on a search to find her mother, Oblivious, Rachel is just happy to have him back.

Quotes

"I sound like someone put tap shoes on a horse and shot it."
—Artie

"You can't feed a child sheet music, Will. I suppose you could, but they'd be dead in a month."
—Bryan Ryan

"You take away glee? You're not just putting out those kids' lights. You're creating thirteen black holes."
—Will

Music List

Daydream Believer

PERFORMED IN *GLEE* BY:	Bryan Ryan (Neil Patrick Harris)
WRITTEN BY:	John Stewart
ORIGINALLY PERFORMED BY:	The Monkees (1967)

Piano Man

PERFORMED IN *GLEE* BY:	Bryan Ryan (Neil Patrick Harris) and Will Schuester (Matthew Morrison)
WRITTEN BY:	Billy Joel
ORIGINALLY PERFORMED BY:	Billy Joel (1973)

Big Spender (from the musical Sweet Charity)

PERFORMED IN *GLEE* BY:	Woman auditioning for *Les Misérables* (Wendy Worthington)
WRITTEN BY:	Cy Coleman (music) and Dorothy Fields (lyrics)
ORIGINALLY PERFORMED ON STAGE BY:	Helen Gallagher, Thelma Oliver, and company (1966)
ORIGINALLY PERFORMED ON SCREEN BY:	Paula Kelly, Chita Rivera, and company (1969)

Dream On

PERFORMED IN *GLEE* BY:	Bryan Ryan (Neil Patrick Harris) and Will Schuester (Matthew Morrison)
WRITTEN BY:	Steven Tyler
ORIGINALLY PERFORMED BY:	Aerosmith (1973)

The Safety Dance

PERFORMED IN *GLEE* BY:	Artie Abrams (Kevin McHale)
WRITTEN BY:	Ivan Doroschuk
ORIGINALLY PERFORMED BY:	Men Without Hats (1982)

I Dreamed a Dream (from the musical Les Misérables)

PERFORMED IN *GLEE* BY:	Rachel Berry (Lea Michele) and Shelby Corcoran (Idina Menzel)
WRITTEN BY:	Claude-Michel Schönberg (music) and Herbert Kretzmer (lyrics)
ORIGINALLY PERFORMED ON STAGE BY:	Patti LuPone (1985)

Dream a Little Dream of Me

PERFORMED IN *GLEE* BY:	Artie Abrams (Kevin McHale)
WRITTEN BY:	Fabian Andre, Gus Kahn, and Wilbur Schwandt
ORIGINALLY PERFORMED BY:	Ozzie Nelson and His Orchestra (1931)
ALSO PERFORMED BY (PARTIAL LIST):	Kate Smith (1931), Frankie Laine (1950), Cass Elliot (1968), Michael Bublé (2010)

Theatricality (1-20)

Original Air Date	Tuesday, May 25, 2010
Written by	Ryan Murphy
Directed by	Ryan Murphy
Glee Club Assignment	GAGA. Which leads to: using theatricality to express what lies within, using Lady Gaga and Kiss as muses.

Tina wears black. Her style is "goth." Therefore, she's in trouble with Figgins because she's *obviously* obsessed with vampires. Or is one. Except that she's not. Then again, Figgins thinks that vampires are real, so his judgment is more questionable than unusual.

While Tina attempts to rock a hoodie, Rachel discovers signs of their imminent destruction. Empty boxes of Christmas lights and shelves bereft of red Chantilly lace can only mean one thing: Lady Gaga. Vocal Adrenaline has decided to go for full theatricality to beat New Directions. What to do? Will grasps at the idea, as he apparently had no assignment planned for the week: Gaga-style theatricality!

Although Will gets excited about all things Gaga, Finn has other ideas for the guys (sans Kurt, who is in full Gaga mode). The girls and Kurt show off their theatrical costumes, most of which are fabulously Gaga-esque. Rachel's is less so, since her dads aren't exactly handy with a sewing machine. One sad costume does not a musical number ruin, however, and Kurt and the six girls kill it on "Bad Romance," in all the best ways.

Walking the halls in their Gaga outfits, Kurt and Tina feel fantastic and empowered—until football players Karofsky and Azimio threaten Tina. Kurt stands up to them and for their right to express themselves, but the thugs warn them that, if they continue to wave their Gaga-esque identities in their face, there will be consequences. But they use much smaller words to say it.

The boys counter Lady Gaga with their "manly" version of over-the-top theatricality: Kiss. Go with the classics. But all is not well in guy-land, and the separation of Kurt from the rest of the boys isn't the only split between him and Finn. Burt and Carole decide to move in together, making Kurt and Finn share a room. Finn is not cool with this, no matter how the room is decorated. The situation deteriorates to the point that Finn, his teenage guy-hood threatened, lashes out, calling Kurt's decorating job "faggy." This does not sit well with Burt, who kicks him out of the house after some choice words.

Kurt's week gets even worse when Karofsky and Azimio go after him, making good on their earlier threat. Enter Finn in all his red-vinyl-shower-

Going Gaga

Each of the Gaga costumes created for "Theatricality" (1-20) was an homage to an actual Lady Gaga costume, rather than an exact replica.

o Brittany wore a version of Gaga's Philip Treacy lobster hat. It took forty-five minutes to get the hat on and off each day, and it restricted her vision to what was directly in front of her.

o Finn's red vinyl floor-length "shower curtain" dress was based on the latex Atsuko Kudo dress Gaga wore to meet Queen Elizabeth II.

o Kurt's outfit was inspired by the Alexander McQueen design that Gaga wears in the "Bad Romance" video.

o The glittery bodysuit and a purple hairbow and wig that Mercedes wore are similar to a look Gaga wore in London in 2009.

o Quinn's outfit was inspired by the Armani Privé orbit dress Gaga wore to the fifty-second Grammy Awards.

o Rachel's first dress was based on Gaga's Kermit the Frog dress.

o Rachel's second dress was based on Gaga's silver mirrored triangle dress.

o Tina's outfit was modeled after the Hussein Chalayan–inspired bubble dress that Gaga wore on her Fame Ball tour.

o Santana's Jeffrey Bryant lace bodysuit, black rose Charlie Le Mindu hat, and lace airbrushed onto her face were based on Gaga's look from the MAC Viva Glam Launch Event.

o Vocal Adrenaline's red Chantilly lace full-body outfits and headpieces were inspired by the Fall 1998 Alexander McQueen dress Gaga wore when she accepted her Best New Artist award at the 2009 MTV Video Music Awards.

Lady Gaga loaned the show her costume designer to help realize the episode's vision.

curtain glory, defending Kurt's right to be who he wants to be. Finn may not be all that bright sometimes, but he can be taught.

Quinn and Puck are on rocky ground as well, with the birth of their daughter imminent. Puck wants to name her Jackie Daniels, giving Quinn yet another good reason to give the baby up for adoption. Puck recruits the rest of the boys to sing "Beth" to her, to show that he could be a good father (actual song lyrics notwithstanding), but Quinn only relents to the point of allowing him to be present at the baby's birth.

As the battle for Regionals looms, Rachel, Mercedes, and Quinn go on reconnaissance to see what their arch-enemies have in store. But Shelby's Streisand lesson makes Rachel realize that she has found her mother at long last. Shelby even makes Rachel a vastly improved Lady Gaga costume. But their dramatic reunion leads to an uncomfortable conversation, causing Shelby to take off.

Will meets with Shelby after he finds out what happened, worrying about the effect the sudden appearance of a mother will have on Rachel, but she has realized that pursuing her daughter may have not been the best idea. Rachel is already a person, a person who doesn't need her. The baby she remembered isn't who Rachel is now. Mother and daughter talk, decide to remain apart, and sing one last duet.

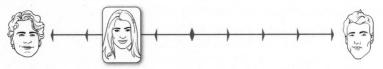

Status quo while Rachel deals with the discovery of the identity of her mother, Shelby Corcoran.

Quotes

"Boys, I don't want to hear about chafing just because you're wearing metal underwear. Not my problem."
—Shelby

"We live in Ohio, not New York...or some other city where people eat vegetables that aren't fried."
—Finn

"While Jackie Daniels is a great name for a powerboat or something, it's not great for a baby girl."
—Puck

Music List

Funny Girl (from the musical Funny Girl)

PERFORMED IN *GLEE* BY:	Shelby Corcoran (Idina Menzel)
WRITTEN BY:	Bob Merrill and Jule Styne
ORIGINALLY PERFORMED ON STAGE BY:	Barbra Streisand (1964)
ORIGINALLY PERFORMED ON SCREEN BY:	Barbra Streisand (1968)

Bad Romance

PERFORMED IN *GLEE* BY:	Rachel Berry (Lea Michele), Brittany (Heather Morris), Tina Cohen-Chang (Jenna Ushkowitz), Quinn Fabray (Dianna Agron), Kurt Hummel (Chris Colfer), Mercedes Jones (Amber Riley), and Santana Lopez (Naya Rivera)
WRITTEN BY:	Stefani Germanotta (a.k.a. Lady Gaga), Nadir Khayat
ORIGINALLY PERFORMED BY:	Lady Gaga (2009)

Shout It Out Loud

PERFORMED IN *GLEE* BY:	Artie Abrams (Kevin McHale), Mike Chang (Harry Shum Jr.), Finn Hudson (Cory Monteith), Noah "Puck" Puckerman (Mark Salling), and Matt Rutherford (Dijon Talton)
WRITTEN BY:	Bob Ezrin, Gene Simmons, and Paul Stanley
ORIGINALLY PERFORMED BY:	Kiss (1976)

Beth

PERFORMED IN *GLEE* BY:	Artie Abrams (Kevin McHale), Mike Chang (Harry Shum Jr.), Finn Hudson (Cory Monteith), Noah "Puck" Puckerman (Mark Salling), and Matt Rutherford (Dijon Talton)
WRITTEN BY:	Peter Criss and Stan Penridge
ORIGINALLY PERFORMED BY:	Kiss (1976)

Poker Face

PERFORMED IN *GLEE* BY:	Rachel Berry (Lea Michele) and Shelby Corcoran (Idina Menzel)
WRITTEN BY:	Stefani Germanotta (a.k.a. Lady Gaga), Nadir Khayat
ORIGINALLY PERFORMED BY:	Lady Gaga (2008)

Funk (1-21)

Original Air Date	Tuesday, June 1, 2010
Written by	Ian Brennan
Directed by	Elodie Keene
Glee Club Assignment	Turn McKinley High into Funky Town

New Directions enters the home stretch feeling good. Confident. Like they could take on Vocal Adrenaline and beat them. Then their rivals come for an intimidation visit, mixing Queen with a full toilet-papering of the choir room. The glee kids slide into a funk, and when Will's divorce becomes finalized, he joins them in the doldrums.

Will tries to help the kids by having them sing funk numbers, since that's Vocal Adrenaline's Achilles heel. Quinn, diving into the assignment, goes first and performs "It's a Man's Man's Man's World," with a pregnant teenage dance troupe, earning the support and sympathy of Mercedes. Puck and Finn don't quite understand the assignment as well as Quinn does; they think Marky Mark and the Funky Bunch counts as funk.

Trying to get out of their funk in their own way, Puck and Finn put aside their differences and dole out a little payback by slashing Vocal Adrenaline's tires. They avoid jail, but they do have to pay for the damage. Their funk deepens as they are forced to work at Sheets-N-Things to make enough money to pay off the debt. The Sheets-N-Things employees share the funk by joining them in song. Because, really, few things can make you feel more loser-like than working in retail. But Terri connects with Finn, making him Assistant Assistant Manager over Howard. She also helps him with his glee club assignment, which might partially explain the Marky Mark selection.

Will tries to get out of *his* funk by getting sweet, sweet revenge on his nemesis, Sue. With the Cheerios about to head to Nationals, Sue is at her most vulnerable. Throwing her off her game now would hurt her chances of winning a sixth straight title. The time is ripe to strike! And strike Will does, using his backside to beguile her, then standing her up and refusing her.

Will's plot works better than he could have dreamed. Sue is humiliated, destroyed, and, well, in a funk, so much so that she refuses to get out of bed. But there are innocent bystanders affected as well: the Cheerios begin to fall apart without Sue's presence. Hair is mussed. Emotions run wild. Shirts are worn backward (okay, that's just Brittany). And if the Cheerios pull out of Nationals, some girls may lose their hard-earned scholarships.

Realizing that the blast area of his attack spread much further than he thought it would, Will apologizes to Sue. She emerges from hiding, wins Nationals, and decides that the gigantic trophy will be set up in the choir room. She also makes Will almost kiss her.

But it's Jesse who earns the Jerk Award of the episode when he lures Rachel to the parking lot and then pelts her with eggs with his teammates. Rachel is shattered. But the New Directions kids have their own revenge when they counter the earlier Queen number with "Give Up the Funk." Their spirits have not been broken! Vocal Adrenaline, soulless automatons that they are, realize that they might be in trouble.

Jesse breaks Rachel's heart.

Quotes

"I'm so depressed, I've worn the same outfit twice this week."
—Kurt

"I have this compulsive need to crush other people's dreams."
—Terri

"Now I just keep having nightmares of all of the mothers of the little baby chicks coming at me for revenge."
—Rachel

Music List

Another One Bites the Dust

PERFORMED IN *GLEE* BY:	Jesse St. James (Jonathan Groff) and Vocal Adrenaline
WRITTEN BY:	John Deacon
ORIGINALLY PERFORMED BY:	Queen (1980)

Tell Me Something Good

PERFORMED IN *GLEE* BY:	Will Schuester (Matthew Morrison)
WRITTEN BY:	Stevie Wonder
ORIGINALLY PERFORMED BY:	Rufus and Chaka Khan (1974)

Loser

PERFORMED IN *GLEE* BY:	Finn Hudson (Cory Monteith), Noah "Puck" Puckerman (Mark Salling), and the Sheets-N-Things staff
WRITTEN BY:	Beck and Carl Stephenson
ORIGINALLY PERFORMED BY:	Beck (1993)

It's a Man's Man's Man's World

PERFORMED IN *GLEE* BY:	Quinn Fabray (Dianna Agron) and the Unwed Mothership Connection
WRITTEN BY:	James Brown and Betty Jean Newsome
ORIGINALLY PERFORMED BY:	James Brown (1966)

Good Vibrations

PERFORMED IN *GLEE* BY:	Finn Hudson (Cory Monteith), Mercedes Jones (Amber Riley), and Noah "Puck" Puckerman (Mark Salling)
WRITTEN BY:	Dan Hartman, Amir "MC Spice" Shakir, Donnie Wahlberg, and Mark Wahlberg
ORIGINALLY PERFORMED BY:	Marky Mark and the Funky Bunch (1991)

Give Up the Funk (Tear the Roof off the Sucker)

PERFORMED IN *GLEE* BY:	New Directions
WRITTEN BY:	Jerome Brailey, George Clinton, and Bootsy Collins
ORIGINALLY PERFORMED BY:	Parliament (1976)

> "Give Up the Funk" is from the album *Mothership Connection*.

Journey (1-22)

Original Air Date	Tuesday, June 8, 2010
Written by	Brad Falchuk
Directed by	Brad Falchuk
Glee Club Assignment	Win or place at Regionals

Regionals has finally arrived, and the very survival of the glee club is at stake. Vocal Adrenaline will be tough to beat, but New Directions thinks they have a real shot at doing it. Well, they think so until Sue announces that she will be one of the judges at the competition.

This crushes the entire club. Their hopes are dashed. They cry over their pizza. It's all very depressing. Even Will bawls in his car when "Don't Stop Believin'" plays on the radio. It's just all-around sad, with the added sadness bonus that Emma is now dating her dentist.

But then Will realizes that the glee club was never about winning. It was about the experience. It was about the journey. And since they sang Journey to start the club, what better way to celebrate how much it's accomplished in its one year of existence? Regionals, like the season, will be all about the Journey. Finn and Rachel have a breakthrough as well: when he confronts her about being positive, she kisses him.

Let's do this! Three teams compete at Regionals: our heroes, Vocal Adrenaline, and a third team called Aural Intensity that we have no reason to care about. The judges make up a mini Who's Who from the season: Josh Groban, Olivia Newton-John, anchorman Rod Remington, and, of course, Sue Sylvester. The team we don't care about starts off the competition, and they throw an early wrench in by singing Josh Groban and Olivia Newton-John songs. No fair!

New Directions take the stage second, but not before Finn tells Rachel that he loves her. Their Journey medley is a huge hit with the audience. New Directions receives a standing ovation and a special backstage visitor: Quinn's mom, who has left her husband and wants her daughter back.

But then Quinn's water breaks, because that's just the sort of thing that happens during season finales. Thankfully, Vocal Adrenaline launches into "Bohemian Rhapsody," which gives her plenty of time to go through labor and give birth to a healthy baby girl.

Then the judging begins. Sue had planned to sabotage New Directions, but the self-centered judges do most of the dirty work for her. Sue finds herself actually defending and ultimately voting for her school's club. The votes are cast, and the decisions are announced. Second place, the "not at all stupidly named" Aural Intensity. And the winner: Vocal Adrenaline. New Directions, our heroes, did not win or place. They lost. The club's death knell sounds.

Knowing their time together is at an end, the students (all of them, even who's-that-guy Matt and Mike the Other Asian) tell Will how much the club has meant to them and sing to their teacher. As she did when glee club began, Sue looks on, but this time she isn't plotting the club's demise. That already happened. Instead, she goes to Figgins to blackmail him into giving New Directions one more year. Her excuse? She wants the chance to beat them again. Will gives the kids the good news and serenades them in return for their song, Quinn and Puck's baby Beth has a new mom in Shelby Corcoran, and all is right with the world.

Until Sue starts to ruin it again.

Rachel kisses Finn. Finn tells Rachel he loves her. Finally!

Quotes

"I realize my cultural ascendance only serves to illuminate your own banality. But face it, I'm legend. It's happened."
—Sue

"Brunettes have no place in show business."
—Olivia Newton-John

"We don't care what the judges say. We won. Because we had you as a teacher."
—Rachel

Music List

AURAL INTENSITY MASHUP:

Magic

PERFORMED IN *GLEE* BY:	Aural Intensity
WRITTEN BY:	John Farrar
ORIGINALLY PERFORMED BY:	Olivia Newton John (1980)

You Raise Me Up

PERFORMED IN *GLEE* BY:	Aural Intensity
WRITTEN BY:	Rolf Løvland and Brendan Graham
ORIGINALLY PERFORMED BY:	Secret Garden (2002)
ALSO PERFORMED BY (PARTIAL LIST):	Josh Groban (2003), Il Divo (2006)

Faithfully

PERFORMED IN *GLEE* BY:	Rachel Berry (Lea Michele), Finn Hudson (Cory Monteith), and New Directions
WRITTEN BY:	Jonathan Cain
ORIGINALLY PERFORMED BY:	Journey (1983)

NEW DIRECTIONS MASHUP:

Any Way You Want It

PERFORMED IN *GLEE* BY:	New Directions
WRITTEN BY:	Steve Perry and Neal Schon
ORIGINALLY PERFORMED BY:	Journey (1979)

Lovin', Touchin', Squeezin'

PERFORMED IN *GLEE* BY:	New Directions
WRITTEN BY:	Steve Perry
ORIGINALLY PERFORMED BY:	Journey (1979)

Don't Stop Believin'

PERFORMED IN *GLEE* BY:	New Directions

Song information listed in "Pilot" (1-1)

Bohemian Rhapsody

PERFORMED IN *GLEE* BY:	Jesse St. James (Jonathan Groff) and Vocal Adrenaline
WRITTEN BY:	Freddie Mercury
ORIGINALLY PERFORMED BY:	Queen (1975)

> The classic Queen song "Bohemian Rhapsody" has been reintroduced to audiences in many ways over the years, most famously by Wayne (Mike Myers) and Garth (Dana Carvey) in *Wayne's World* (1992), and, more recently, as a viral video starring the Muppets (2009).

To Sir, With Love

PERFORMED IN *GLEE* BY:	New Directions
WRITTEN BY:	Don Black and Mark London
ORIGINALLY PERFORMED BY:	Lulu (1968)

Over the Rainbow (from the film The Wizard of Oz)

PERFORMED IN *GLEE* BY:	Will Schuester (Matthew Morrison) with Noah "Puck" Puckerman (Mark Salling)
WRITTEN BY:	Harold Arlen (music) and E.Y. Harburg (lyrics)
ORIGINALLY PERFORMED BY:	Judy Garland (1939)
ARRANGEMENT USED IN *GLEE* ORIGINALLY PERFORMED BY:	Israel Ka'ano'I Kamakawiwo'ole (1993)

GLEE CAST BIOGRAPHIES

Main Cast

Dianna Agron as Quinn Fabray

Agron is no stranger to television; she had in recurring roles in the third season of *Veronica Mars* as well as the second season of *Heroes*, playing—you guessed it!—a cheerleader. Speaking of *Heroes*, she also co-starred in a short comedy series made for American Eagle Outfitters called "It's a Mall World," which aired on MTV during *The Real World* and was directed by Milo Ventimiglia, *Heroes'* Peter Petrelli. You might have also caught Agron on the TV shows *CSI: NY*, *Shark*, and *Numb3rs*, or the films *TKO* and *Dinner with Raphael*. She's a person of many talents, as she also wrote, directed, and starred in the short film "A Fuchsia Elephant."

Chris Colfer as Kurt Hummel

A novice and the youngest cast member, Colfer had no professional performance experience prior to *Glee*. He originally auditioned for the role of Artie, but Ryan Murphy and the creative team wrote the role of Kurt just for him after his initial audition, naming him after the character from *The Sound of Music*.[1] But while he may not have the professional credits, he has the drive to perform. Case in point: at his high school, he re-wrote, directed, and starred in a version of *Sweeney Todd* he called *Shirley Todd*.[2] Not only that, but when his high school wouldn't allow him to sing "Defying Gravity" in their talent show (sound familiar?), his grandmother, a reverend, had him sing it at her church.[3] He was also a speech and debate champion and president of his high school's writers club. His audition song for the show was the same as Kurt's: "Mr. Cellophane."[4]

[1] Goldberg, Lesley, *Just One of the Guys*, Advocate.com, http://advocate.com/Arts_and_Entertainment/Television/Glees_Chris_Colfer__Just_one_of_the_guys (October 2009).
[2] Ibid.
[3] Zuckerman, Blaine, Glee's *Chris Colfer Reveals Real-Life Story Behind Kurt's Diva Moment*, http://tvwatch.people.com/2009/11/12/glees-chris-colfer-reveals-real-life-story-behind-kurts-diva-moment (November 2009).
[4] Hendrickson, Paula, *Casting the Keys to Glee*, http://www.emmys.com/articles/casting-keys-glee (November 2009).

Jessalyn Gilsig as Terri Schuester

Gilsig was primarily a stage actress before moving to television, with major roles in *The Tempest* and *Tartuffe* in Cambridge, as well as appearing in various Off-Broadway plays. Her first starring role in television, as teacher Lauren Davis in David E. Kelley's *Boston Public*, was written specifically for her. She's also has recurring roles in many TV shows, including *Heroes*, *Friday Night Lights*, *Prison Break*, and *NYPD Blue*. Ryan Murphy fans would know her as Gina Russo in his F/X show, *Nip/Tuck*.

Jane Lynch as Sue Sylvester

If you've seen the Christopher Guest mockumetaries *Best in Show*, *A Mighty Wind*, and *For Your Consideration*, then you know Jane Lynch already. Or you may know her from *The 40-Year-Old Virgin*, or *Julie & Julia*, or one of the many other films she's been in over the past twenty years. Don't go to movies? Lynch was Aileen Poole in *MDs*, Constance Carmell in *Party Down*, and had recurring television roles in *Criminal Minds*, *Two and a Half Men*, *Boston Legal*, *The L Word*, and *Help Me Help You*. She has made guest appearances on over fifty television shows since 1993, so you've likely seen her onscreen *somewhere*. Her roots are on the stage; she was part of the Second City comedy troupe, she starred as Carol Brady in *The Real Live Brady Bunch*, and she both wrote and starred in the play *Oh Sister, My Sister*. Off-Broadway, she appeared in *Love, Loss, and What I Wore*. She was a Golden Globe nominee for *Glee*.

Jayma Mays as Emma Pillsbury

A cheerleader and a self-proclaimed "math nerd" in high school, Mays' film debut was in the thriller *Red Eye*.[5] Since then, she has appeared in films such as *Epic Movie*, *Flags of Our Fathers*, and *Paul Blart, Mall Cop*. Her television appearances include *Joey*, *Six Feet*

---

[5] Sternberg, Alix, *EXCLUSIVE INTERVIEW: Jayma Mays (Emma) from Glee*, The TV Chick, http://thetvchick.com/exclusive-interviews/exclusive-interview-jayma-mays-emma-from-glee/ (December 2009).

Under, Entourage, How I Met Your Mother, House, M.D., *Pushing Daisies*, and *Ghost Whisperer*. She has two recurring television roles that have something in common: she appeared as a character named Charlie on both *Ugly Betty* and *Heroes*. She is slated to appear in 2011's *The Smurfs*.

Kevin McHale as Artie Abrams

Before *Glee*, McHale was best known as a member of the boy band NLT (short for "Not Like Them"), who released their first single, "That Girl," in 2007. The band made a guest appearance in *Bratz: The Movie*, and then disbanded in 2009. McHale's previous television appearances include *The Office*, *True Blood*, and *Zoey 101*. *Glee* choreographer Zach Woodlee calls McHale "the best dancer on the show."[6]

Lea Michele as Rachel Berry

There's more to her name: it's actually Lea Michele Sarfati. She's best known for her Broadway work, which she began as a child, including appearances in *Les Misérables* (Young Cosette/Young Eponine) and the original cast of *Ragtime* (Little Girl). Next she took on the Broadway revival of *Fiddler on the Roof* (Shprintze, understudy for Chava). Her first starring role on Broadway was as Wendla in the original cast of *Spring Awakening*, for which she was a Drama Desk Award nominee. Since she originated the roles, she can be heard on the original Broadway cast recordings of both *Ragtime* and *Spring Awakening*, as well as the revival cast recording of *Fiddler*. She then moved to Los Angeles, but her first role on the West Coast was the older version of a role already familiar to her: she played Eponine in the special concert performances of *Les Misérables* at the Hollywood Bowl in 2008, along with future *Glee* guest star John Lloyd Young. Her first television appearance was on *Third Watch*, but most of her television performances have been theater-related, such as the Tony Awards

[6] Das, Lina, *Join the Glee Club! A Who's Who of the TV Sensation and Why Everyone Should Be an Addict*, Mail Online, http://www.dailymail.co.uk/tvshowbiz/article-1269892/Glee-After-The-Power-Of-Madonna-guide-latest-TV-sensation.html (April 2010).

and the Macy's Thanksgiving Day Parade. She was nominated for a Screen Actors Guild Award, a Teen Choice Award, and a Golden Globe Award, and received the 2009 Satellite Award for *Glee*.

Cory Monteith as Finn Hudson

Monteith dropped out of school in ninth grade.[7] He has worked various jobs while pursuing acting, including a WalMart greeter, taxi driver, school bus driver, and roofer.[8] The Canadian had guest-starring roles in several Vancouver-based shows, including *Stargate: Atlantis*, *Supernatural*, and *Smallville*. *Stargate* fans may also remember him as the younger version of Cameron Mitchell (Ben Browder) on the 200th episode of *Stargate SG-1*. He co-starred on the MTV series *Kaya* and had a recurring role on *Kyle XY*. Like Finn, he had no singing or dancing experience prior to *Glee*, but he does know his way around a drum set.

Matthew Morrison as Will Schuester

Morrison hasn't always been a Broadway star. In high school, he both played soccer and performed in musicals.[9] He even worked at The Gap.[10] The boy-band LMNT (pronounced "element") snapped him up in 2001, but that didn't last, and he was replaced before their album was released; he calls that experience the "worst year of his life."[11] He made his Broadway debut as a dancer and understudy in *Footloose*, then joined the chorus of the revival of *The Rocky Horror Show* as a Phantom. His first starring role on Broadway was as heartthrob Link Larkin in the original cast of *Hairspray*, the role that Zac Ephron played in the movie version. After a hugely successful run,

---

[7] Wagner, Curt, *Fans Gleek Out for "Showmance" Episode of* Glee, http://www.chicagonow.com/blogs/show-patrol/2009/07/fans-gleek-out-for-showmance-episode-of-glee.html (July 2009).
[8] Strachan, Alex, *Cory Montieth Is Gleeful About* Glee, *The Vancouver Sun*, http://www.vancouver-sun.com/entertainment/movie-guide/Cory%20Monteith%20gleeful%20about%20Glee/1937809/story.html (August 2009).
[9] *Broadway Star Morrison Leaps To TV With* Glee, NPR, http://www.npr.org/templates/story/story.php?storyId=112711680 (September, 2009).
[10] Gostin, Nicki, *Glee Star Matthew Morrison Recalls "Worst Year" Ever*, Popeater.com, http://www.popeater.com/2010/01/15/glee-star-matthew-morrison (January 2010).
[11] Ibid.

he originated the role of Fabrizio Nacarelli in the musical *The Light in the Piazza*, for which he was nominated for a Tony Award, a Drama Desk Award, and an Outer Critics Circle Award. He has popped up in television over the years as well: he appeared in one episode of *Sex in the City*, briefly appeared on *As the World Turns*, and played Sir Harry in the 2005 Disney-produced television movie adaptation of *Once Upon a Mattress*, starring Carol Burnett, Tracey Ullman, and Zooey Deschanel. His film appearances include *Encino Man*, *Music and Lyrics*, and *Dan in Real Life*, among others. He was nominated for a Golden Globe Award and was winner of a Satellite Award for *Glee*.

Amber Riley as Mercedes Jones

Can you imagine *American Idol* turning her down? That's exactly what happened when Riley auditioned for the show in 2005. Worse, she was turned away by the producers and never even met the judges.[12] That didn't stop her, as she worked a day job at Ikea and sang backup at clubs while continuing to go to auditions.[13] Before *Glee*, her television credits consisted of the Ryan Murphy–penned *St. Sass* pilot and appearances on *Cedric the Entertainer Presents*. On stage she has performed in Los Angeles productions such as *A Midsummer Night's Dream*, *Into the Woods*, and *Alice in Wonderland*. She learned about the *Glee* audition through a friend's roommate and won the role of Mercedes when she was asked to sing a few lines from the song "And I Am Telling You I'm Not Going" during the audition, a song she had never sung before in her life.

Mark Salling as Noah "Puck" Puckerman

As a teenager, Salling co-starred in the film *Children of the Corn: The Gathering* and appeared in an episode of *Walker, Texas Ranger*. Later he appeared in the film *The Graveyard*. A native of Dallas, he is a singer, songwriter, guitarist, bassist, drummer, and pianist. His debut album

[12] Access Hollywood, Glee *Star Amber Riley on* Idol *Rejection: "I Still Work on FOX and Get Paid,"* http://omg.yahoo.com/news/glee-star-amber-riley-on-idol-rejection-i-still-work-on-fox-and-get-paid/28788 (October 2009).
[13] Ingrassia, Lisa, Glee's *Amber Riley: "I Love My Body," People* Magazine, http://www.people.com/people/archive/article/0,,20367254,00.html (May 2010).

of all original music, *Smoke Signals*, was released in 2008 under his stage name, Jericho. Before *Glee*, he gave guitar lessons to make extra money. He volunteers for the James Hunter Wildlife Rescue.

Jenna Ushkowitz as Tina Cohen-Chang

Born in South Korea and adopted by American parents as a baby, Ushkowitz appeared on *Sesame Street* and *Reading Rainbow* as a child.[14] She also appeared on *As the World Turns*. Her first Broadway role was in a revival of *The King and I*, and she understudied Martha, Thea, and Anna in the original Broadway production of *Spring Awakening* with Lea Michele and Jonathan Groff. She is the only cast member who was a member of her high school's glee club.

Recurring Cast

Brad Ellis as Brad the Accompanist

Ellis accompanied hundreds of actors through the *Glee* audition process with no idea that he too would appear on the show. But Ryan Murphy had other ideas. In fact, Ellis appeared in every episode of the show's first season. Outside of *Glee*, he is an acclaimed pianist, music director, and composer, and has worked with stars ranging from Dizzy Gillespie to Idina Menzel to Billy Joel. His band, the Brad Ellis Little Big Band, was Kristin Chenoweth's band for her cabaret show. He has long worked with the Off-Broadway satire *Forbidden Broadway* as it continually evolves, and he and Jason Alexander created the medley *Seven Broadway Shows in Seven Minutes*. He also cowrote the opening number for Hugh Jackman's Emmy-winning 2009 Academy Awards hosting performance.

---

[14] Jann, Janice, *Jenna Ushkowitz*, http://iamkoream.com/jenna-ushkowitz (August 2009).

Patrick Gallagher as Ken Tanaka

Think he looks familiar? That might be because he played Attila the Hun in both of the *Night at the Museum* films. His other film appearances include *Master and Commander: The Far Side of the World* and *Sideways*. You may also have seen him in one of his many television guest appearances on shows including *Forever Knight*, *Stargate SG-1*, *Stargate: Atlantis*, *Dark Angel*, *Battlestar Galactica*, and *Cold Case*. He has a recurring role as the vampire Chow in *True Blood*.

Heather Morris as Brittany

Morris went for her big break when she auditioned for the second season of Fox's *So You Think You Can Dance*, but she didn't make it onto the show. Despite that, she built herself a stellar dance career. She performed with Beyoncé on her tour *The Beyoncé Experience* in 2008, including performances at the American Music Awards, on *Saturday Night Live*, *Ellen*, *The Today Show*, and MTV's *Total Request Live* finale in 2008. She was also a backup dancer for Beyoncé and Tina Turner at the fifthieth Grammy Awards in 2008, and for Usher in a promotional clip for the 2008 MTV Movie Awards. With her Beyoncé credentials, Morris was initially brought in to *Glee* only to

The Fox Connection

Several of the dancers who have appeared on *Glee* have also been finalists on the Fox reality show *So You Think You Can Dance*, including Brandon Bryant, Comfort Fedoke, Courtney Galiano, Jason Glover, Lauren Gottlieb, Janette Manrara, Kherington Payne, Jonathan Platero, Melissa Sandvig, Katee Shean, and Nathan Trasoras.

In addition, three songs performed on *Glee* were originally performed by American Idol winners: "My Life Would Suck Without You" (season one champion Kelly Clarkson), "Last Name" (season four champion Carrie Underwood), and "No Air" (season six champion Jordin Sparks).

teach the choreography for "Single Ladies," but she was hired on when they needed an additional cheerleader.[15] The rest is Brittany history, and she was added as a regular for the second season. Hopefully Brittany will finally get a last name.

Mike O'Malley as Burt Hummel

As one of the stars of the CBS comedy *Yes, Dear* for six seasons, O'Malley is well known to television audiences. He also played the dual role of spy Raymond Carter/buddy Tom Grady opposite Christian Slater in the short-lived *My Own Worst Enemy*. But long before that, he created, executive produced, and starred in *The Mike O'Malley Show* for NBC in 1999. It only lasted two episodes. On the big screen, he appeared in *Deep Impact, Pushing Tin, 28 Days, Meet Dave,* and *Leatherheads,* among others. He also appears in Time Warner Cable advertisements in some markets, confusing those who might be fast-forwarding through commercials on their TiVos and DVRs.

Naya Rivera as Santana Lopez

In high school, Rivera joined the choir in her freshman year at her mother's insistence, but she quit after a few weeks.[16] Her focus was acting, which she started at an early age, co-starring on the television show *The Royal Family* when she was four years old. She had a recurring role on *The Bernie Mac Show* and made guest appearances in *The Fresh Prince of Bel-Air, Family Matters, Baywatch, Smart Guy, Even Stevens, 8 Simple Rules,* and *CSI: Miami,* among others.

Romy Rosemont as Carole Hudson

This veteran actress has appeared in over forty television shows, including *Boston Legal, Babylon 5, Crossing Jordan, Grey's Anatomy, Nip/Tuck, Dirt, Eastwick,* and *Prison Break.* She co-starred with James

---

[15] *Young Entertainers Get a Taste of Hollywood*, My Buffalo, http://www.mybuffalo.com/_Young-Entertainers-Get-a-Taste-of-Hollywood/blog/1663704/85283.html (December 2009).

[16] Simpson, Melody, *Meet Cory Monteith and Naya Rivera of Glee*, HollywoodTheWriteWay.com, http://www.hollywoodthewriteway.com/2009/03/meet-cory-monteith-naya-rivera-of-glee.html (March 2009).

Woods on the television show *Shark* and had a recurring role in the original *CSI: Crime Scene Investigation* from 2002 to 2005.

Harry Shum Jr. as Mike Chang (a.k.a. "Other Asian")

You know those dancing silhouettes in iPod commercials? Shum was the first. He started his career as the only male dancer on BET's *Comic View*. He's been the lead dancer for Beyoncé, Mariah Carey, Jennifer Lopez, and Jessica Simpson, and he serves as both featured dancer and choreographer for the group Legion of Extraordinary Dancers, or LXD. He's appeared in the dance films *Stomp the Yard*, *You Got Served*, *Step Up 2: The Streets*, and *Step Up 3-D*, and has made multiple television appearances, including *Boston Public*, *Viva Laughlin*, and *iCarly*. He has also been a teacher at dancing conventions for kids.[17]

Josh Sussman as Jacob Ben Israel

Prior to *Glee*, Sussman was best known as Hugh Normous in *Wizards of Waverly Place*. He has also appeared on television shows such as *What About Brian*, *The Suite Life of Zack and Cody*, and *Bones*. He fully admits that he can't sing, and he used that lack of singing talent when he did a spoof for *The Tonight Show with Jay Leno* as an *American Idol* "contestant," singing "Ring of Fire"[18]

Dijon Talton as Matt Rutherford

As a child, Talton has a small role in the film *L.A. Without a Map*, which starred future *Doctor Who* star David Tennant. Talton has also appeared in two ads for McDonald's, including one with Tyra Banks. His cousin Meagan Good is an actress, and his cousin La'Myia Good is an actress and singer.

---

[17] Lin, Shannon, *Harry Shum Is Full of* Glee, Asiance Magazine, http://www.asiancemagazine.com/2009/09/02/harry-shum-is-full-of-glee (September 2009).
[18] Elkin, Michael, *Of* Glee *I Sing*, The Jewish Exponent, http://www.jewishexponent.com/article/19027 (June 2009).

Iqbal Theba as Principal Figgins

Born in Pakistan, Theba has a degree in Construction Engineering Management from the University of Oklahoma.[19] He arrived in Hollywood with only $37 in his pocket.[20] His first onscreen performance was in *Indecent Proposal*, and his other film appearances include *BASEketball, Blind Dating*, and *Frankenhood*. Theba has appeared in over fifty television shows, including *L.A. Law, Seinfeld, Roseanne, Ellen, Friends, ER, The West Wing, Joan of Arcadia, Alias, The Tick, Weeds*, and *Chuck*. He played a character with the same name as his own in *Married... with Children, Life With Bonnie*, and *Kitchen Confidential*. His longest character name to date: Inzamamulhaq Siddiqui, a recurring role in *The George Carlin Show*.

Stephen Tobolowsky as Sandy Ryerson

Tobolowsky performed in musicals in his hometown of Dallas, including *Godspell* and *Whispers on the Wind*. He also plays piano and guitar.[21] He has over two hundred film and television credits under his belt. His films include *Spaceballs, Thelma and Louise, Basic Instinct, Groundhog Day, The Insider, Memento, Freddy Got Fingered, Wild Hogs*, and *The Time Traveler's Wife*; his television appearances include *Heroes, Entourage, Deadwood, The Drew Carey Show, Seinfeld, Roswell, Will & Grace, Malcolm in the Middle, Cagney & Lacey, Curb Your Enthusiasm*, and the unaired pilot episode of *Buffy the Vampire Slayer* as Principal Flutie.

---

[19] *NEAL B. EXCLUSIVE: Interview with Iqbal Theba aka PRINCIPAL FIGGINS!*, Neal B in NYC, http://nealbinnyc.wordpress.com/2009/12/04/neal-b-exclusive-interview-with-iqbal-theba-aka-principal-figgins (December 2009).

[20] *Curry Bear Interviews Glee's Iqbal Theba (Principal Figgins)*, Currybear.com, http://www.currybear.com/wordpress/?p=3566 (October 2009).

[21] *Stephen Tobolowsky*, Moviehole.com, http://www.moviehole.net/200921844-stephen-tobolowsky (2009).

Notable Guest Stars

Kristin Chenoweth as April Rhodes

One of the current divas of the Broadway stage, Chenoweth's roles include Sally in *You're a Good Man, Charlie Brown,* for which she received a Tony Award, a Drama Desk Award, and an Outer Critics Circle Award for the role; originating the role of Glinda in *Wicked,* for which she won a Tony, Drama Desk, and Outer Critics Circle nominee; Eve/Princess Barbara/Ella and Passionella in *The Apple Tree,* for which she won a Tony, Drama Desk, Drama League, and Outer Critics Circle nominee; and Fran Kubelik in *Promises, Promises.* She has appeared in many films, including *Bewitched, The Pink Panther, RV, Running With Scissors,* and *Deck the Halls.* No stranger to television, her roles as a series regular include Kristin Yancey in *Kristin,* Annabeth Schott in *The West Wing,* and Olive Snook in *Pushing Daisies,* for which she was awarded the Emmy for Best Supporting Actress in a Comedy Series in 2009. When a television tackles a musical, she often gets the call: she appeared as Lily St. Regis in *Annie* (also starring Victor Garber), Marian Paroo in *The Music Man* (also starring several other future *Glee* guest stars), and Cunegonde in *Candide* for *Great Performances.* She has also had a recurring role on *Sesame Street* as Mrs. Noodle since 2003.

The Music Man 2003 Reunion

Four actors who have guest-starred on *Glee* also appeared in the 2003 made-for-television movie of *The Music Man* that starred Matthew Broderick: Kristin Chenoweth (Marian Paroo), Victor Garber (Mayor Shinn), Debra Monk (Mrs. Paroo), and Molly Shannon (Mrs. Eulalie Mackechnie Shinn).

Eve as Grace Hitchens

Eve's first album, *Let There Be Eve…Ruff Ryders' First Lady*, was the second hip-hop album by a woman to enter the Billboard 200 at number one. Her other albums include *Scorpion*, *Eve-olution*, and *Lip Lock*, and she has also been featured in singles with Gwen Stefani, Amerie, Keyshia Cole, Teairra Mari, and Kelly Rowland. Eve was named NAACP Outstanding New Artist in 2000, and won a Grammy in 2002 for Best Rap/Sung Collaboration as well as an MTV Music Video Award in 2001 for Best Female Video for "Let Me Blow Ya Mind" with Gwen Stefani. She has received multiple Grammy nominations, MTV Music Video Award nominations, and Image Award nominations, among others. Her film appearances include *xXx*, *Barbershop*, *Barbershop 2: Back in Business*, *The Cookout*, *The Woodsman*, and *Whip It*. She starred in the UPN sitcom *Eve*, which ran for three seasons, and her television guest appearances include *Third Watch* and *Numb3rs*. Her full name is Eve Jihan Jeffers.

Victor Garber as Will's Father

Long before Garber became a stage and screen star, he formed a folk band in 1967, with Peter Mann, Laurie Hood, and Lee Harris, called The Sugar Shoppe. They performed on *The Ed Sullivan Show* and *The Tonight Show Starring Johnny Carson*. Garber moved to the stage after that, and his big break came when his stage performance as Jesus in the first Canadian production of *Godspell* led to his first on-screen starring role: reprising the role for the film version in 1973. After that, Broadway called, and he has been a mainstay there to this day. He originated the role of Anthony Hope in *Sweeney Todd* and was also in the original Broadway casts of *Deathtrap* (as Clifford Anderson) and *Noises Off* (as Garry Lejeune). He was in the original Off-Broadway cast of Stephen Sondheim's *Assassins*, starring as John Wilkes Booth, in 1990. His best-known film role to date was ship builder Thomas Andrews in James Cameron's *Titanic*, but he has played many other historical figures as well, including the Marquis de Lafayette in *Valley Forge*, Ernest Hemmingway in *The Legendary*

Life of Ernest Hemingway, John Dickenson in *Liberty! The American Revolution*, and Mayor George Moscone in *Milk*. In another real-life role, he was nominated for an Emmy for his portrayal of Liberace in *Liberace: Behind the Music* in 1998. His other films include *Sleepless in Seattle*, *Legally Blonde*, *The First Wives Club*, *Kung-Fu Panda*, and *Tuck Everlasting*, among others. On television, Garber made the rounds in made-for-television musicals, including King Maximillian in 1997's *Cinderella*, Daddy Warbucks in 1999's *Annie*, and Mayor Shinn in 2003's *The Music Man*. His best-known television role was as Jack Bristow in J.J. Abrams' spy drama *Alias*. He also starred in the television shows *I Had Three Wives* and *Justice* and had regular or recurring roles on *Eli Stone*, *ReGenesis*, and *E.N.G.* Continuing his association with Abrams, Garber was cast as a Klingon interrogator in 2009's *Star Trek*, but his scenes were deleted from the final version of the film. Matthew Morrison was thrilled that Garber had been cast as his character's father, as he is a big fan.[22] However, despite his talents and singing experience, Garber did not sing in his (to date) one-episode appearance on the show.

Josh Groban as Himself (sort of)

As a teenager, Groban was discovered by producer David Foster and worked for him as a rehearsal singer for high-profile events and as a stand-in for Andrea Bocelli. Groban released his first solo album, the self-titled *Josh Groban*, in 2001, and that same year he appeared in *Ally McBeal* as Malcolm Wyatt, a role that gave him the opportunity to showcase his singing talents. It was after that appearance that his career exploded. He has so far sold nearly twenty million albums in the United States alone and was the bestselling artist of 2007. He has sung at many high-profile events, including the closing ceremonies of the Salt Lake City 2002 Winter Olympics, in the pregame ceremonies of Super Bowl XXXVIII, and for the 2009 Presidential

---

[22] Brioux, Bill, *Canadian Cast Members Are Glee-ful About Success of Hot New Musical TV Show*, The Canadian Press, http://www.kamloopsnews.ca/article/GB/20090903/CP05/309039875/-1/KAM-LOOPS/canadian-cast-members-are-glee-ful-about-success-of-hot-new-musical&template=cpArt (September 2009).

inauguration. His four solo albums (*Josh Groban*, *Closer*, *Awake*, and *Noël*) have been certified multi-platinum, and his performances have been nominated for over a dozen awards, including an American Music Award, Grammy Awards, a Juno Award, a People's Choice Award, and an Academy Award (for "Believe" from *Polar Express*). Recently he starred as Anatoly in *Chess in Concert* for *Great Performances* opposite fellow *Glee* guest star Idina Menzel. Groban has also found projects that let him showcase his sense of humor: he lent his voice to *The Simpsons* and *American Dad*, sang in Jimmy Kimmel's video skits "Panda Love" in 2007 and "I'm F***ing Ben Affleck," and performed a medley of twenty-five television theme songs at the sixtieth Emmy Awards in 2008, including the themes to *The Love Boat*, *South Park* (complete with a Cartman impression), *Baywatch*, *Cops*, *The Fresh Prince of Bel-Air*, and *The Muppet Show*. He also appeared on Adult Swim's *Tim and Eric Awesome Show, Great Job!*, singing "Casey's Greatest Hits," which included "Hamburgers and Hot Dogs" and "(I Want to Ride) In a Choo Choo Train," in his signature style. He even asked the *Glee* producers to make his character on the show a jerk.[23]

Jonathan Groff as Jesse St. James

Groff debuted on Broadway in 2005 in the musical *In My Life*, but his first starring stage role was when he originated the role of Melchior Gabor in *Spring Awakening*, playing opposite Lea Michele. He was nominated for a Drama Desk Award and a Tony Award for that role. He and Michele became best friends, and it was Groff who introduced her to *Glee* creator Ryan Murphy in 2007.[24] Also in 2007, Groff played Henry Mackler on the soap opera *One Life to Live* and appeared in the Macy's Thanksgiving Day Parade. He starred as Claude in the Shakespeare in the Park production of *Hair*, and then moved to the big screen to play Woodstock organizer Michael Lang

[23] *Josh Groban: Glee Is for Theater Geeks—Like Me*, People.com, http://tvwatch.people.com/2009/10/23/josh-groban-glee-is-for-theater-geeks-like-me (October 2009).
[24] Wieselman, Jarett, *Jonathan Groff: Jesse Really Complicates Life for the Glee Club*, New York Post, http://www.nypost.com/p/blogs/popwrap/jonathan_groff_ZCsO1zhbFRlYvCL1ohWSZK (April 2010).

in Ang Lee's *Taking Woodstock*. He is slated to appear in Robert Red-ford's film *The Conspirator*. *Glee* will always be a part of him: he has a five-inch scar on his arm from an injury suffered during the filming of "Bohemian Rhapsody" in the episode "Journey."[25]

Neil Patrick Harris as Bryan Ryan

A television star since childhood for his Golden Globe–nominated role in *Clara's Heart* and his starring role in the series *Doogie Howser, M.D.*, Harris has now become a star of stage, screen, and internet. His Broadway roles include the balladeer and Lee Harvey Oswald in *Assassins*, Hal in *Proof*, and the Master of Ceremonies in *Cabaret*. On stage, he played Mark in the second national touring company of *Rent*, Toby in the 2001 concert version of *Sweeney Todd* (starring Patti LuPone and George Hearn), and Mozart in the Hollywood Bowl production of *Amadeus*. He's even dabbled in Shakespeare, playing Romeo in *Romeo and Juliet* in 1998. His films include *Starship Troopers, The Proposition, Undercover Brother*, the Harold and Kumar series, the upcoming *The Smurfs* (starring alongside Jayma Mays), and a slew of made-for-television movies. Harris has lent his voice to numerous animated projects, including *Cloudy with a Chance of Meatballs, The Penguins of Madagascar, Capitol Critters*, and iconic comic book characters like Peter Parker and Dick Grayson/Robin. His guest appearances on television include *Blossom, Roseanne, The Simpsons, Quantum Leap, Homicide: Life on the Street, Oz, Will & Grace, Touched by an Angel, Boomtown, Numb3rs, Family Guy, Sesame Street* (as the Fairy Shoeperson), and *Robot Chicken*. Reality television has had a healthy dose of NPH as well: he has appeared on *Celebrity Poker Showdown, Dinner: Impossible, Top Chef Masters*, as a celebrity contestant on *Jeopardy!*, and as a guest judge on *American Idol*. He also co-starred in the series *Stark Raving Mad* with Tony Shalhoub. Harris took on the role of Barney Stinson in 2005 on the sitcom *How I Met Your Mother*, a role which has earned him multiple Emmy Award nominations. On the internet, NPH is a superstar: in 2008 he had

---

[25] Marino, Mark, *Jonathan Groff Left with Five-Inch Scar After Glee Injury*, CNN, http://marquee. blogs.cnn.com/2010/06/08/jonathan-groff-left-with-5-inch-scar-after-glee-injury (June 2008).

the title role in Joss Whedon's Emmy-winning *Dr. Horrible's Sing-Along Blog*, he had a featured role in *Prop 8: The Musical*, and in 2009 he battled (and ultimately beat) John Barrowman for the highly-touted-on-Twitter title of Gay/Bisexual Man of the Decade. He has also become a sought-after host, having guest-hosted *Live with Regis & Kelly* several times and hosted the Creative Arts Emmy Awards, the World Magic Awards, and the TV Land Awards, among others. In 2009 he hosted *Saturday Night Live*, then hosted both the Tony Awards and the Emmy Awards, performing musical numbers as well. He followed that up by performing the opening number at the 2010 Academy Awards. He returned to one of his first major stage shows by directing a special production of *Rent* for the Hollywood Bowl.

Idina Menzel as Shelby Corcoran

The musical *Rent* turned Menzel from an unknown with no professional credits to a Broadway star when she originated the role of Maureen in 1996. During her time playing Maureen, she received a Tony nomination and also met her husband, Taye Diggs. She also originated the role of Elphaba in *Wicked*, starring opposite Kristin Chenoweth; she won the Tony Award for that role. She took over the role of Amneris for a time on Broadway in *Aida*, and Off-Broadway she has starred in *The Wild Party*, *Summer of '42*, and *The Vagina Monologues*. She reprised the role of Maureen in the film adaptation of *Rent*, and later co-starred in the Disney film *Enchanted* as Nancy Tremaine. Her other films include *Just a Kiss*, *Kissing Jessica Stein*, *Tollbooth*, and *Water*. She starred as Florence in *Chess in Concert* for *Great Performances* (2009) with Josh Groban and fellow *Rent* cast member Adam Pascal. Menzel writes her own music and has released three albums: *Still I Can't Be Still*, *Here*, and *I Stand*. She appeared at Lilith Fair in 1998, sang on the soundtrack of *Beowulf* (2007), and has contributed songs to *Desperate Housewives*. She is not actually related to Lea Michele. Really.

Debra Monk as Will's Mother

Born and raised in Ohio, Monk created her own "big break" when she co-wrote, co-directed, and starred in *Pump Boys and Dinettes*, which hit Broadway in 1982. Her Broadway work also includes *Prelude to a Kiss, Nick & Nora, Picnic, Company, Steel Pier, Ah, Wilderness!, Thou Shalt Not,* and *Chicago.* She starred with another future *Glee* guest star, Victor Garber, in the Off-Broadway cast of *Assassins* in 1990. She won a Tony Award for *Redwood Curtain* and was a Tony nominee and Drama Desk winner for *Curtains.* Her film work includes *Prelude to a Kiss Fearless, Quiz Show, The Bridges of Madison County, Jeffrey, The First Wives Club, The Devil's Advocate, In & Out, Bulworth, Center Stage,* and *The Producers.* On television, she co-starred in 2003's made-for-television *The Music Man,* playing the mother of Kristin Chenoweth's character. Monk won an Emmy Award in 1999 for *NYPD Blue* and has recently had recurring roles on *Damages* and *Grey's Anatomy.* She has also appeared on *Law & Order* three times—in 1994, 2002, and 2005—as three different characters. She played Kristin Chenoweth's mother on one episode of the sitcom *Kristin.*

Olivia Newton-John as Herself (sort of)

Born in England and raised in Australia, Newton-John formed an all-girl singing group at the age of fifteen. Then she went solo, recording her first single in 1966 and her first album, for which Bob Dylan wrote the title track, in 1971. She was recruited for the group Toomorrow by Monkees creator Don Kirshner. Toomorrow recorded an album in 1970 and starred in a science-fiction musical film by the same name. The group flopped, but Newton-John's career took off. She has released twenty-four studio albums and seven compilation albums, including Greatest Hits albums in 1977 and 1982. She's had five number-one singles on the Billboard Hot 100 ("I Honestly Love You," "Have You Never Been Mellow," "You're the One That I Want" [with John Travolta], "Magic," and "Physical"), and ten additional Top Ten hits, winning Grammy Awards for both the pop and country genres. Onscreen, her best-known film roles are Sandy in *Grease* and

Kira in *Xanadu*. She played Bitsy Mae Harding in both *Sordid Lives* and *Sordid Lives: The Series* and made a cameo appearance in *Madonna: Truth or Dare*. Newton-John co-owns the Gaia Retreat & Spa in Australia. A cancer survivor, she is an active advocate for breast cancer research and research for other health issues.

Molly Shannon as Brenda Castle

Born and raised in Ohio, Shannon was a *Saturday Night Live* cast member from 1995 to 2001, which was the record for a female cast member at the time. Her best known *SNL* character was catholic school student Mary Katherine Gallagher, which led to the film *Superstar*. Shannon's television work also included a recurring role on *Will & Grace* and a starring role in the short-lived American version of *Kath & Kim*. She appeared in the video for Sheryl Crow's "A Change (Will Do You Good)" and guest-starred on *Seinfeld*, *Scrubs*, and *Pushing Daisies*. She co-starred in 2003's made-for-television *The Music Man*, playing Mrs. Eulalie Mackechnie Shinn, the wife of Victor Garber's character. Her film work includes *A Night at the Roxbury*, *My Boss's Daughter*, *Good Boy!*, *Marie Antoinette*, *Evan Almighty*, and *Year of the Dog*.

John Lloyd Young as Henri St. Pierre (a.k.a. The Thumbless Shop Teacher)

After college, Young worked his way up in regional and Off-Broadway theater. His first role on Broadway was a big one: the starring role of Frankie Valli in *Jersey Boys*. Young is the only American actor in history to receive a Tony Award (for Lead Actor in a Musical), a Drama Desk Award, an Outer Critics Circle Award, and a Theatre World Award for a Broadway debut. He performed excerpts from the role at the White House, Carnegie Hall, Radio City Music Hall, the New York City Marathon, Yankee Stadium, and the Macy's Thanksgiving Day Parade. Young's solo concert debut at Lincoln Center sold out in one day. He played Marius in the special concert performances of *Les Misérables* at the Hollywood Bowl in 2008, performing opposite Lea Michele's Eponine. His debut single was released on Valentine's Day 2010.